WYATT, SURREY AND TUDOR POETRY

LONGMAN MEDIEVAL AND RENAISSANCE LIBRARY

Published titles:

Piers Plowman: An Introduction to the B-Text
James Simpson

Shakespeare's Mouldy Tales: Recurrent Plot Motifs in Shakespearian Drama
Leah Scragg

The Fabliau in English
John Hines

English Medieval Mystics: Games of Faith
Marion Glasscoe

Speaking Pictures: English Emblem Books and Renaissance Culture
Michael Bath

The Classical Legacy in Renaissance Poetry
Robin Sowerby

Regaining Paradise Lost
Thomas Corns

English and Italian Literature from Dante to Shakespeare: A Study of Source, Analogue and Divergence
Robin Kirkpatrick

Shakespeare's Alternative Tales
Leah Scragg

The Gawain-*Poet*
Ad Putter

Donne's Religious Writing: A Discourse of Feigned Devotion
P. M. Oliver

Images of Faith in English Literature 700–1500: An Introduction
Dee Dyas

Courtliness and Literature in Medieval England
David Burnley

Wyatt, Surrey and Early Tudor Poetry
Elizabeth Heale

Elizabeth Heale

WYATT, SURREY AND EARLY TUDOR POETRY

LONGMAN
LONDON AND NEW YORK

Addison Wesley Longman
Edinburgh Gate
Harlow
Essex CM20 2JE
England
and Associated Companies throughout the world.

Published in the United States of America
by Addison Wesley Longman Inc., New York

First published 1998

ISBN 0 582 09353 8 CSD
ISBN 0 582 09352 X PPR

British Library Cataloguing-in-Publication Data

A catalogue record of this book is available from the British Library

Library of Congress Cataloging-in-Publication Data

Heale, Elizabeth, 1946–
Wyatt, Surrey, and early Tudor poetry / Elizabeth M. Heale.
p. cm. -- (Longman medieval and Renaissance library)
Includes bibliographical references (p.) and index.
ISBN 0-582-09353-8 (csd : alk. paper). -- ISBN 0-582-09352-X (ppr)
1. English poetry--Early modern, 1500–1700--History and criticism.
2. Wyatt, Thomas, Sir, 1503?–1542--Criticism and interpretation.
3. Surrey, Henry Howard, Earl of, 1517?–1547--Criticism and interpretation. 4. Great Britain--History--Tudors, 1485–1603.
5. Renaissance--England. 6. Tudor, House of. I. Title.
II. Series.
PR521.H43 1998
821' .209--dc21 97-15377
CIP

Set by 7 in 10.5/12 Bembo
Produced by Longman Singapore Publishers (Pte) Ltd.
Printed in Singapore

Contents

Abbreviations

CSP (Spanish)	*Calendar of State Papers, Spanish*
Jones	Jones, E. (1964) *Henry Howard, Earl of Surrey: Poems*. Clarendon Medieval and Tudor Series. Oxford: Clarendon Press.
LL	Muir, K. (1963) *Life and Letters of Sir Thomas Wyatt*. Liverpool: Liverpool University Press.
LP	Brewer, J. S., Gairdner, J. *et al.*, eds (1862–1932) *Letters and Papers, Foreign and Domestic, of the Reign of Henry VIII, 1509–1547*. 21 vols, London: HMSO.
M&T	Muir, K. and Thomson, P., eds (1969) *Collected Poems of Sir Thomas Wyatt*. Liverpool: Liverpool University Press.
Nott	Nott, G. F., ed. (1815–16) *The Works of Henry Howard, Earl of Surrey and of Sir Thomas Wyatt the Elder*. 2 vols, London: Longman, Hurst, Rees, Orme and Brown.
Padelford	Padelford, F. M., ed. (1928) *Poems of Henry Howard, Earl of Surrey* (revised edn). Seattle: University of Washington Press.
Reb.	Rebholz, R. A., ed. (1978) *Sir Thomas Wyatt: The Complete Poems*. Harmondsworth: Penguin.
Rollins	Rollins, H. E., ed. (1928–9) *Tottel's Miscellany (1557–1587)*. 2 vols, Cambridge, Mass.: Harvard University Press.

Note on early and modernized spelling

Any attempt to present early modern texts to a modern audience must confront the problem of early spelling and punctuation. Changes in pronunciation and orthography mean that for readers unused to Tudor texts, Tudor spelling can often make a relatively straightforward text seem obscure and difficult to follow. Spelling was not standardized in the sixteenth century and scribal or printers' variations give the spellings of surviving texts little or no authorial authority. In addition early punctuation, especially in manuscripts, is often either non-existent or consists of very light indications of pauses, often permitting considerable flexibility of interpretation, but sometimes making the sense difficult to follow for modern readers. On the other hand, early spelling, as well as indicating pronunciation and allowing on occasion for puns, presents the texts to us in some approximation to the form in which they were read in the sixteenth century, retaining some sense of historical difference and distinctiveness that is lost with modernization. My solution offers a compromise which is not consistent, but which tries to combine clarity with some indication of the different pronunciation and potential flexibility of meaning that come with Tudor spelling.

On the whole I have followed the spelling of the copy text I am using. When quoting from a manuscript, from an early edition or from a modern early-spelling edition, I have modernized some aspects of Tudor orthography and convention, altering 'u's and 'v's, 'i's and 'j's and, usually, 'y's, to conform to modern usage. Where the sense of a word seems unclear I have added a gloss alongside the text. I have usually followed the punctuation of the edition or manuscript I am following. On a few occasions, when quoting from prose, I have decided to modernize spelling and punctuation even when quoting from an early-spelling text in order to clarify the sense. When I have done this, I have indicated it in a footnote.

All the poetry I quote is in early-spelling form with the exception of Wyatt's poems, for which I have normally used R. A. Rebholz's modern-spelling edition of Wyatt's *Complete Poems*. Ideally I would have liked to have used an early-spelling version of Wyatt's poems, but the only available editions are either unsatisfactory or not as readily available to readers. Rebholz provides an excellent edition with superb notes and it seemed perverse not to use this as my standard text. Early-spelling versions of Wyatt's poems, with modern punctuation, can most readily be found in the edition of the *Collected Poems* by Kenneth Muir and Patricia Thomson (M&T).

Acknowledgements

In the course of writing this book I have benefited from the ideas and suggestions of more scholars, colleagues and students than I can adequately acknowledge. To a few I owe a particular debt of gratitude. Dr Janette Dillon read early drafts of much of this book and very generously shared her own research and expertise with me. My colleagues Dr Ralph Houlbrooke, David J. Williams, Philippa and Christopher Hardman and Dr Diane Purkiss have helped to shape my understanding of the early modern period and of the work of Wyatt and Surrey in particular. Professor Cedric Brown has been unfailingly encouraging and, through his organization of the triennial Early Modern History and English conferences at Reading, provided a pleasurable and stimulating forum for a rich exchange of ideas on the history and literature of the period. Professor Neil Keeble, editor responsible for the Renaissance titles in the Longman Medieval and Renaissance Library series, has also provided generous encouragement throughout the writing of this study.

My greatest debts, quite unrepayable, are to my family who have sacrificed so much to help me. Without their stoic patience and support, and the discriminating advice of my husband, Dr Graeme Watson, this book would not have been written. To him and to my daughters this book is dedicated with gratitude.

To
Graeme, Beatrice and Matilda

Introduction

> In the latter end of [King Henry VIII's] raigne sprong up a new company of courtly makers, of whom Sir Thomas Wyatt th'elder & Henry Earle of Surrey were the two chieftaines, who having travailed into Italie, and there tasted the sweete and stately measures and stile of the Italian Poesie . . . they greatly pollished our rude & homely maner of vulgar [vernacular] Poesie, from that it had bene before.

Thus wrote an arbiter of Elizabethan taste, George Puttenham, looking back from the 1580s.[1] For his generation, Wyatt and Surrey were 'the chief lanternes of light to all others that have since employed their pennes upon English Poesie',[2] glamorously aristocratic and Italianate models who first showed how to 'polish' what had previously been 'rude and homely'.

Puttenham's assessment has been shared by many later writers, but his emphasis on the Henrician poets' later influence distorts our perception of the poetry and ignores the vital relationship it has to the period of dramatic cultural and political change within which it was written. It may be that in our own 'post-modern' world we can, with particular interest, look back to the writing of the early Tudor period, to find, in their world of change and adjustment, striking parallels with our own. Modern developed Western society is one in which work brings intense pressures but also glamorous and enticing privileges, where those in elite professions are networked in a global intimacy from which the underclass are excluded, and where individuals are judged, valued and rewarded by performance, and easily expendable. This experience may encourage us to look with renewed interest and a livelier sympathy at texts produced within a court that was privileged and privileging, but also rapidly changing and, in the idiom of the day, 'slippery'; as pressurized, uncertain, lavish and cruel to its denizens as the modern world of international market forces now seems to us. The writings of Wyatt and Surrey, ambitious and politically prominent participants in that distant Henrician courtly world, can speak to us with extraordinary vividness of the desires and terrors, the manoeuvres and evasions, that attended success or failure in their world, and perhaps occasionally provide us with a perspective on the myths and bogies we construct to ease a passage through our own.

Of course, by thus looking back at the past through the perspective of our own concerns in the present, we, as did Puttenham, re-read and redefine. Such a process is continuous and unavoidable and may, indeed, be a gesture of profound indebtedness. Surrey began the process of reinterpretative homage in a series of elegies written immediately after Wyatt's death (see my discussion below, pp 19–21). In turn, Puttenham and his generation appropriated and mythologized Surrey himself, sometimes turning his writings to unforeseeable ends (for a brief account, see my Epilogue). In turn, readers of the late twentieth century may find, in these distant upper-class men who served an autocratic monarch in a world effectively bound by the limits of western Europe, unforeseen points of contact with our own experience.

In attempting to reinterpret the past, however, we must also respect its 'otherness', its difference from our own. A seductive version is offered by the 'heritage industry' which provides us with a powerful lens with which to look at a sanitized and picturesque past of costume drama clichés. Wyatt and Surrey could readily figure in a blockbuster epic or a mini-series, shot on location in carefully preserved Tudor palaces, with the characters, to include all six of Henry VIII's wives, dressed in accurately detailed period costume. There would be an abundance of lurid incident, almost to excess: ambassadorial adventures at the courts of foreign potentates, battles in the trenches before Boulogne, periodic imprisonments in the Tower, and many beheadings, including, in January 1547, that of Surrey himself, days before the old king's death. Poring over the material remnants of the past, the jewellery, palaces, paintings and texts, we must beware of constructing fantasy versions of ourselves in fancy dress.

I do not claim for my own approach a clear-eyed objectivity which keeps itself pure from ventriloquized voices and selective rearrangements of the facts. This study aspires to take its place in that process of re-reading and reinterpretation that is also, in a process that began with Surrey's elegy on Wyatt, an act of homage. The questions I ask have inevitably been shaped, sometimes no doubt in ways of which I am unaware, by my own place as a woman in a late twentieth-century Western urban culture, but I have also tried, as far as possible, to pay attention to the differences, cultural, historical and semantic, of the past.

My own reading has inevitably been shaped by previous studies, especially of Wyatt's poetry which, more than Surrey's, has absorbed the attention of twentieth-century readers. Earlier twentieth-century critics valued the sense the poetry yielded of Wyatt the man, a flawed but intense personality. For E. K. Chambers in the 1930s, Wyatt was a lover/poet 'watching his own emotions in detachment, with a finger on the burning pulse'.[3] H. A. Mason, twenty-five years later, thought Wyatt was better able 'to focus his whole personality' in the moral poems, the satires and the classical and biblical translations.[4] Most recently, Alastair Fox, in a highly biographical account of the man and his work, finds Wyatt in a 'perpetual search for some kind of emotional stability' within the exploitative power structures of the Henrician court.[5]

Such readings of Wyatt's poetry tend to identify the speaking voice of the poetry with that of the historical Wyatt. Focusing on the expressive 'I' speaker, they lose sight of the careful crafting of his voice, and of the conventions that govern his attitudes.[6] In the last few decades there has been a loss of critical faith in individual cultural and historical agency, a view influentially formulated in the work of Stephen Greenblatt whose chapter on Wyatt in *Renaissance Self-Fashioning* (1980) reads the poetry as deeply implicated in the discourses of its own time, fashioning a 'literary and social identity' within the constraints of the Henrician court.[7] Greenblatt's sympathetic readings of Wyatt's poems have themselves been criticized, however, for a slippage of critical point of view into identification with that of the poems' male personae and their often strongly misogynist attitudes.[8] As I shall argue in Chapter 2, there is some evidence that early sixteenth-century female readers were in fact the first sceptical critics of the poetry of Wyatt and his courtly contemporaries, as resistant as modern feminists to their persuasive male fictions.

Surrey's poetry has attracted less twentieth-century attention, perhaps because of modern, meritocratic discomfort with his princely social status. His poetry has sometimes seemed to modern tastes, in contrast to that of Wyatt, to epitomize 'the polished, the polite, and hence the trivial'.[9] The metrical smoothness and decorous sentiments of much of Surrey's verse, unlike the perceived 'roughness' of Wyatt's, have been felt to veil that sense of a raw personality, so sympathetic to modern taste. Earlier centuries, however, valued precisely the elegance and social status that we reject.

Surrey's name, rather than Wyatt's, appears on the title page of the first major printing of their poetry, Richard Tottel's *Songes and Sonettes* (1557), and until the early nineteenth century Surrey was regarded as pre-eminent, 'Wyatt's master in poetic composition'.[10]

Alongside critical fascination with Wyatt and Surrey as distinctive personalities and poetic innovators, much valuable work has been done on the conventions in which their poetry is embedded: the extent to which forms and topics must be understood in terms of literary genres, traditions, and the social contexts in which the poetry, particularly the courtly lyrics, circulated and were performed.[11] An important recent discussion is Arthur Marotti's study of the manuscript circulation of Renaissance lyrics, in which he emphasizes that the poems of Wyatt, Surrey and their courtly contemporaries were not written for print publication, but copied for circulation and exchange in manuscript form.[12] In this system, verses were sometimes ascribed to an author, sometimes not, and were often altered or appropriated to suit the tastes or purposes of copyist or collector. Such a system implies that we need to rethink the very concept of the author as someone who controls and authenticates the meaning of her or his text. Poems in manuscript circulation were not necessarily, or primarily, valued as biographical expressions of a known author, but as reusable texts, belonging to a shared culture: 'In the early modern era, especially in the manuscript environment, works were regarded as intrinsically open to supplementation, revision, excerpting, parody, and poetic answering and rejoinder.'[13]

A partial modern analogy might perhaps be found in the modern 'pop' song, collected, memorized, quoted, imitated and appropriated because of its ability to articulate the aspirations and the angst of a particular 'generation' rather than primarily as the production of any single songwriter. Of course some songwriters establish a reputation as particularly successful and accomplished, and in early Tudor manuscript collections of verse, Wyatt's name figures more frequently than any other named writer. Clearly Wyatt, and later Surrey, won reputations as successful and distinctive producers of verse. Nevertheless, the social embeddedness of courtly Tudor verse and its circulation through manuscript copying and collection reminds us of the shared, communal, if elitist, culture that these poems articulated.

Like modern 'pop' songs, amateur courtly verse of the 1530s and 1540s often deals with overtly political as well as conventionally amorous topics, and is integrally concerned with self-promotion and public image-making. The analogy serves to remind us that in unexpected ways our own culture may find points of contact with that distant culture of the Henrician court. In the following study, my argument will be that by trying to understand early Tudor poetry within its social contexts, we will gain a renewed sense of its vitality and the very modern-seeming anxieties and accommodations which it negotiates. In my first chapter, I shall examine the ideology of service at the Henrician court and the roles within it of Wyatt, the career courtier, and Surrey, a scion of a high nobility under threat from increasingly centralized government and the competing claims of 'new blood'. In Chapter 2, I shall turn to the arts of courting and ways in which courtly verse could register acute anxieties about a masculine identity forced to adapt to the demands of peacetime careers and the whims of royal favour. In Chapter 3, I shall consider the significance of choices of form and genre, and the kinds of voices and gestures offered by the fashionable Italian poetic 'kinds' available to aristocratic courtly poets in the 1530s and 1540s. Chapter 4 extends this enquiry to examine the genres and topics of the classical plain style, especially the epigram and satire, posing questions about the status and connotations of such genres and their power to shape and articulate weighty, virtuous and politically usable personae. Chapter 5 concludes the main body of this study by examining, within the context of the major religious changes of the period, the emergent genre of the vernacular psalm paraphrase and the very different, but equally political, uses to which it was put by Wyatt and Surrey. In a brief epilogue, I look forward to the immediate legacy of the poetry and reputations of Wyatt and Surrey, and some of the surprising transformations they underwent later in the sixteenth century.

NOTES

1. Puttenham, G. (1968) *The Arte of English Poesie (1589)*. Menston, Yorks.: The Scolar Press, p 48.
2. Ibid, p 50.
3. Chambers, E. K. (1933) *Sir Thomas Wyatt and Some Collected Studies*. London: Sidgwick & Jackson, p 130. For a useful anthology of twentieth-century criticism, see Thomson, P., ed. (1974) *Wyatt: The Critical Heritage*. London: Routledge & Kegan Paul; and for a brief survey, Foley, S. M. (1990) *Sir Thomas Wyatt*. Twayne English Authors series. Boston: G. K. Hall & Co., pp 108–10.
4. Mason, H. A. (1959) *Humanism and Poetry in the Early Tudor Period: An Essay*. London: Routledge & Kegan Paul, p 234.

5. Fox, A. (1989) *Politics and Literature in the Reigns of Henry VII and Henry VIII*. Oxford: Basil Blackwell, p 284.
6. This point is made very effectively by Crewe, J. (1991) *Trials of Authorship: Anterior Forms and Poetic Reconstruction from Wyatt to Shakespeare*. Berkeley and Los Angeles: University of California Press, ch 1.
7. Greenblatt, S. (1980) *Renaissance Self-Fashioning: From More to Shakespeare*. Chicago: University of Chicago Press, p 154.
8. Waller, M. (1989) 'The empire's new clothes: refashioning the Renaissance'. In *Seeking the Woman in Late Medieval and Renaissance Writings. Essays in Feminist Contextual Criticism*, eds S. Fisher and J. E. Halley. Knoxville: University of Tennessee Press, pp 160–83.
9. I quote Crewe (1991) p 24, summarizing others' views.
10. Quoted from Rollins 2 p 66. For my abbreviated references to a few commonly cited editions, see p vii. Tottel's volume is commonly known as *Tottel's Miscellany*. I shall normally refer to it in my text by this title.
11. See especially the studies by Thomson, P. (1964) *Sir Thomas Wyatt and His Background*. London: Routledge & Kegan Paul; Stevens, J. (1961) *Music and Poetry in the Early Tudor Court*. London: Methuen; Southall, R. (1964) *The Courtly Maker: An Essay on the Poetry of Wyatt and his Contemporaries*. Oxford: Basil Blackwell. Mason, H. A., ed. (1986) *Sir Thomas Wyatt: A Literary Portrait*. Bristol: Bristol Classical Press, provides very useful introductions and notes to a number of Wyatt's poems.
12. Marotti, A. (1995) *Manuscript, Print and the English Renaissance Lyric*. Ithaca, NY, and London: Cornell University Press.
13. From Marotti, A. (1989) 'Manuscript, print and the English Renaissance lyric'. In *The New Cultural History*, ed. L. Hunt. Berkeley: University of California Press, pp 209–21 (p 218).

Chapter 1

The King's Service

'IN COURT TO SERVE'

Although we are now familiar with the names of Sir Thomas Wyatt and Henry Howard, Earl of Surrey as poets, the writing of verse or, as they would have termed it themselves, balet-making, was only a very incidental part of their activities – a social grace to amuse friends, or a gesture (within the limits of manuscript circulation) of public self-presentation and self-definition.[1] The same is true for those other male courtly balet-makers whose names will, from time to time, figure throughout this book, men such as Sir Francis Bryan (*c.*1492–1550), George Boleyn, Viscount Rochford (*d.* 1536), George Blage (1512/13–1551) and Sir Edmund Knyvet (*c.*1508–51).[2] The primary calling and justification of such men was service to the commonwealth and the king: 'it is farre from the institucion of a gentleman to thinke himselfe borne to idlenes, to fede the belly and cloth the backe, to hawking, hunting, and receiving of rentes'; rather, 'shal such gentlemen be profitable to others, wel deservers of the comune welth, and worthy to possesse such landes and inheritaunce as god hath prepared for them'.[3] When Wyatt, in the penultimate line of his epigram 'Tagus, farewell' writes: 'My king, my country, alone for whom I live' (Reb. lx), he is, on one level, doing no more than giving fervent expression to an orthodox view of his vocation as a gentleman, dedicated to a public and royal service whose active fulfilment justified his privileged status and income.[4]

Although their names and poetry are commonly linked together, Wyatt and Surrey occupied distinctively different social positions within the ruling elite. Wyatt was the son of a man who had risen in Henry VII's service as an agent and administrator, fought under Henry VIII at the battle of the Spurs in 1513, and been appointed Keeper of the King's Jewels. For these services Sir Henry Wyatt, Thomas's father, was rewarded with a knighthood and an estate at

Allington Castle in Kent.[5] Surrey was the son of the premier nobleman in England and the grandson of the victor of Flodden. He was described in 1539 as 'the most folishe prowde boye that is in Englande'.[6] His writings and behaviour show him to have had, as did Henry VIII himself, an idealizing and romantic conception of history and chivalry, inherited in large part from the Burgundian chivalric culture that dominated the English court in the early part of the century.[7] Surrey's ancestry and abilities should by rights, in his own view, have given him a central place among the noble ruling elite. In this chapter, I shall review some aspects of the career of each man in order to suggest ways in which their distinctive ideologies of class and service helped to shape their verse. In different ways the writings of each are marked by the contradictions and tensions of service to the Tudor state and its king.

Traditionally, the role of the knight had been primarily military. A thirteenth-century treatise by Ramon Lull, translated as *The Book of the Ordre of Chyvalry* in 1484 by the printer Caxton, defined the office of the knight as 'to maintene and deffende his lord worldly or terrein' and 'to maintene the londe'.[8] Such service could be, and often was, administrative as well as military, but the highest prestige accrued to the armed knight whose 'noblesse of courage', or magnanimity, was demonstrated in the joust and on the battlefield.[9] Alongside this tradition, which stressed nobility of birth, was another, not necessarily in conflict, which emphasized the primacy of virtue over noble lineage.[10] Antagonism from the 'old nobility' was aroused, however, when such virtue was administrative and 'new' men were raised for their skill with the pen rather than with the sword. In the early sixteenth century humanist education produced able men who could not always boast a knightly ancestry, or distinguish themselves in the joust or on the battlefield, but who, through their education and service, claimed a right to gentle status. 'True nobility', wrote Henry's Latin secretary, the humanist Richard Pace, 'is made by virtue rather than a long pedigree.'[11]

The superior prestige of lineage and the traditional knightly service of arms remained, however, a powerful force. Mervyn James notes that 'even in peace the way of honour was the way of the sword, whose prestige was such that those who rose by other callings were often more than ready, given the opportunity, to take it'.[12] The gifted, but low-born, royal administrator Thomas Cromwell (*c.*1485–1540), for example, felt obliged to appear at the head of his men, armed at his own cost, for musters in 1539.[13] As late as 1555, the author of *The Institucion of a Gentleman* complained that gentlemen of the tongue and pen 'are nowe called upstartes, a terme lately invented by such as pondered not the groundes of honest meanes of rising', and asked 'whether maye a man be more worthely brought to dignitie by giftes of the mind or giftes of the body? I thinke no reasonable man will denye but that corporall giftes are not to be compared with giftes of the mind.'[14]

Sir Thomas Wyatt served Henry VIII as a local administrator in Kent, and as an ambassador, but he was also expected to behave as an armed knight, serving from 1528 to 1530 as High Marshal of the garrison city of Calais, and twice, after periods of disgrace in 1536 and 1541, called upon to give military service.[15] Thomas Becon, incumbent of the neighbouring Kentish parish of Brensett in 1538, felt it appropriate to dedicate his treatise *The New Pollicie of Warre* to Wyatt as a man 'apt for the godly administration of the public weal, no less in the perfect knowledge of the diversity of languages, than in the activity of martial affairs'.[16] For most of the knightly class and the nobility there continued to be no clear demarcation between military and administrative service. Surrey's father, the third Duke of Norfolk, repeatedly led Henry's armies, but he also gave service as a local magnate, ensuring the administration of Tudor power in his own area of Norfolk as well as serving as a privy councillor through much of the reign and, at one delicate moment in early 1540, as an ambassador.[17]

One of the political successes of the early Tudor monarchy was the transformation of a 'cult of chivalry . . . into a cult of service'.[18] Nevertheless tensions remained. A code that associated gentlemanly honour with masculine assertiveness existed alongside the client courtier's need for deference, flexibility and, on occasion, tolerance of humiliation – a conflict, in Richard McCoy's words, between 'aristocratic self-esteem and autonomy and the demands of obedience and duty to the monarch'.[19] A chivalric code, rooted in violence, was increasingly questioned and undermined by the more civic virtues and moral codes taught by Christian humanism and the new Reformed religion. Honour was the traditional mark of masculine prestige, but when its primary source was royal favour, definitions of honour old and new, communal and individual, might be brought into conflict.

Service to the king involved attendance at court, traditionally perceived as a place of idleness, vice and insecurity.[20] This perception was fuelled in the early sixteenth century by a humanist ideal of scholarly and virtuous freedom of mind which might be compromised by courtly service. Asked why he did not seek wealth and honour at the hands of kings, Raphael Hythloday, in Sir Thomas More's *Utopia*, replies: 'As it is, I now live as I please, which I surely fancy is very seldom the case with your grand courtiers.'[21] In place of the court, humanists sometimes recommended a life of virtuous retirement to the country to enjoy good conversation, liberty and a moderate diet.[22] Thus a popular Spanish treatise by Antonio de Guevara, translated into English by Sir Francis Bryan (like Wyatt a courtier and diplomat, and the dedicatee of two of Wyatt's poems), and published in 1548 as *A Dispraise of the life of a Courtier, and a commendation of the life of the labouryng man*, praised the gentleman who, retiring to his country estate, was 'all free and not su[b]jecte to any lord . . . without doing any homage or service to any man'.[23] There he would have 'time enough to study, time to visite his frendes, time to go a hunting'. The court, on the contrary, is a 'faire prison' where 'men employe the time so evil that from the time the courtier doeth arise, til he go to bed, he occupieth him selfe aboute nothing but in asking of newes, jetting about stretes, write letters, speake of the warres, entertein them that be in favor, counsell with bandes, make as he were in love and lese alwayes the time' (fol. d.iv^{v}). Even so, the treatise is uneasy about advocating withdrawal from the court, warning its readers against 'men that forsake the court to be more idle at home'(d.iv^{v}). Vigorous hunting, good reading and the conversation of sage friends should bolster virtue against the corruptions of idleness.

Wyatt's satire 'Mine own John Poyntz' takes its ironic place within the terms of such an opposition between virtuous retirement and corrupting courtly service. It is to a life strikingly close to that praised by Guevara, on the 'liberties' of his own estate and free from the newsmongering of the court, that Wyatt withdraws his disgruntled courtier:

> This maketh me at home to hunt and hawk
> And in foul weather at my book to sit;
> In frost and snow then with my bow to stalk.
> No man doth mark whereso I ride or go;
> In lusty leas in liberty I walk.
> And of these news I feel nor weal nor woe.
>
> (Reb. cxlix ll. 80–5)

The decision of Wyatt's speaker to quit the court and its corruptions is, however, complicated by the fact that in the country he has a 'clog' at his heels. A 'clog' was a block attached to the leg of a prisoner and here apparently refers to Wyatt's own enforced rustication to his father's estates in Kent, following a period of imprisonment after Anne Boleyn's fall in 1536. The choice, then, to leave the court is not as voluntary as it may at first appear. Within months, Wyatt was setting out to Spain to serve as Henry's resident ambassador at the court of the Emperor Charles V.[24] Sir Francis Bryan, the translator of Guevara's treatise dispraising the courtier's life, was also a lifelong courtier, notorious for rendering Henry sometimes venial service.[25] *The Dispraise of the Courtier's Life* and 'Mine own John Poyntz' should be seen primarily as satires, directing their attack on the court and its vices through the tactical lens of its opposite, a life of virtuous retirement. The texts work less as serious recommendations of a country life of self-indulgence than as the satirical jibing of insiders, expressing the frustrations and discontents attendant on a royal service which duty and ideology as much as economic self-interest forced upon them.

WYATT: THE DEVELOPING CAREER

Thomas Wyatt's father, Sir Henry, was clearly aware of how best to groom his eldest son for royal service in the new conditions of the Tudor monarchy. He gave him a thoroughly good humanist education, evident in the younger Wyatt's lifelong interest in translation and imitation of classical and prestigious continental models, as well as his command of languages: Latin, French and Italian, and probably Spanish.[26] His prose translation of an essay by the Greek stoic writer Plutarch, *The Quyete of Mynde*, published in 1528, probably at the instigation of Queen Katherine of Aragon, is one of the first of that series of translations from classical texts which marks the humanist educational endeavour in England.[27] His grooming for royal service was not, however, confined to an excellent education. In 1516, at the age of thirteen, he served as 'Sewer Extraordinary' (ceremoniously supervising the serving of dishes at table) at court. In 1524 he was made Clerk of the King's Jewels and by 1525 was an esquire of the royal body (one of Henry's closest personal servants) (*LL* p 4). At Christmas 1524, the chronicler, Edward Hall, records that Wyatt took part with other courtiers, including his brother-in-law, Sir George Cobham, Sir Francis Bryan and John Poyntz, in an elaborate tournament over a number of days. Its fiction, a defence of the Castle of Loyalty in which four ladies of the court were placed, was the stuff of romance and literary chivalry, but the fighting itself was evidently serious practice for real wars.

On this occasion it got out of hand when some of the participants began hurling stones at their opponents, hurting some bystanders in the process.[28]

This incident demonstrates a violent and aggressive edge to such courtly entertainment. The ladies in the castle and the queen herself, presiding among the spectators, were there to add grace and romance, part of the fictional display. They were neither the real occasion nor the primary audience, who, on this occasion, were Scottish ambassadors in London to negotiate a treaty. In a similar assault on a 'château vert' in 1522, the figure of Perseverance had been played by Anne Boleyn, the daughter of a Kentish neighbour of the Wyatts, who had returned from France in 1521 after a number of years spent acquiring courtly polish at two of the most sophisticated courts of Europe, the Netherlandish court of Margaret of Austria, Charles V's sister, and the French court itself.[29] As I shall suggest in the next chapter, the courtly lyrics and balets with which Wyatt, like other courtly gentlemen, entertained friends and potential patrons in quieter moments and on less explicitly aggressive occasions, may be understood in a similar context of a need to assert masculine credentials in aggression and competitive display. Like tournaments, balets were designed as much to vaunt the machismo and display the skill of the writer, as to please and divert an ostensibly female audience.

Accomplished performance in the various pastimes of the court was a necessary prelude to promotion in the royal service, but once in post, effective action was expected. Wyatt was given an opportunity on a brief embassy to France in the company of Sir Thomas Cheney in 1526, where he showed he had 'as much wit to mark and remember everything he seeth as any young man hath in England' (*LL* p 6). In January 1527 he made his own opportunity when he met Sir John Russell at the outset of an embassy to the papal court and on the spur of the moment decided to 'aske leave, get mony and goe with you'.[30] A readiness to take advantage of opportunities, even with a certain recklessness, seems to have been characteristic of Wyatt throughout his career. On this occasion, Wyatt was able, when Russell broke his leg, to take his place, carrying to Venice proposals for a league against Spain. While in Italy, Wyatt set off, in spite of the dangerous and unsettled condition of the northern Italian states, 'to see the countries' before returning to Rome. He was captured by Spanish troops after visiting Ferrara, but soon freed. He left Rome shortly before its sack by Imperial troops in May 1527 (*LL* pp 6–8).

Wyatt's promising career developed steadily. His post, from late 1528 to November 1530, as high marshal of Calais, the English garrison town in France, was a prestigious one. The historian S. J. Gunn remarks that 'senior offices [there] were much in demand among peers and courtiers, selling for considerable sums' partly because they paid well and partly because good service there (involving some military service) could lead to advancement.[31] By the end of 1530, however, he was back at court resuming his place as esquire of the royal body (*LL* p 25). By this point he was probably already giving service to Thomas Cromwell in the latter's bid, through client landowners in Kent, to extend government control of the county.[32] Cromwell was to remain a powerful and valuable patron until 1540, when his fall threatened Wyatt's fortunes. Meanwhile, as a young courtier about town, Wyatt seems to have behaved with the aggressive bravado typical of his class and gender in the early modern period. Involved in a 'great affray' with the 'serjeants of London' in 1534, in which one of them was killed, Wyatt was briefly imprisoned (*LL* p 25). Such incidents may be seen as a manifestation of the 'competitive assertiveness' of the contemporary male honour code.[33]

For Wyatt, as for many at Henry's court, 1536 proved a climactic year. Queen Anne Boleyn's fall in May, accused of adultery with a number of courtiers, including her brother, led to Wyatt's imprisonment, probably on suspicion of being one of her lovers. For some reason, possibly Cromwell's patronage, he did not suffer the fate of the queen and the other accused 'lovers', but was rusticated to his father's safe-keeping in the country. In one of those vertiginous turns of fortune so typical of courtly service in the latter part of Henry's reign, a mere month or two later Wyatt was trusted to lead a command of Kentish men against the uprising known as the Pilgrimage of Grace (*LL* p 36), and in January 1537, as we have noted, was appointed to the crucially important post of resident ambassador at the court of the Holy Roman Emperor, Charles V, in his dominions in Spain. Wyatt was said to have commented on these dizzying turns of fortune: 'Goddes bloud, the kinge sett me in the tower and afterwarde sent me for his embassadoure. Was not this, I praye you, a pretie way to gett me credet?' (*LL* pp 200–1).

The experiences of 1536 must have confirmed for Wyatt the old truisms about the inconstancy of courts and of favour, repeatedly figured in literature, by the rule of a wilful, duplicitous female:

> For why, when one commeth new to the court, my lady dame gorgious, ledes him a traine, she entertaines him, she makes muche on

> him, she calles him: but when she spieth him to lacke, she sendes him to pasture in the bare fieldes.[34]

In subsequent chapters I shall argue that much of Wyatt's poetry can be understood in terms of its negotiation between what was conceived of as the dangerous charisma of a riggish court, and a defensive rhetoric of male self-determination and honour. In the following section, I shall focus on Wyatt's diplomatic service, and especially the central importance for it of a skilful mastery of language. The wily verbal manipulation we find in Wyatt's diplomatic letters and in his 'Defence', written in 1541, helps us to a better understanding of Wyatt's crafty dexterity in his poems.

WYATT'S DIPLOMACY

In his elegy on Wyatt, Surrey praised the elder poet's tongue:

> that served in forein realmes his king;
> Whose courtous talke to vertue did enflame
> Eche noble hart; a worthy guide to bring
> Our English youth by travail unto fame.
>
> (Jones no. 28 ll. 17–20)

As the stanza moves from 'forein realmes' to 'English youth', it opens a gap between the teaching of virtue and forcign service. The virtue seems an additional and separate effect of Wyatt's tongue, not a result of his ambassadorial duties. Garett Mattingly has associated the growing use of resident ambassadors at the end of the fifteenth and beginning of the sixteenth centuries with the growth of the nation-state and a shift from a rhetoric of the public good of Christendom to one of service to master and country first; the ambassador becomes, in a famous *bon mot* of a later ambassador, Sir Henry Wotton, 'an honest man sent to lie abroad for the good of his country'.[35] The continuing presence of an idealized rhetoric of the public weal of Christendom continues to be everywhere apparent in the official prose of Wyatt's ambassadorial instructions, but it is found alongside more nationally self-interested considerations. When in November 1539, for example, Wyatt was sent to resume his post as resident ambassador to Charles V, he was told to congratulate the emperor on his accord with the French king, Francis I, and declare that Henry VIII 'cannot a little rejoice to see those two Princes, being both his friends, allies and confederates, so happy both towards themselves and toward the public weal of Christendom as they seem to be'.[36] In spite of such amiable expressions,

Wyatt's real business, as the letter made clear, was, with his fellow ambassador Edmund Bonner, 'to bend, and use all their wisdoms and dexterities to ensearch and investigate by all ways and means to them possible, how things do stand and shall proceed between the Emperor and the French King . . . and by what means the said Princes have been brought at this time together'.[37] After his break with Rome, Henry VIII was dangerously isolated in Europe, and any alliance between the two most powerful Catholic monarchs in Europe, Charles and Francis, was bad news.

An ambassador represented the dignity of his king and might act as a counsellor as well as, within tight controls, a negotiator on important matters of state. He was expected to behave in a manner and live in a fashion consonant with his king's status and pretensions, albeit with inadequate resources, irregularly supplied.[38] When Edmund Bonner accused Wyatt of treason in 1538 and again in 1541, one of Wyatt's counter-accusations was that his fellow ambassador was 'meter to be parrishe preste' than the king's representative, and that his 'unmanerly behaviour . . . made ye a laughehing stocke to all men that came in your companye and me sume time to swete [sweat] for shame to see you' (*LL* pp 203–4). In his turn Bonner clearly found Wyatt's courtly ease with the emperor galling, accusing him of going on jaunts with Charles to 'a place of nunnes, wher the fest and solempnite was kept, talking with themperour all the waye, and after such mery sorte and fashion that expostulation was turned to oblivion' (*LL* p 66).

Back-biting and the spying of fellow diplomats was only one of the dangers attendant on service abroad. If the ambassador was embraced and favoured when things were going well diplomatically, equally he could be excluded and humiliated when things went badly. As Wyatt's correspondence makes painfully clear, the position of resident ambassador was one usually occupied by a gentleman or churchman of a middling sort, with little claim to dignity in his own right. On royal journeys and at the meetings of kings, the ambassadors of other monarchs ranked low, with no thought being taken for their need for horses or for their lodgings. Wyatt complained of trotting 'throughe heate and stinke' in Nice in 1538 or wading 'with much ado apon plow horse in the diepe and fowle way' in France in 1539 (*LL* pp 181, 104).

Nevertheless an ambassadorial post brought with it considerable opportunities for an ambitious man, as well as risks and hardships. A willingness to do his king bold service in the murky world of European diplomacy, even to the point of foolhardiness, seems to have been particularly characteristic of Wyatt. A decision to send his secretary Mason into the enemy camp to 'sucke out' information from the English traitor, Cardinal Pole, in 1538 helped to land Wyatt in the Tower on treason charges in 1541. Other risky initiatives included a 'practise that is offerd me for Italy, to kendle ther a fier' too secret to be communicated except by word of mouth (*LL* pp 92–3). Wyatt wrote in his own defence in 1541: 'If a mane shulde be dreven to be so scrupulouse to do nothinge withowt warrant, manye occasions of good service shulde schape [escape] him' (*LL* p 184).

An incident that illustrates both Wyatt's ambitious recklessness and his ability to extricate himself through a deft command of language occurred in 1540. Wyatt and Bonner plotted to arrest, on French soil, one of Pole's agents, an extraordinary character known as Robert Brancestor.[39] The plot failed, causing an international incident, and Wyatt's long letter of explanation and excuse, written to Henry VIII, is a masterpiece of self-glorification and self-justification (*LL*, letter no. 20). Wyatt casts himself initially as the hero of the hour, stalking Brancestor to his room where he stumbled on the threshold, hurting his leg, 'that in dede I fere me will not be hole this month'. Nevertheless, Wyatt 'reched to have set hand apon lettres that he [Brancestor] was writing, but he cawght them afore me and flang them bak ward in to the fire. Yet I overthrew him and crached [crushed?] them owt' (*LL* p 117). Unfortunately Brancestor got away and went to Charles V, then a guest in France, for protection. With professional thoroughness Wyatt gives a verbatim account of his subsequent, and undoubtedly humiliating, interview with the emperor: 'And I tell yow againe, it was not well done off yow to do him to be taken' (*LL* p 123). Nevertheless, as the letter progresses, Wyatt is able to recover from this debacle to salvage an interpretation designed to flatter Henry by suggesting that the emperor's 'evill handling of your subjectes' (his own dressing-down) should be seen as a tit-for-tat action revealing the emperor's fear of Henry's own alliance with the Germans: 'to this me thinketh partainith the rownd wordes he givith me'. Wyatt finally shifts into the rhetoric of the counsellor: 'Iff it plesid your maiestie to command me to say my simple opinion in this matter . . .' (*LL* p 128).

On 3 February 1540, Wyatt was summoned from his sick bed, his head so painful that he was 'able skant to write iii lines togider', to face Charles's anger once again, 'not ons or twise, but offten, he clippid my tale with imperius and brave wordes enow' (*LL* pp 139,

134). Henry, through Wyatt, had accused him of 'ingratitude' in harbouring an English traitor. Charles testily replied that he could not be 'Ingrate. The inferiour may be Ingrate to the greter, and the terme is skant sufferable bitwene like' (*LL* p 135). In an acutely precedent-conscious world, this could be used to open a can of worms, and Wyatt spotted the potential for discord. The Duke of Norfolk was at once sent to Francis I to tell him of Charles's words, which must mean he 'aims at monarchy', and ask for French advice in formulating a reply to Charles.[40] The word was clearly being used to aggravate strains already becoming apparent between Francis and the emperor. On hearing the words, Norfolk reported, Francis gratifyingly showed signs of displeasure: 'he altered something in gesture, looking very earnestly at him'.[41] In turn, the emperor wrote to Francis putting a different interpretation on his words.[42] The word 'ingrate', manipulated by the English to do as much damage as possible to Franco-Spanish relations, passed back and forth in diplomatic correspondence between various main powers for the rest of February and into March.[43]

Wyatt's verbal alertness and his sense of shifts of meaning in the subtle nuancing of words are again evident in his effort to extricate himself from the consequences of an earlier recklessness. Edmund Bonner's charges, first made in 1538, accused him of, among other matters, treasonable association with Cardinal Pole (*LL* pp 63–9). In 1538, Cromwell proved a 'good lord' to his client Wyatt and managed to block any potential damage to Wyatt's reputation and career. With Cromwell's fall and execution in July 1540, the charges were revived. In January 1541, Wyatt was arrested and taken, bound and fettered, to the Tower. Feeling, no doubt, that now, if ever, was a time for persuasive words, Wyatt composed in the Tower a 'Defence' which he seems to have hoped would have been seen or heard by his judges, and perhaps by the king himself. No trial ever took place, but the 'Defence' survives in manuscript and demonstrates, not only Wyatt's consummate skill with words, but also his extraordinary awareness of the slipperiness of words and the mobility of meaning.

The 'Defence' is a lengthy document and is reprinted in whole by Kenneth Muir in *LL* (pp 187–209). I shall focus on Wyatt's answer to only one of Bonner's accusations, that 'Mr. Wyat . . . forbereth not to make exclamations and after this sorte. "By goodes bludde, ye shall see the kinge our maister cast out at the carts tail, and if he soo be served, by godds body, he is well served" ' (*LL* p 67), or, as Wyatt himself repeats it, 'the kinge shulde be caste owte of a Cartes arse'. The accusation has credibility because it clearly draws on Wyatt's mode of speech: 'by cawse I am wonte some time to rappe owt an othe in an erneste tawlke, looke how craftilye theye have put in an othe . . . to maike the matter seme mine' (*LL* p 199). But supposing he had spoken some such words, what was meant by them? 'What say my accusares in thes wordes? Do theye swere I spake them traiterously or maliciously?' Do all the witnesses agree about the precise words Wyatt was supposed to have used? If not, 'let us here the woordes theye varie in. For in some littell thinge may apere the truthe'. Besides, small variations in words may make significant differences:

> For in this thinge 'I fere', or 'I truste', semethe but one smale syllable changed, and yet it makethe a great differaunce, and may be of an herer wronge conceaved and worse reported, and yet worste of all altered by an examiner. Againe 'fall owte', 'caste owte', or 'lefte owte' maketh differaunce, yea and the settinge of the wordes one in an others place may maike greate differaunce, tho the wordes were all one – as 'a mill horse' and 'a horse mill'. I besiche you therfore examen the matter under this sorte. Confere theire severall sayinges togither, confer th'examinations upone the same matter and I dare warrante ye shall finde misreportinge and misunderstandinge.
>
> (*LL* pp 196–7)

Words are indeed slippery things, especially proverbs. Even had he used such a proverb, what did it mean? Not, 'which god forbede shulde be thought of anye man – that by throwinge owte of a cartes ars I shulde mene that vile deathe that is ordained for wretchede theves' (alluding to the practice of hanging men by pushing them off the back of a cart). No, Wyatt explains, this is 'a commen proverbe . . . and it is taken upon packinge gere togither for cariage. That that is evell taken heede to, or negligently, slippes owte of the carte and is loste'. All he would have meant (had he used the words) was that Henry VIII would be left out of a treaty concluded at Nice in 1538 between Charles V and Francis I, 'And in communication with some paradventure castinge this parrels I might say "I fere for all these menes faier promises the kinge shalbe lefte owte of the cartes ars" and lament that mainye good occasions had bene lett slipe of concludinge with one of ther princes'.[44] Wyatt claims innocence and transparency for his own words (had he ever spoken them), while with a finely honed art he attributes distortion and malice to his enemies.

In his sonnet 'There was never file half so well filed' (Reb.

xxxii), Wyatt represents the 'I' speaker as the victim of the dishonest manipulation of others:

> There was never file half so well filed
> To file a file for every smith's intent
> As I was made a filing instrument
> To frame other, while I was beguiled.

The paradox is that the speaker's own filed eloquence undermines, even as it crafts, his verbal innocence. Wyatt's poetry, as does his prose, negotiates a world of sliding signifiers in which there is no transparency.

Wyatt was freed in March 1541. It is an appropriately ironic comment on the Henrician world Wyatt's writings evoke that his freedom was not won by this bold and skilful 'Defence', but by means of his monarch's amorous obsession with his latest wife, Katherine Howard. As she sailed down the Thames with her husband, she pleaded for Wyatt's pardon, perhaps through the intervention of her cousin, the Earl of Surrey.[45] Wyatt was pardoned on condition that he take back the wife from whom he had been separated for 'upwards of fifteen years' (*LL* p 209). Katherine Howard's own marital infidelities were to be discovered eight months later, but there was no pardon for her.

SURREY, WYATT AND ELEGY

Wyatt's well-honed words may have helped him indirectly. If Henry Howard, Earl of Surrey did prompt his cousin to speak to the king on Wyatt's behalf, he may have been responding to a poem by Wyatt, 'Sometime the pride of my assured truth' (Reb. cclxvii), probably addressed to Surrey and sent to him with a psalm paraphrase, which implies that the poet needed help in the face of injustice and malice.[46] Patronage was extended by Surrey to Wyatt's son, Sir Thomas Wyatt the Younger, who appears on records as Surrey's companion in 1543, and under his command at Boulogne in 1545–6. When Wyatt died in October 1542 while riding to meet a Spanish envoy at Falmouth, Surrey took the unprecedented step for an aristocrat of publishing his own elegy, 'Wyatt resteth here' (Jones no. 28), with three elegaic sonnets (Jones nos. 29, 30, 31) which appeared within weeks of Wyatt's death. Surrey was almost certainly also instrumental in the production and publication of a series of elegaic poems on Wyatt, written and published in the same period by the humanist scholar and antiquarian Leland.[47]

Unlike Leland, who imagines the gods of war and poetry, Mars and Phoebus, fighting over their claim to Wyatt's spirit and who stresses Wyatt's status as a local magnate by invoking his estates and provincial offices, Surrey represents Wyatt as a man of language and the pen. Only very passing attention is paid to Wyatt as soldier in the single line (29) 'his valiant corps, where force and beawty met'. Instead, Surrey's elegy 'emblazons' (in origin a heraldic figure, describing armorial bearings) Wyatt as a humanist, substituting head, face, tongue and hand for the more traditional symbols of chivalry and lineage.[48] Wyatt's hand, 'that taught what might be said in ryme', is firmly associated with the pen, not the sword.

The Wyatt that emerges from Surrey's elegy is a model of a certain kind of service to the state: counsellor, diplomat and writer, devoted selflessly to the common weal:

> A hed, where wisdom misteries did frame;
> Whose hammers bet still in that lively brain — *bet: beat*
> As on a stithe, where that some work of fame — *stithe: anvil*
> Was daily wrought to turne to Britaines gain . . .
>
> (ll. 5–8)

However, such service was not properly rewarded:

> W. resteth here, that quick could never rest;
> Whose heavenly giftes encreased by disdain
> And vertue sank the deper in his brest:
> Such profit he by envy could obtain.
>
> (ll. 1–4)

Wyatt's 'rest'lessness suggests vitality and activity, but also the exhausting demands made on him by the state; he was not allowed to rest. The word 'profit' is also barbed, especially in the light of Wyatt's own satirical epistle to Bryan which represents the rewards of royal service as 'honest poverty' (Reb. cli, l. 86). By the end of Surrey's elegy, Wyatt has become a saint-like, self-sacrificing figure of virtue. Tromly suggests the wording of the final lines echoes the description, in Paul's Epistle to the Hebrews, of those 'witnesses' of faith '"Of whom the world was not worthy" (Hebrews 11.38)' and who 'encourage the living to "run with patience the race that is set before us" (Hebrews 12.1)':[49]

> But to the heavens that simple soul is fled,
> Which left with such as covet Christ to know
> Witnesse of faith that never shall be ded;
> Sent for our helth, but not received so.

Thus, for our gilte, this jewel have we lost.
The earth his bones, the heavens possesse his gost.

(ll. 33–8)

Surrey's version of Wyatt has a polemical purpose. He shapes a model of truthful and unself-seeking effort for the common weal which implicitly reflects on other rising office-holders in royal service, men who like Wyatt serve through the pen rather than the sword, but who unlike Wyatt are rapacious and self-seeking. In the present age, the poem implies, Wyatt's example of faithful service is an isolated one. His race has been run in spite of others, 'happy, alas, to[o] happy, but for foes' (l. 30) whose envious vices and venial ambitions now seem to prevail. The obverse of Surrey's praise of Wyatt is his remark, during his trial in 1547, to the highly educated but low-born Secretary of State Sir William Paget, 'the kingdom has never been well since the King put mean creatures like thee into the government'.[50]

Surrey's own role in relation to the virtuous Wyatt is more fully developed in three elegaic sonnets which accompanied the longer elegy. In 'Divers thy death' (Jones no. 29), Surrey differentiates himself from those who 'Yeld Cesars teres uppon Pompeius hedd', identifying his own voice as that of the sole true mourner. In the second, Surrey and 'Wyattes frendes' can only yield tears to honour Wyatt, unlike past ages which, 'ruder' in sophistication but greater in spirit, deified those who 'taught / Artes to reverte to profite of our life' (Jones no. 30). The third, 'The great Macedon' (Jones no. 31), again looks back to a previous age, and the rich 'ark' in which Alexander placed Homer's *Iliad*, to ask 'What holly grave, what wourthy sepulture / To Wyates Psalmes shulde Christians then purchase?' No modern monarch will similarly honour Wyatt's poems:

Where Rewlers may se in a mirrour clere
The bitter frewte of false concupiscense,
How Jewry bought Urias deathe full dere.
In Princes hartes Goddes scourge yprinted depe
Might them awake out of their sinfull slepe

If present rulers, and one in particular, will not honour Wyatt's psalms then Surrey will take on Alexander's role through his elegaic poems. Surrey represents himself complexly as the patron and protector of a wise and saintly Wyatt, but also as a kind of apostle, bearing witness to Wyatt's 'witnesse of faith'.

It is no accident that a number of Surrey's finest poems are elegies. The elegy, like the complaint, another genre which Surrey repeatedly uses, voices nostalgia and alienation, bewailing loss and disempowerment in the present while looking back to a former happiness identified in Surrey's poems with an idealized, and in many respects conservative, social and moral order. Such a pattern is particularly clear in a poem, 'So crewell prison' (Jones no. 27), which is both a complaint on present imprisonment and an elegy on the friend of Surrey's early youth, Henry Fitzroy, Duke of Richmond, the illegitimate son of Henry VIII, who died of consumption at the age of seventeen in July 1536.[51] As in the elegy on Wyatt, with which it shares its stanzaic form, the poet represents himself as an isolated witness of a virtue that has gone. Fitzroy, however, exemplifies for Surrey a very different class and kind of action from that embodied by Wyatt.

Surrey sets the poem in Windsor where Richmond and Surrey spent some of their teenage years between 1530 and 1536, recreating an aristocratic world of privileged pastime in which the chivalric idealism of the youths merges into a golden world of literary romance:[52]

> The graveld ground, with sleves tied on the helme, — *a lady's sleeve tied on the helmet as a favour*
> On fominge horse, with swordes and frendlie hertes,
> With chere as thoughe the one should overwhelme,
> Where we have fought and chased oft with dartes . . .
>
> The secret groves, which ofte we made resound
> Of pleasaunt plaint and of our ladies praies, — *praies: praise*
> Recording soft what grace eche one had found,
> What hope of spede, what dred of long delayes.
>
> (ll. 17–20, 25–8)

Richmond's death deprived Surrey of a beloved companion, with all that term's chivalric connotations of mutual love and loyalty.[53] The timing of the death, coinciding as it did with the disgrace and execution of Surrey's cousin, Queen Anne Boleyn, and Henry's new marriage to Jane Seymour, must have dealt Surrey's ambitions and status a severe blow. In 'So crewell prison' Surrey looks back on his golden companionship with Richmond from a changed perspective, with his 'fredome' (unrestrained aristocratic will, as well as 'liberty') forcibly curtailed:[54]

> Thus I alone, where all my fredome grew,
> In prison pine with bondage and restraint.
>
> (ll. 51–2)

Nearly ten years after Richmond's death, Surrey had an image of himself painted leaning against a broken pillar on which is written 'Sat super est' ('enough survives'). In the background is the outline of ruins. The painting seems to allude to Richmond's death and the potential ruin of Surrey's early ambitions.[55]

SURREY: FINDING A ROLE

Aristocratic pride, and disdain of the newly ennobled Seymours, is displayed in an oblique poem, 'Eache beeste can chuse his feere', attributed to Surrey by Tottel, which uses heraldic animal imagery apparently to refer to aspects of Surrey's own biography.[56] A proud but 'gentill' lion 'which seemid well to leade the race' (lions featured on the Howard heraldic shield) is scorned by a wolf (perhaps an allusion to the arms of Anne Stanhope, who had married Edward Seymour). The lion boasts of coming from a 'race, / That with his pawes a crowned kinge devoured in the place' (an apparent reference to Surrey's grandfather, the victor of Flodden, where James IV of Scotland was killed). The poem also seems to allude to Surrey's uncle, Lord Thomas Howard, who died in the Tower in 1537 where he had been imprisoned for forming an engagement, without permission, with the king's niece, Margaret Douglas:

> my blood is not untrew;
> Ffor you your self dothe know, it is not long agoe,
> Sins that, for love, one of the race did end his life in woe
> In towre both strong and highe, for his assured truthe.
> Wheare as in teares he spent his breath, alas! the more the ruthe
> (ll. 34–8)[57]

The Howard lion is of a superior, wilder, breed than the wolf, who is associated both with a craven nature and with effeminate/feminine courting behaviours:

> My kind, is to desire the honour of the field,
> And you, with blood to slake your thurst of suche as to you yelde.
> Wherefore I wolde you wist, that for your coy lookes *wist: knew*
> I am no man that will be traind, nor tanglid bye suche hookes;
> And thoughe some list to bow, wheare blame full well they might,
> And to such beastes a currant fawne, that shuld have travaile bright,
> I will observe the law that nature gave to me,
> To conqueare such as will resist, and let the rest go free.
> (ll. 51–8)

This is the ideology of aristocratic 'noblesse of courage' proper to the chivalric knight: 'Chivalry and Fraunchise accorden togider . . . for the knight must be free and franke'.[58]

Richmond's death seems to have caused a serious loss of direction to Surrey's career. In July 1537, Norfolk, writing to Cromwell from the north of England where he was engaged in reasserting royal military control after the Pilgrimage of Grace, referred to his concern for his son's health: 'his nature running from him abundantly . . . he was in that case a great part of the last year, and as he showed me came to him for thought of my lord of Richmond, and now I think is come again by some other thought. He is there with his wife, which is an ill medicine for that purpose.'[59] The allusion to Surrey's wife seems to suggest that Norfolk felt his son was behaving with too much womanish weakness. He asked leave to send for Surrey, perhaps believing that he needed to see some active, manly service.

For Surrey, and those like him who shared an ideology of masculine knightly 'noblesse of courage', a reputation for sloth or womanishness was a potentially serious stain to honour.[60] Nine years later, Sir William Paget warned Surrey: 'if you should now tarry at home within a wall . . . it would be thought abroad I fear, that either you were desirous to tarry in a sure place of rest, or else . . . that you were taken here for a man of [little] activity and service'.[61] Restless activity in his country's service was above all what Surrey praised in Wyatt. Opportunities for honourable activity seem, however, to have repeatedly eluded Surrey, and his own poetry often gives voice to a sense of frustrated restlessness. In a sonnet, probably written at the same time as 'So crewell prison', during a period of imprisonment or confinement in 1537, Surrey's body is forced into inactivity: Windsor's walls 'sustained my wearied arme, / My hand my chin, to ease my restless hedd' (Jones no. 26). The only action that seems possible is to let himself fall, 'And I half bent to throwe me down withall'. The poet's 'restless hedd' fretfully recalls scenes of restlessness, 'the hateles shorte debate, / The rakhell life that longes to loves disporte' in which honourable activity contrasts with his present dishonourable confinement.

In the mid- and late 1530s, Surrey's opportunities for active service were meagre. Signs of frustration, or perhaps of the behaviour that made his king wary of employing him, are evident in repeated incidents such as that which put him in prison at Windsor in 1537, or that in 1542, when he was imprisoned in the Fleet prison for challenging one John a Leigh.[62] Even more serious was an incident in 1543 when Surrey, accompanied by Sir Thomas Wyatt's son and other friends, went on the rampage in London 'with four stone bows, and tarried forth till after midnight . . . breaking of glass windows, both of houses and churches, and shooting of men in the streets'.[63] He could scarcely have helped himself by claiming, as he does in the satire 'London hast thow', that he acted as the instrument of God's vengeance on the city (see my discussion below). In a letter to the Privy Council following the incident involving John a Leigh in 1542, Surrey's submission is mixed with a certain amount of aristocratic self-justification: 'Yet, let my youth unpractised in durance obtain pardon.'[64] A gentleman such as he is only needs a 'gentle warning to learn how to bridle my heady will'. Here we can see Surrey drawing on the same aristocratic sense of a 'free and franke' nature as an aspect of his noble birth that we saw in 'So crewell prison' and 'Eche beeste can chuse his feere'. Indeed, he represents his violence, due 'to the fury of rechless youth', as evidence of the courage and boldness which would make him fit for royal service: 'this simple body rashly adventured in the revenge of mine own quarrel, shall be without respect always ready to be employed in his service'.

A chance for such military service came in 1543 when Henry VIII, now in alliance with Charles V, agreed to wage war against France. The excitement of Surrey and his sovereign at the prospect of war with France was undoubtedly encouraged by chivalric romance and such chronicle histories as Froissart's account of English fourteenth-century campaigns in France which had been translated, at the request of Henry VIII himself, by Sir Francis Bryan's uncle and Surrey's half-uncle, John Bourchier, Lord Berners. 'What pleasure shall it be to the noble gentlemen of England to see, behold and read the high enterprises, famous acts and glorious deeds done and achieved by their valiant ancestors?' wrote Berners in his preface.[65] Evidence that such sentiments influenced hardened captains in the field is provided by the leader of the English forces in the 1543 campaign, Sir John Wallop, who challenged the French garrison of Thérouanne 'to a six-a-side jousting match'.[66] It is through such a romantic lens that Surrey views the Trojan war in his balet 'When raging love':

> I call to minde the navye greate
> That the grekes brought to Troye towne . . .
>
> And how that in those ten yeres warre
> Ful manye a bloudie dede was done,

And manye a lord, that came full farre,
There caught his bane, alas, to sone,
And many a good knight overronne,
Before the Grekes had Helene wonne.

(Jones no. 1 ll. 7–8, 13–18)

Surrey's birth and ancestry placed him squarely within such an ideology of chivalric military prestige. On 9 October 1543, Surrey was sent by Henry VIII to join the English and Imperial armies besieging Laundrecy so that 'by experience of war . . . [he] may succeed to the honourable qualities of his relatives'.[67] The camps at Laundrecy, however, did not entirely live in the chivalric world evoked by the complimentary language of their leaders. While there, Surrey inspected the latest ballistic weaponry, 'artificial bullets' which on landing 'leaped from place to place, casting out fire; and within a while after, burst forth, and shoot off guns out of him an hundreth shot'.[68] Even here, as a fêted young star, there are signs of impolitic action on Surrey's part. A note in cipher from the Imperial ambassador in England refers to a 'foolish letter' from Surrey to Henry of which the king did not approve and concerning which the emperor might justifiably demand an apology.[69]

Malcolm Vale, in his study of chivalry and war at the end of the Middle Ages, argues that while the trappings and language of chivalry remained vital into the sixteenth century, the military knightly class in fact showed themselves able and willing to adapt to the new technologies of war. Both the language of chivalry, and a professional interest in the modern technologies of war, are clearly evident in Surrey's writings in connection with the 1544–6 campaigns in France. In the epitaph 'Norfolk sprang thee', the death of Surrey's companion, Thomas Clere, is transformed into a trumpeting chivalric blazon:

Norfolk sprang thee, Lambeth holds thee dead,
Clere of the County of Cleremont though hight; *hight: named*
Within the wombe of Ormondes race thou bread,
And sawest thy cosine crowned in thy sight.
Shelton for love, Surrey for Lord thou chase:
Ay me, while life did last that league was tender;
Tracing whose steps thou sawest Kelsall blaze,
Laundersey burnt, and battered Bullen render.
At Muttrell gates, hopeles of all recure,
Thine Earle halfe dead gave in thy hand his Will

(Jones no. 35 ll. 1–10)

Here the chivalric ideals of the mutual bond of trust between the squire and his lord, and his faithful service to a lady, are set in the context of a roll-call of famous battles. The epitaph successfully disguises the grimmer realities of modern warfare: the retaliatory, unopposed burning of Kelso in 1543, the capitulation of Boulogne through the efforts of mining and ballistics experts in 1544, and Clere's probable death from dysentery or a similar disease, caught in the rain-sodden trenches before Montreuil where illness decimated the English troops.[70]

Surrey's excitement at military command and his professional interest in the modern science of war is evident in letters he wrote to Henry when, in 1545, on the sudden deaths of two commanders in the field, he was appointed Henry's 'Lieutenant General of the King on Sea and Land' for England's continental possessions, based in Boulogne.[71] From Surrey's point of view, he had for once been in the right place at the right time, and through the autumn of 1545 his 'lucky succeedings . . . prospered'.[72] However, Surrey's opportunity was beset by political problems. Henry's Privy Council in London, aware of the huge financial burden of defending Boulogne, urged Surrey to 'animate not the King too much for the keeping of Boulogne'.[73] Surrey's agent Hussey reported to Surrey that his father, Norfolk, a member of the Council, had been heard to say 'he had rather bury you and the rest of his children before he should give his consent to the ruin of this realm, not doubting but that ye should be removed in spite of your head, work what ye would'.[74]

Surrey's letters from Boulogne in late autumn 1545, however, show how much he relished his commission. The language of restlessness and marginalization that is characteristic of the poems of the late 1530s and early 1540s is displaced by a sense of purpose and confident achievement. Surrey's dispatches are full of activity, of the excitement and glory of sudden sallies and fierce skirmishes, and of the technology of warfare, of interlaced trenching, of 'plats' (maps) and the details of shipping and revictualling. On 4 December, in an account of a carefully planned ambush of enemy reinforcements, Surrey reported a successful charge, redolent of the tournament yard, and culminating with a hubristic flourish:

> [We] assembled our horsemen upon the hill, and drew our footmen upon the skantling [limited space] of the hill as nigh as we could, not to be discovered; and Mr. Marshall and the cavalry offered the charge upon them . . . At which charge Mr. Marshall very honestly and hardily brake his mace upon a Frenchman; Mr. Shelly brake his staff upon a tall young gentleman of Monsieur De Botyer's band, and took him

prisoner: and in effect, all the men at arms of this town brake their staves.

staves: lances; Casady explains the phrase 'to break a stave' as the 'jargon of the tournament'[75]

A less glorious perspective on Surrey's military leadership is, however, provided by the chronicles of a soldier posted at Calais, Elis Gruffydd. On 5 January 1546, Surrey ordered his troops to attack a superior French force. After some initial success the English were routed, with fourteen of Surrey's best and most eminent captains slain or missing. Gruffydd writes with hostility of Surrey's unwillingness to listen to advice or take heed of the hunger and demoralization of his soldiers. In spite of his scholarship, noted Gruffydd, Surrey followed 'the practice of the captains of this time and generation [which] was to upbraid the soldiers with vain, contemptuous words'.[76] In Gruffydd's view 'most sensible men' attributed the rout to 'the earl their leader, whose head and heart were swollen with pride, arrogance and empty confidence in his own unreasoning bravery'.[77] Surrey's account to the king, signed by the whole Privy Council at Boulogne, tells a rather different story of 'loss and victory on both sides', with the English cavalry performing with 'great courage and . . . good order'. 'If any disorder there were, we assure your Majesty there was no default in the rulers, nor lack of courage to be given them, but a humour that sometime reigneth in Englishmen' (Nott 1 p 201; Casady p 157). The Council's up-beat version was delayed in reaching England by a storm and the resultant rumours clearly did Surrey no good. Charles V's ambassador in England reported to his master on 13 January that 'the Earl of Surrey has . . . lost greatly in reputation, and there is considerable discontent at these heavy losses'.[78] At the Imperial court, Henry's own ambassador, Stephen Gardiner, showed what was expected of a diplomat by fictionally embellishing the events with an entirely invented successful all-night raid on the French baggage by the English. 'We "kept the ground of truth" and fashioned it with circumstances', he reported back on 27 January.[79]

Surrey had been appointed lieutenant-general on the unexpected deaths of commanders in the field, he was inexperienced, and his commission had been for a winter garrison during the non-campaigning season. It is therefore unsurprising that he was replaced for the large-scale summer campaign. The announcement, in mid-February, following hard on the January defeat, that Edward

Seymour, Earl of Hertford was to replace him, could not, however, have been pleasing. His Privy Council ally of the moment, Sir William Paget, warned him that his replacement 'shall touch your honour . . . [which] the world would much muse at, and, though there be no such matter, think you were rejected upon occasion of some either negligence, inexperience, or such other like fault'. Paget urged Surrey to write at once to Henry for some other position of honour in the army 'which should be to your reputation in the world' (Nott 1 pp 225–6; Casady p 161).

Surrey was not given another position of honour and by late March 1546 was back in London, tarrying 'at home within a wall' as Paget had warned back in February. Surrey's sensitivity to his own reputation and status is evident in his response to a dispute with his successor at Boulogne, Lord Grey of Wilton, a mere 'Captain of Boulogne', who had accused Surrey, 'the King's Lieutenant', of trafficking in places for personal gain: 'there be in Boulogne too many witnesses that Henry of Surrey was never for singular profect corrupted; nor never yet bribe closed his hand: which lesson I learned of my Father; and wish to succeed him therein as in the rest' (Nott 1 p 230; Casady p 176). Surrey was never to succeed his father. Six months later he was beheaded by the executioner's axe, accused of treason in a struggle with Edward Seymour over precedence and power in the crucial months preceding Henry's death.[80]

'RESTLESS REST'

Surrey's birth and family helped to define his public role as a scion of the 'old nobility', freighted with an ideology in which pre-eminence of blood was justified and demonstrated by acts of courage and virtue, most prestigiously on the battlefield. But if warfare beckoned as a fitting public role, in which he might figure as an informed military strategist and a bold and active leader, Surrey's poetry interestingly explores a very different range of roles, characterized by virtuous isolation, endurance and suffering. Surrey's translations of Books 2 and 4 of the *Aeneid* epitomize the heroic subjects of many of Surrey's poems. In Book 2, Aeneas is forced into the position of an anguished onlooker as Troy is betrayed and burned. His only effective action is to flee the flames, tragically leaving behind his loved wife and the city in which his honour and identity are rooted, but bearing forward into exile a burden of loyalty and hope in the persons of his father and son. Book 4 provides another key model, that of the lamenting woman, Dido, whose restless mind can find no outlet but words leading to suicide.[81] A female voice, which he adopts in a number of poems, may have seemed to Surrey a legitimate vehicle for his favourite themes of marginalization, powerlessness and loss.[82] Even in many of the male-voiced complaints (e.g. Jones nos. 21, 25 and 26), restlessness of mind is brought into conflict with an enforced or voluntary passivity of body. For Surrey, a subject position of alienation and mourning may have provided a means of exploring and expressing conflicts which shaped his life as, on the one hand, an idealized aristocratic ideology of honour rooted in lineage was replaced by the 'new' politic conditions of Henrician courting, and, on the other, a chivalric cult of violence was questioned by the new Christian humanist values of suffering and patience.[83]

Restlessness of body and mind could be, in the Henrician period, a sign of purposeful vigour or the condition of exhausting service. The word echoes through two interrelated poems by Wyatt and Surrey. In 'Of Carthage he' (Reb. xlvi), Wyatt reflects on some of the frustrations of royal service in Spain:

> So hangeth in balance
> Of war my peace, reward of all my pain.
> At Monzòn thus I restless rest in Spain.

Surrey echoes Wyatt's 'restless rest' in a sonnet, 'The fansy which that I have served long', set in Boulogne which concludes:

> Where I am now, as restlesse to remain,
> Against my will, full pleased with my pain.
>
> (Jones no. 10)

Both poems deal with the dissatisfactions and frustrations of their poets' royal service. Wyatt's poem derives from a Petrarchan sonnet in which the Italian poet had urged his friend, Colonna, on to further military action, unlike the Carthaginian general Hannibal who did not know how to use his victory well ('non seppe usar poi / ben la vittoriosa sua ventura').[84] Wyatt's speaker, on the contrary, is compared to Hannibal because he too fails to make use of his success:

> Of Carthage he that worthy warrior,
> Could overcome but could not use his chance.
> And I likewise, of all my long endeavour,
> The sharp conquest though fortune did advance,
> Could not it use.

The context of Monzòn suggests Wyatt's great task is a diplomatic one. He was in Monzòn in 1537 with the Imperial court, engaged in negotiating peace between two warring monarchs: 'So hangeth in balance / Of war my peace, reward of all my pain'.[85] On this reading, Wyatt's long, patient, diplomatic activity, 'the long endeavour', though fortunate, is finally unsuccessful, perhaps through the evasiveness of one or other or both of the monarchs between whom he acts. Or perhaps the speaker cannot use his diplomatic success to gain any personal reward; he cannot 'use his chance'. Wyatt aggrandizes his diplomatic service by likening it to the military conquests of the soldier Hannibal, but on the other hand his position is one of frustration, impotence and enforced patience: 'At Monzòn thus I restless rest in Spain.'

Wyatt's phrasing, however, playfully recalls another 'worthy warrior' of Carthage, Aeneas, who left Dido, Queen of Carthage, for sterner service in Italy. On this reading the conquest is amorous. Wyatt has been torn away just as he was on the point of reaping the rewards of his 'long endeavour' (perhaps a reference to his mistress Elizabeth Darrell, to whom he seems to have formed a strong attachment just before leaving on diplomatic service in 1537).[86] Aeneas's abandonment of Dido was to found Rome, for the national good, but Wyatt represents his own fate as a misfortune. The Wyatt of this poem is restlessly confined, divided between heroic models of bold conquest on the one hand and self-denial on the other, but, in whichever reading one follows, frustrated, unrewarded and 'unpossessed'.

Surrey's sonnet also enacts a scenario of frustration and impotence, but its logic is significantly different from Wyatt's. Surrey develops a series of paradoxes through the poem which evoke a sense of radical uncertainty and alienation, but these are the result of the speaker's own divided mind rather than of an enforced posting abroad, as in Wyatt's poem. The sonnet opens with the speaker determined to quit the 'fansy' which has long kept him confined in a crowded and faithless place ('enmie to mye ease'). Instead he determines to follow 'Som other way, till I saw faith more strong'. Looking back, his life seems wasted, 'those dayes / In vain were spent, to runne the race so long'.[87] At this point, a 'guide'

> Out of the way wherin I wandered wrong
> Brought me amiddes the hilles in base Bullayn;
> Where I am now, as restlesse to remain,
> Against my will, full pleased with my pain.
>
> (ll. 11–14)

'Base Bullayn' was the lower town of Boulogne, attached to the fortress which it was part of Surrey's commission to defend in 1545–6. In 'Base Bullayn', however, he still finds himself 'restlesse', his divided mind suggested by the paradoxes of the final couplet.[88] Service 'amiddes the hilles in base Bullayne' proves as contradictory and riven as service to 'fansy' amidst the 'throng' in the poem's opening. The poem circulates within its own terms, its final restless 'pain' taking us back to the 'painfull hart' with which it began, dramatizing the speaker's irresolution.

The poems of Wyatt and Surrey, like those of many courtly contemporaries, need to be understood within the context of their primary occupations as servants of the king and the commonwealth. In many respects Wyatt and Surrey represent two very different responses, shaped by class and attitude, to that context. Wyatt's family fortunes were built on outstanding service to the Tudors, a service that, in the poet's case, depended on his politic skill with words. Surrey felt himself to belong to a family which should command power and privilege in its own right, and saw his own role primarily in the traditional chivalric terms of military service to the crown. Nevertheless in different ways, the poetry of both men is shaped by the conflicts and changes of their place and time: conflicts between the demands of obedience and those of an ideology of masculine self-assertion; between hubris and dependency; and over the changing forms and requirements of royal service as the nation moved from medieval to modern forms of government. The poetry of Wyatt and Surrey reveals the extraordinary range of complex fictions and forms within which such conflicts could be shaped and defused. In 'Of Carthage he' Wyatt places himself at the premier continental court and chooses the latest, sophisticated continental form, the eight-line Italian *strambotto*, modelled on a sonnet by Petrarch, in order to represent himself as a loser. Surrey crafts within the difficult and sophisticated form of the sonnet a circular dilemma in which 'Bullayn', whose name resonated so proudly in the chivalric epitaph to Clere, is rendered as double and as uncertain as the thronged court he fled. In the next chapter I shall examine in more detail that court and the poetry of 'fansy' and frustration that it produced.

NOTES

1. On the term 'balet', its meaning and use, see Stevens, J. (1961) *Music and Poetry in the Early Tudor Court*. London: Methuen, pp 120–1. I shall use the

term interchangeably with 'verse' and 'poem' and, occasionally, for variety, the unhistorical 'lyric', throughout this book.

2. Further biographical information about these men will appear in the course of my discussion. For an anthology of early Tudor verse, including other courtly balet-makers of the period, see Tydeman, W., ed. (1970) *English Poetry 1400–1580.* London: Heinemann. See Rollins 2 pp 65–85 for biographical information on some known contributors to *Tottel's Miscellany.*

3. Anon. (1555) *The Institucion of a Gentleman,* sig. Dvi^{v}. For the long history of such sentiments and for identification of commonwealth with crown, see especially Ferguson, A. B. (1960) *The Indian Summer of English Chivalry: Studies in the Decline and Transformation of Chivalric Idealism.* Durham, NC: Duke University Press, pp 106–8 and 118–20; and James, M. E. (1986) *Society, Politics and Culture: Studies in Early Modern England.* Cambridge: Cambridge University Press, pp 327–9 and 375–81.

4. For the erotic overtones which complicate this orthodox sentiment, see Ch 2 p 60 below.

5. For Sir Henry Wyatt, see Foley, S. M. (1990) *Sir Thomas Wyatt.* Twayne English Authors series. Boston: G. K. Hall & Co., pp 4–13; Conway, A. (1932) *Henry VII's Relations with Scotland and Ireland, 1485–1498.* Cambridge: Cambridge University Press, passim; and Richardson, W. C. (1952) *Tudor Chamber Administration, 1485–1547.* Baton Rouge, La: Louisiana University Press, esp. pp 94–7.

6. The comment was recorded by George Constantyne in testimony relating to a conversation with John Barlow, Dean of Westbury, in August 1539. The full text is transcribed in Amyot, T. (1831) 'Transcript of an Original Manuscript, containing a Memorial from George Constantyne to Thomas Lord Cromwell'. *Archaeologia* 23: 50–78.

7. See Kipling, G. (1977) *The Triumph of Honour: Burgundian Origins of the Elizabethan Renaissance.* Leiden: Leiden University Press. The Tudor translator of Froissart, one of the central texts for the dissemination of Burgundian knightly culture, was Surrey's half-uncle, John Bourchier, Lord Berners.

8. Lull, Ramon (1926) *The Book of the Ordre of Chyvalry,* trans. William Caxton. Early English Text Society, OS 168, ed. T. P. Bayles. London: Oxford University Press, pp 29 and 32.

9. Lull (1926) p 89; Vale, M. (1981) *War and Chivalry: Warfare and Aristocratic Culture in England, France and Burgundy at the End of the Middle Ages.* London: Duckworth, pp 20–1, 79; and James (1986) pp 310–12.

10. For the two traditions, see Cooper, J. P. (1983) 'Ideas of gentility in early-modern England'. In *Land, Men and Beliefs: Studies in Early-Modern History,* eds G. E. Aylmer and J. S. Morrill. London: The Hambledon Press, pp 46–50, and James (1986) pp 376–9.

11. Quoted by Cooper (1983) pp 49–50.

12. James (1986) pp 312–13.

13. Miller, H. (1986) *Henry VIII and the English Nobility.* Oxford: Basil Blackwell, pp 35, 61.

14. *Institucion* sig. Ciiii^{v}.
15. *LL* pp 36, 210–16.
16. Becon, T. (1843) *The Early Works*, ed. J. Ayre. The Parker Society. Cambridge: Cambridge University Press, p 236. *The New Pollicie of Warre* was first published in 1542, but seems to have been written not long after the Pilgrimage of Grace in 1537.
17. For the third Duke of Norfolk's life and career, see Robinson, J. (1982) *The Dukes of Norfolk: A Quincentennial History*. Oxford: Oxford University Press, ch 3.
18. Gunn, S. J. (1991) 'Tournaments and early Tudor chivalry'. *History Today* 41: 15–21. See also Gunn, S. J. (1990) 'Chivalry and the politics of the early Tudor court'. In *Chivalry in the Renaissance*, ed. S. Anglo. Woodbridge, Suffolk: The Boydell Press, pp 107–28.
19. McCoy, R. (1989) *The Rites of Knighthood: The Literature and Politics of Elizabethan Chivalry*. Berkeley and Los Angeles: University of California Press, ch 1 (p 14). For the impact of new humanist and Protestant ideas on the traditional codes of chivalry, see esp. James (1986) ch 8 passim.
20. For the anti-court tradition, see Anglo, S. (1977) 'The courtier. The Renaissance and changing ideals'. In *The Courts of Europe: Politics, Patronage and Royalty 1400–1800*, ed. A. G. Dickens. London: Thames and Hudson, pp 33–53 (pp 33–5). For an influential study of the close association of power and personal attendance on the king, see Starkey, D. (1987) 'Intimacy and innovation: the rise of the Privy Chamber, 1485–1547'. In *The English Court: From the Wars of the Roses to the Civil War*, ed. D. Starkey. London: Longman, pp 71–118.
21. More, Sir T. (1965) *Utopia*, trans. G. C. Richards. In *The Yale Edition of the Complete Works of St. Thomas More*, vol 4, eds E. Surtz and J. H. Hexter. New Haven, Conn.: Yale University Press, p 57.
22. The classical sources for the 'beatus ille' topic of blessed retirement in the country are to be found in Horace's second epode, which begins with the phrase 'Beatus ille qui'; Satire II.6, which Wyatt uses in his second satire, 'My mother's maids', and Epistle I.10. See Sowerby, R. (1994) *The Classical Legacy in Renaissance Poetry*. London: Longman, pp 150–1, 356.
23. Guevara's *Menosprecio de Corte* was first published in 1539. Bryan's translation was republished as *A Looking glasse for the court* in 1575. I quote here from sigs. e.iii^{r-v} and e.iv^{v} of Bryan's 1548 version; the location of subsequent references is given in the text in parentheses.
24. The fullest account of Wyatt's life, with an edition of the letters and the 'Defence', written in 1541, are in *LL*. For these events, see pp 28–36. For fuller discussion of 'Mine own John Poyntz', see Ch 4 pp 131–35 below.
25. For Sir Francis Bryan's biography and reputation, see Brigden, S. (1996) '"The Shadow That You Know": Sir Thomas Wyatt and Sir Francis Bryan at court and in embassy'. *The Historical Journal* 39(1): 1–31; Starkey, D. (1982) 'The court: Castiglione's ideal and Tudor reality, being a discussion of Sir Thomas Wyatt's satire addressed to Sir Francis Bryan'. *Journal of the Warburg and*

Courtauld Institutes 45: 232–9 (pp 235–6). See also Bindoff, S. T., ed. (1982) *The House of Commons, 1509–1558.* 3 vols. *The History of Parliament.* London: published for the History of Parliament Trust by Secker & Warburg, 1 pp 527–9. For discussion of the satire addressed to him, see Ch 4 pp 136–39 below.

26. It is often suggested that Wyatt attended St John's College, Cambridge, which was a humanist foundation and helped to spread humanist educational ideas at Cambridge. However, Foley (1990) p 114 n 37 points out that there is no documentary evidence linking Wyatt with St John's.
27. See Bolgar, R. R. (1954) *The Classical Heritage and its Beneficiaries.* Cambridge: Cambridge University Press, appendix 2, which lists 'The translations of the Greek and Roman Classical Authors Before 1600'. See also Sowerby (1994) pp 4–5.
28. On the incident, see Hall, E. (1965) *Chronicle, Containing the History of England* (reprint of the 1809 edn). New York: AMS Press Inc., pp 689–90. On tournaments as serious practice for war, see Vale (1981) esp. p 80.
29. Ives, E. W. (1986) *Anne Boleyn.* Oxford: Basil Blackwell, pp 47–8.
30. Loades, D. M., ed. (1968) *Papers of George Wyatt Esquire of Boxley Abbey in the County of Kent.* Camden Fourth Series, vol 5. London: Royal Historical Society, p 27 (I have slightly adjusted the spelling and punctuation to make the passage easier to understand). The story is told by George Wyatt, the poet's grandson, who claims he had it from Russell's son.
31. Gunn, S. J. (1987) 'The French wars of Henry VIII'. In *The Origins of War in Early Modern Europe*, ed. J. Black. Edinburgh: John Donald Publishers Ltd, pp 28–51 (p 41).
32. Clark, P. (1977) *English Provincial Society from the Reformation to the Revolution: Religion, Politics and Society in Kent, 1500–1640.* Hassocks, Sussex: Harvester Press, pp 50–2. Foley (1990) p 15 points out that in 1532, Wyatt served as justice of the peace in Essex.
33. James (1986) p 309.
34. Guevara, A. de (1548) *A Dispraise of the life of a Courtier, and a commendation of the life of the labouryng man*, trans. Sir Francis Bryan. London: R. Grafton, sig. L.ii.^{v}.
35. Mattingly, G. (1962) *Renaissance Diplomacy.* London: Jonathan Cape, pp 64, 109, 239. Isaac Walton reported that Wotton's sentence, in Latin, was written in the album of Christopher Flecamore: see Walton, I. (1973) *The Lives.* Oxford: Oxford University Press, p 121.
36. Quoted by Nott 2 p 517. *LP* xiv (2), 524 summarizes the letter.
37. Nott 2 p 516.
38. For example, *LL* p 132.
39. For an account of Brancestor's extraordinary career, see Scarisbrick, J. J. (1961) 'The first Englishman round the Cape of Good Hope?' *Bulletin of the Institute of Historical Research* 34: 165–177.
40. *LP* xv 145.

41. *LP* xv 222.
42. *LP* xv 257.
43. For example, *LP* xv 223 and 285, and *LL* p 139.
44. Habenicht, discussing John Heywood's very different use of the same proverb, suggests it is 'an allusion to the cart's tail: to which offenders were tied to be whipped': see Habenicht, R. E., ed. (1963) *John Heywood's 'A Dialogue of Proverbs'*. Berkeley: University of California Press, l. 491 and note.
45. The suggestion that Queen Katherine Howard intervened at the instigation of her family was made by Thomson, P. (1964) *Sir Thomas Wyatt and His Background*. London: Routledge and Kegan Paul, p 73.
46. For the *strambotto* form, see p 83 below.
47. For a discussion of the significance of these elegies as part of a deliberate project by Surrey to redefine prevailing notions of nobility and honour, see Sessions, W. A. (1994) 'Surrey's Wyatt: Autumn 1542 and the new poet'. In *Rethinking the Henrician Era: Essays on Early Tudor Texts and Contexts*, ed. P. C. Herman. Urbana and Chicago: University of Illinois Press, pp 168–92. Muir prints an English translation of Leland's elegy in Appendix A of *LL*. A subtle discussion of Surrey's elegy, whose conclusions differ from mine, but to which I am indebted, is that of Tromley, F. B. (1980) 'Surrey's fidelity to Wyatt in "Wyatt Resteth Here" '. *Studies in Philology* 77: 376–87.
48. Compare Surrey's more traditionally heraldic use of the blazon in his epitaph on Thomas Clere (Jones no. 35), discussed above, p 26.
49. Tromley (1980) p 384. The word 'witnesses' is used in Tyndale's translation of Hebrews 12.1. Surrey's Wyatt 'ran the race that nature set' at l. 31 of the elegy.
50. For Surrey's remark and Paget's background, see Gunn, S. J. (1995) *Early Tudor Government, 1485–1558*. British History in Perspective. Basingstoke: Macmillan, p 21.
51. The most likely date for Surrey's imprisonment seems to be 1537, when Surrey was threatened with having his right hand amputated, the standard punishment for striking someone within the precincts of the court. Edmond Bapst speculated that the occasion may have been a quarrel with Edward Seymour following a slur on Surrey's and Norfolk's loyalty to the crown, cited in a discussion of the evidence by Casady, E. (1938) *Henry Howard, Earl of Surrey*. New York: The Modern Language Association of America, pp 60–3.
52. They passed 1532–3 together at the splendid Renaissance court of Francis I at Fontainebleau. Richmond was married to Surrey's sister Mary, but the relationship was never consummated.
53. On the bond of 'chamber companionship', see James (1986) p 330.
54. Jones p 122 points out the chivalric meaning of 'fredome' ('nobility' or 'courtesy').
55. For discussions of the portrait, its iconography, and the vexed question of its dating, see Sessions, W. (1991) ' "Enough Survives". The Earl of Surrey and European culture'. *History Today* 41(6): 48–54, and the discussion by Hearn,

K. (1995) *Dynasties: Painting in Tudor and Jacobean England, 1530–1630.* Tate Publishing, pp 50–2 (this is the catalogue for the Tate Gallery exhibition of the same title).

56. Padelford no. 34. For evidence that Surrey's disdain of the Seymours was not so great as to preclude their dining together on a number of occasions, see Susan Brigden's important article on Surrey's final year: Brigden, S. (1994) 'Henry Howard, Earl of Surrey and the "Conjured League" '. *The Historical Journal* 37: 507–37 (pp 520–1).
57. The line 'In towre both strong and highe', describing Howard's imprisonment, is strikingly close to a line in a poem probably by Douglas, 'this tower ye se is strong and hie', which may refer to her own imprisonment. See Heale, E. (1995) 'Women and the courtly love lyric: the Devonshire MS (BL Additional 17492)'. *Modern Language Review* 90: 296–313 (p 309 n 32). The phrase, however, may be merely conventional.
58. Lull (1926) pp 89, 116.
59. *LP* xii (2) 248, quoting directly from Norfolk's letter.
60. For example, Lull (1926) pp 36–7, and Caxton's epilogue, pp 122–3.
61. Nott 1 p 226.
62. Casady (1938) pp 88–91. The reason for the challenge is not known.
63. *LP* xviii (1) 327 (2); Casady (1938) pp 97–9.
64. The letter is reprinted in Nott 1 pp 167–9.
65. Quoted from Berners' preface, Froissart, J. (1913) *The Chronicles,* trans. John Bourchier, Lord Berners, ed. G. C. MacCauley. London: Macmillan and Co., p xxix.
66. Gunn (1987) p 40.
67. *LP* xviii (2) 243; Casady (1938) p 103.
68. Nott 1 appendix xii, p xl. See *LP* xviii (2) 310.
69. *CSP (Spanish)* vi (2) 250.
70. For the argument that in spite of its militaristic resonances, Clere in fact died of a disease caught at Montreuil, see Zitner, S. (1983) 'Truth and mourning in a sonnet by Surrey'. *English Literary History* 50: 509–29.
71. Casady (1938) p 131; *LP* xx (2) 140, 162, 208, 209, 252.
72. The phrase is that of Surrey's agent, Thomas Hussey: see Casady (1938) p 136.
73. Casady (1938) p 135.
74. Casady (1938) p 137.
75. Nott 1 pp 182–3. The letter is transcribed by Casady (1938) p 141 in a rather more modernized version. In the following pages I shall quote letters from Nott's edition, giving references to both that and Casady's version in parentheses.
76. Davies, B. M. (1959–60) 'Surrey at Boulogne'. *Huntington Library Quarterly* 23: 339–48 (p 344).
77. Davies (1959–60) p 345.

78. *CSP (Spanish)* viii 184.

79. *LP* xxi (1) 128. The *LP* summary quotes from the original letter.

80. For a detailed account of the events leading up to his death, see Brigden (1994). For my discussion of Surrey's psalm paraphrases in relation to these events, see Ch 5 pp 173–84 below.

81. Sessions, W. A. (1986) *Henry Howard, Earl of Surrey*. Twayne English Authors Series. Boston: G. K. Hall, pp 79–82 and 129 suggests that Dido is an important model for a number of Surrey's poems.

82. The gendered connotations of complaint have to some extent been explored by Kerrigan, J., ed. (1991) *Motives of Woe: Shakespeare and "Female Complaint". A Critical Anthology*. Oxford: Clarendon Press, esp. pp 8–12, and Schmitz, G. (1990) *The Fall of Women in Early English Narrative Verse*. Cambridge: Cambridge University Press, esp. pp 227–30. For a suggestive discussion of literary uses of female-voiced complaint, see Wall, W. (1993) *The Imprint of Gender: Authorship and Publication in the Renaissance*. Ithaca: Cornell University Press, pp 250–60, esp. her fn 23. For fuller discussion of Surrey's female-voiced complaints, see Ch 2 pp 62–63 below.

83. For a highly suggestive discussion of the changing concept of honour in the sixteenth century, see James (1986) ch 8.

84. Petrarch, *Rime* 103. All quotations from Petrarch are from Petrarca, F. (1951) *Rime, Trionfi, e Poesie Latine*, eds F. Neri, G. Martellotti, E. Bianchi and N. Sapegno. La Letteratura Italiana. Storia e Testi vol 6. Milano e Napoli: Riccardo Ricciardi Editore. In every instance when quoting from Petrarch I have checked this text against the 1525 edition of *Le Volgari Opere . . . con la espositione di Alessandro Vellutello da Lucca*. Venice: Giovanniantonio & Fratelli da Sabbio, such a text as Wyatt might himself have used (see Ch 4 fn 59 below) and found no significant differences of wording. However, for ease of reference I quote from, and refer to the (standard) numbering of, the modern edition.

85. Wyatt's instructions at Monzòn were very specifically to offer Henry's mediation between Charles V and Francis I to 'frame some good peace . . . between them': Nott 1 appendix viii, p 462; *LP* xii (2) 869.

86. For Elizabeth Darrell, see *LL* p 84. For a strongly autobiographical reading of this and other poems, see Fox (1989) pp 256–85.

87. Compare Surrey's use of the same image, whose source may be biblical or Virgilian, in l. 31 of his elegy on Wyatt (Jones no. 28). See Jones's notes and my p 20 above.

88. Casady (1938) p 163 relates the sonnet to Surrey's unsuccessful requests to have his wife join him at Boulogne, and suggests the sonnet was written 'to tell his wife of his disappointment'. See my discussion of the close relationship between a language of erotic and political desire for stability in Ch 2 below.

Chapter 2

Courtly Service and Courtly Verse

'ENTERTAINMENT FOR THE LADIES'

Service to the king involved service at court, a 'quesy', 'unstable' place, commonly associated, as we have seen, with women and a threatening effeminacy.[1] The transition from 'courting' as a kind of behaviour suitable for courts where entertainment of women was an important indicator of accomplished behaviour, to 'courting' in its modern sense of wooing, was one easily made, and a semantic shift seems to have occurred in the early Tudor period.[2] When the musician Thomas Whythorne (1528–96), remembering his own youthful apprenticeship in the mid-1540s to the interlude writer John Heywood, described 'courting' as a kind of game with the ladies 'to talk with them, to jibe and jest with them', the term easily encompassed both meanings.[3]

The association of courtly arts with women is found in the seminal Renaissance courtly conduct book, Baldassare Castiglione's *Il Libro del Cortegiano*, first published in Italian in 1528 and translated into English as *The Book of the Courtier* in 1561 by Sir Thomas Hoby, brother of a diplomatic colleague of Wyatt's. *The Courtier* provides a fictive, but highly influential, account of the court of Urbino in the early years of the sixteenth century. The Duchess of Urbino presides over the evening pastime of her courtiers, a series of debates on the behaviour and functions of the ideal courtier and his counterpart, the ideal female courtier. A major function of the courtier is to please women. In the first book, Count Lodovico advises that the aspiring courtier 'be very well acquainted with the poets . . . and also skilled at writing both verse and prose, especially in our own language; for in addition to the satisfaction this will give him personally, it will enable him to provide constant entertainment for the ladies, who are usually very fond of such things'.[4] In the same vein, he praises the art of singing and playing on an instrument '. . . especially at Court where . . . many things are done to please the ladies, whose tender and gentle souls are very susceptible to harmony and sweetness' (p 94). The lurking fear that such entertainment may be effeminately trivial is immediately made explicit by the misogynist Pallavicino: 'I think that music, like so many other vanities, is most certainly very suited to women, and perhaps also to some of those who have the appearance of men, but not to real men who should not indulge in pleasures which render their minds effeminate and so cause them to fear death' (p 94). Pallavicino voices the long-standing opposition between the 'manly' activities, connected with military courage and honour, and the perceived 'womanishness' of mere aesthetics and the cultivation of social graces. Lull in the thirteenth century expressed his contempt of such unmanliness: 'If . . . for to holde the mirrour in the hand / and other Jolitees / shold a squier be adoubed knight . . . thou mightest chese wimmen to be knightes.'[5]

Verse writing was accounted a central grace of courting. The most usual early Tudor term for such courtly verses, often, but not always, suitable for singing, was 'balet', a term used to describe a range of usually stanzaic poems, including medieval forms such as the rondeau or the carol, but also a range of freer and newer forms, sometimes with a refrain, but often not. The term may well have been used by contemporaries to describe Wyatt's and Surrey's amorous sonnets. What links these diverse forms is their social nature, the internal or external evidence we have that they form part of a courtly exchange, contributing to the pastime of the court and sharing in the familiar courtly discourse of love, either in its praise or dispraise. Queen Anne Boleyn, with a brave courtly wit, punned on the similarity of balet and pallet (a straw bed or mattress) when imprisoned in the Tower in May 1536. Told that her supposed 'lovers', including her brother, the Earl of Rochford, who had a reputation as a versifier, had been imprisoned without menial servants to care for their basic needs, she commented that they 'might make balettes well now, bot ther is non bot [Rochfor]de can do it'. 'Yes,' said Lady Kingston, the wife of the Constable of the Tower, 'Master Wyett [can],' and Anne Boleyn seems to have agreed.[6]

Anne Boleyn's words, and the circumstances in which she spoke them, bring together a number of the themes of this chapter. They suggest how central balet making was to the courtly identity of her brother and of Wyatt, both in her own mind and in that of Lady Kingston. Her punning joke, uttered in the dire circumstances of May 1536, also displays a brave skill in the performance of the witty rallying expected of the courtly woman. Ann Rosalind Jones has described the particular difficulties a social role at court imposed on women each of whom was required 'to be a member of the chorus prompting men to bravery in tournaments and eloquence in conversation; she was expected to be a witty and informed participant in dialogues whose subject was most often love. Rather than prohibiting amorous repartee to women, the courtly code elicited it from them'.[7] But such courtly repartee potentially brought her into conflict with Christian moral codes in which a woman's chastity was closely associated with her silence and self-effacement. The dangerous tightrope courtly women had to tread between wit and scandal is suggested by the daunting advice of Giuliano in *The Courtier*: 'Thus she must observe a certain difficult mean, composed as it were of contrasting qualities, and take care not to stray beyond certain fixed limits.'[8]

In her frantic attempts in the Tower to recollect incidents that might have led to the accusations against her, Anne Boleyn recalled a series of exchanges whose exact position on the continuum between courtliness and amorous courting it is now impossible for us to judge. On one occasion, seeing Mark Smeaton, a low-born musician attached to her chamber, look downcast, she had said, 'You may not look to have me speak to you as I should do to a noble man, because you be an inferior person.' 'No, no, madam,' he answered, 'A look sufficed me, and thus fare you well.'[9] This exchange provided evidence that helped to bring both Smeaton and Boleyn to the scaffold in May 1536.

Anne Boleyn's mockery of balets within the grim walls of the Tower may draw on their association with triviality, a perception (in part due to their association with women) that has been embraced by some twentieth-century critics. John Stevens, in an important study of music and poetry at the Henrician court, described Wyatt's courtly balets as 'verse of lighter weight . . . ephemeral', and, in a well-known judgement, H. A. Mason commented:

> many of these poems of Wyatt's are simply strung together from [conventional] phrases into set forms. There is not the slightest trace of poetic activity . . . Wyatt, like the other court writers, was merely supplying material for social occasions.[10]

While Stevens and Mason are right to insist on the social and occasional context of courtly balets, Mason's conclusion, that 'most of Wyatt's "lyrics" are not poems at all', is excessively reductive, limiting 'poetic activity' to a very confined sphere predicated on modern ideas of authorship in which poems are valued primarily as the unique, self-expressive utterances of individuals.[11] If we are prepared to modify such assumptions, we can begin to appreciate the courtly balets of the Henrician court as in fact highly accomplished, and at times emotionally powerful, artefacts which mythologize the ideals, and strive to displace the tensions, of a whole social class.

WOMEN AND THE DEVONSHIRE MANUSCRIPT

The central role women played as the objects, collectors and, perhaps, composers of courtly verse is vividly suggested by a manuscript collection of courtly balets compiled in the 1530s and early 1540s. The Devonshire MS (BL Add. MS 17492) has often been invoked as a context for Wyatt's courtly verse, many examples of which it contains.[12] I invoke it again because its use by a group of women can both be traced in more detail, and is more significant and revealing, than has previously been acknowledged.[13]

Its association with one woman, Lady Margaret Douglas, niece to Henry VIII, is relatively well known. The manuscript contains a group of poems relating to a liaison between Douglas and Surrey's uncle, Lord Thomas Howard.[14] When the liaison was discovered in the aftermath of Anne Boleyn's fall, the two lovers were imprisoned in the Tower. Some poems seem to refer to this period. They provide striking evidence of the vitality of the conventional posturings of courtly love. One, which speaks of the lover's pain at seeing 'her daily whom I love best / in great and untollerabel sorows strong', has 'margrt' written underneath (fol. 26^{v}). In another, the speaker refers to himself as the husband, though lower in degree, of a lady whose 'gentill letters' he cannot 'aquite / In rime and meter elegantly' (fol. 29^{r}). It has the initials T.H. (Thomas Howard) worked into the final stanza. Most of these poems are spoken by a man, but one at least is in a woman's voice, 'I may well say with Joyfull hart' (fol. 28^{v}), and could well be by Margaret herself.[15] Its speaker appeals to a code of honour derived from romance to justify disobedience to patriarchal and dynastic rules:

> Who shall let me then off right
> onto myself him to retane
> and love him best both day and night
> in recompens off his great paine[16]

The sentiment of the poems relating to the Douglas/Howard affair are conventional, but the inserted names and initials give the platitudes immediacy, and what is known of their biographies suggests that, with dangerous boldness, Douglas and Howard took the platitudes seriously.

Quite different from the romantic and idealizing note of these poems are contributions by another woman, Mary Shelton, a cousin of Anne Boleyn's and in attendance on her at court.[17] For example, after one poem, 'Suffring in sorow in hope to attain' (M&T no. ccli), she has written a tart comment: 'ondesiard fansies / requier no hiar [undesired fancies require no payment] / mary mary Shelton'. The poem itself, copied by an unidentified hand, is an acrostic: the first letter of each of its seven stanzas spells out SHELTUN. Elsewhere in the manuscript, sometimes alternating with Douglas, she has copied out lines and stanzas from what seem to be popular songs and rhymes, often adopting a woman's point of view.[18] One balet may be adapting a male-voiced poem for female use. When it was later printed in Tottel's *Miscellany* (1556) and *The Gorgeous Gallery of Gallant Inventions* (1578) it appeared as a complaint against a hard-hearted mistress:

> I see how she doth wry, *wry: swerve away; or grimace*
> When I begin to mone:
> I see whan I come nie,
> How faine she wold be gone.[19]

Throughout Shelton's version, the pronoun 'she' appears as 'the' [they], generalizing the complaint so that it could apply to men, or to the speaker's guardians or friends, but also to women:

> I se how the do wry
> wan I begen to mon
> I se wan I com by
> how ffare the wuld be gun.

(fol. 68^r; Muir (1947) no. 32)

Shelton's contributions do not always show an interest in a woman's point of view: she also copied a misogynist balet by her brother-in-law Sir Edmund Knyvet.[20] In fact throughout the manuscript, cheek by jowl with woman-voiced warnings of male infidelity are balets such as Wyatt's 'Is it possible' (Reb. cxlv) or 'What no perdy' (Reb. viii) with their cynical view of women. A typical example by Richard Hattfeld depends for its effect on ambiguous punctuation. The sense changes according to whether the reader pauses at the end of each line or lets the sense run on, as in the manuscript punctuation below, into the following line:

All women have vertues noble and excelent
Who can percive that / they do offend
Daily / they serve god with good intent
Seldome / they displease there husbandes to their lives end
Always /. to plese them they do intend
never /. man may find in them s[h]rewdnes
comonly /. suche condicions they have more and lese.

(fol. 18^{v}; Muir (1947) no. 5)

This poem neatly demonstrates the close relationship between the idealization and the misogynist dispraise of women. What the Devonshire MS shows is that such poems, part of the repertoire of courtly dalliance, were collected by women who seem to have felt free, on occasion, to reply, or at least to collect poems which replied, in kind.

Particularly remarkable is a series of stanzas, possibly for reference and subsequent use, copied at the very end of the manuscript. Many of these utter with considerable force a woman's view of the dangers and doubleness of male protestations of love. In one example the rhetoric of insult and instability so often directed against women is turned on men: 'she that them loveth shall them finde as fast / as in a tempest is a rotten maste' (fol. 91^{r}; Muir (1947) no. 49). The codes of courtly love often led male poets to represent their lack of success as fate or cruel fortune, but this posture acquires a social immediacy when used by a woman:

thereto we wretched women nothing conne — *conne: can; also, perhaps, learn the skill*
whan to us is wo / but wepe and sit and thingke
our wreake is this / our owne wo to drinke — *wreake: care (reck), but also, perhaps, downfall (wreck)*

(fol. 91^{v}; Muir (1947) no. 52)

However vividly these stanzas seem to express a woman's experience, their sources and the uncertainty of the copyist's identity teach caution, for all have been shown to derive from works printed as Chaucer's in Thynne's 1532 edition of the *Workes.*[21] The stanzas have clearly been selected to give a perspective sympathetic to women. On one occasion, the copyist has changed Thynne's version to turn misogynist lines inside out. The manuscript version reads:

iff all the erthe were parchment scribable
spedy for the hande / and all maner wode — *wode: wood*
were hewed and proportioned to pennes able
al water inke / in damme or in flode
every man being a parfite scribe and goode

the faithfulnes yet and praise of women
cowde not be shewed by the meane off penne
(fol. 90ʳ; Muir (1947) no. 45)

The penultimate line of Thynne's original, a rendering of Ovid's *Remedia Amoris*, has 'The cursidness yet and disceite of women'.

It would be pleasing to be able to claim that these stanzas were copied by a woman, sifting through the 1532 Chaucer for language with which to enunciate a woman's experience of courtly love. It is, however, entirely possible that they were noted and copied out by Lord Thomas Howard or by another man, whether to amuse and please their female acquaintances or as a source for poems of their own.[22] It is possible that none of the poems in women's voices, not even those copied by Margaret Douglas and Mary Shelton, were actually written by women. The only poem the manuscript contains in the hand of Mary Howard, Duchess of Richmond, Surrey's sister, is, interestingly, a version of her brother's poem 'O happy dames', a female-voiced complaint. Nevertheless it is clear that many of the poems copied into the manuscript show a particular interest in a rhetoric, spoken in a woman's voice, of defence against misogynist attack, or in articulating an idealized female view of courtly love.[23] Whether composed by men or by women, in a system of manuscript copying, appropriation and adaptation the question is less one of the name or gender of an originating author than of the kinds of voices and gestures the available discourses make possible to copiers and readers of both sexes.

However cautious we must be about the claim that poems that speak in the voice of a woman were in fact written by women, the Devonshire MS gives us some vivid glimpses of the role women might play, as recipients, as selectors, as commentators, very probably, on occasion, as adapters and composers of courtly verses. The amount of identifiable female involvement in this manuscript is unusual amongst those that survive, but we can, I think, assume that the active part they are seen to play in the manuscript accurately reflects their centrality to the genre as a whole.[24] Douglas and Shelton played a lively, and sometimes perilous, part in the game of 'jesting and jibing' for which many of these balets were written, collecting, circulating, and perhaps even singing, highly misogynist efforts alongside poems that articulated or defended a woman's perspective. Even in the apparently conventional exchange between Douglas and Lord Thomas Howard, Douglas seems not only to have made the clichés of romantic love her own, but to have found in them, as Joan Kelly argued, 'liberating implications', and transformed their assertions of the lady's obligations to a faithful lover into a kind of rebellion against the patriarchal system which controlled her own and her lover's marriage choices.[25]

While it is clear that such women as Douglas and Shelton were not merely the silenced and fragmented objects of male fictions, the contest of courtly 'jibing and jesting' between the sexes in which they participated was by no means an equal one. The Devonshire MS testifies to the great popularity in the period of courtly misogynist verse.[26] Utley, whose study of the tradition of satire and defence of women in medieval literature finishes at 1563, notes that 'the last 68 years we have to treat contribute some 250 of our 400 pieces', the majority of them anti-feminist, a statistic confirmed by Louis B. Salomon who comments, in his study of rebellious lover poetry, that what he calls the 'anti-amorous sentiment seems to have accumulated gradually during the first half of the sixteenth century, until Wyatt and Surrey finally opened the sluice gates and let out the flood'.[27] In the following section, I shall explore some of the possible reasons for the vitality of misogynist topics in the courtly verse of this period.

MISOGYNISM AND COURTLY VERSE

Utley argues that misogynist poetry was often designed for a mixed audience.[28] Evidence of the resilience which courtly women were expected to show in the face of perennial misogynist jokes is abundant. Henry VIII's sister, Margaret Tudor, for example, when married to King James V of Scotland, had a ribald piece, 'Madame, our men said thay wald rid[e]', dedicated to her by Dunbar.[29] At her brother's court, songs such as 'Blow thy horn hunter' seem to have particularly suited the taste of the ruling elite.[30] This balet makes great play with the pun on deer and the erotic symbolism of arrows:

> Sore this deer stricken is
>   And yet she bleeds no whit;
> She lay so fair, I could not miss;
>   Lord, I was glad of it!
>
> . . . .
>
> He to go and I to go,
>   But he ran fast afore;
> I bad him shoot and strike the doe,
>   For I might shoot no more.

To the covert both they went,
For I found where she lay;
An arrow in her haunch she hent;
For faint she might not bray.

I was weary of the game,
I went to the tavern to drink;
Now, the construction of the same –
What do you mean or think.

There is no reason to think such songs would not have been performed in the presence of women, perhaps during such youthful displays of vigour as a progress in 1511 when the king daily exercised himself 'in singing, daunsing, wrasteling, casting of the barre, playing at the recorders, flute, virginals, and in setting of songes, making of balettes . . . in hunting, hawking and shoting'.[31]

Henry's queen at the time, Katherine of Aragon, was no doubt expected to respond to such material with the graceful tolerance shown by Castiglione's Duchess of Urbino in *The Book of the Courtier* to Gaspare Pallavicino's recycling of some of Boccaccio's lewder stories about the sexual trickery of women, and his openly misogynistic view that 'there are few men of worth who have much respect for women by and large, though occasionally for their own purposes they pretend the contrary'. To all this, the exemplary duchess replied playfully by making a sign, at which 'a large number of ladies present rose to their feet and, laughing, they all ran towards signor Gaspare as if to rain blows on him and treat him as the Bacchantes treated Orpheus, saying at the same time: "Now you shall see whether we care whether evil things are said about us." '[32]

Such an analogy, however playful, between the duchess and her ladies and the frenzied, irrational Bacchantes who tore Orpheus apart, reveals an ambivalence about the nature of women which runs through Castiglione's work and is given fuller scope in the prolonged debate about women which continues from Book 2 into Book 3. In this debate the speakers are all male. The women function, in Thomas Greene's words, as part of the 'drama of containment' which he traces in Castiglione's text, managing its tone, turning aside the more bitterly misogynist comments with wit and mirth, confining potentially disruptive ambitions and resentments within the rules of courtly game and pastime.[33] Women at the Henrician court were no doubt similarly expected to deflect with grace disruptive anxieties and ambitions. Their role went beyond containment, however: they might also embody, or act as scape-goats for, deep-seated masculine fears and resentments, displacing the competition for royal service into an often antagonistic game-world of amorous service. Through their pretend authority as courtly mistress, women were constrained to fulfil, both socially and figuratively, a regulatory role in the social hothouse of the court, absorbing and diverting energies and behaviours which might otherwise have proved socially, perhaps even politically, trouble-some.

The popularity of anti-feminist topics in the early years of the sixteenth century may have to do with changes in the nature and conditions of royal service in the early Tudor court. Centralized power and the growing bureaucracy of the Tudor state gave the court ever-increasing importance as the focus for gentlemanly aspir-ations and the forum for day-to-day business. Within the court, accomplished verbal performance and graceful display could help a gentleman catch the king's eye and recommend the performer as a man suitable for service. Military prowess continued to be an im-portant avenue to advancement, but it was not the only one, or even, in itself, sufficient.[34] Physical vigour and ability were judged not only by success on the battlefield but also in the tournament, on the tennis court and on the hunting expedition, where it formed part of the social and courtly game-playing in which social cour-tesies and finesse might be just as important as strength and skill.[35]

Attendance at court could be for an aspiring gentleman an op-portunity and, potentially, a mark of favour, but it could also bring with it the threatening stigma of corruption and effeminacy. Through a discourse of misogyny, however, balet-making, singing, the exchanges of erotic dalliance, the very marks of that feared effeminacy could be wrested to assert a male solidarity and scorn of women. The threat of dishonour could be commuted from royal service to amorous service, bringing with it the imagined possibility of retaliation and the returned insult. Desires and resentments aroused by the fickle favours of monarchs could be explored and expressed in balets in terms of a feminized Dame Fortune, or fickle mistress. By strenuously asserting his own masculine trustiness in the face of a feminized treachery and betrayal, the courtier could dis-play his own reliability and virtue. In such ways a poetic discourse of misogyny could displace into safer forms the frustrations and re-sentments of courtly life.[36]

A glimpse of the potentially reassuring solidarity of a shared dis-course of misogyny is afforded by a manuscript of the fourteenth-century poem, *Les Lamentations of Matheolus* (BL Royal MS 20 B xxi), apparently owned by George Boleyn, Earl of Rochford. The *Lamentations* were, in Bloch's view, the 'most virulent antifeminist vernacular work of the Middle Ages'.[37] The satirical poem ridicules a married man who is at the mercy of a libidinous and faithless wife who is taken as typical of all wives and described with obscene relish. The manuscript seems to have been passed around a courtly group of men who left their mark with scribbled names. The name 'Wyat' in different spellings appears three times, also [Poyns] and 'Marc S', who may be the Mark Smeaton who was executed with Rochford in 1536 as one of Anne Boleyn's 'lovers'. The names are accompanied by a number of mottoes and proverbs which, given the nature of the manuscript's contents, have suggestive sexual innuendos. Next to Wyatt's name has been written 'presto para servir' [ready to serve] followed by 'forse' [perhaps] three times. The double possibilities of 'serve' (political and amorous) were, as we have seen, ready to hand. Another proverbial jotting is in French:

> qui asne est et cerff cuide bien estre
> a sallir une fosse on le puit bien cognostre.
>
> (He/she who is an ass, and thinks him/herself a hind, on leaping the ditch will realize the truth.)[38]

Thomson suggests the pun on 'asne' [ass] and Anne might make it more specifically a comment on Anne Boleyn, whether at the beginning or end of her relationship with Henry VIII.[39]

WYATT AND FICKLE MISTRESSES

A fantasy of retaliation, whose violence is contained in graceful epigrammatic form, may be found in a witty poem by Wyatt, 'She sat and sewed' (Reb. xli), which was copied by an unidentified hand into the Devonshire MS. The male speaking voice is initially represented as innocent and aggrieved, expressing itself in plaintive song. By the end of the poem's brief span, the plaintiveness is replaced by aggressive sexuality:

> She sat and sewed that hath done me the wrong
> Whereof I plain and have done many a day,
> And whilst she heard my plaint in piteous song
> Wished my heart the sampler as it lay.
> The blind master whom I have served so long,
> Grudging to hear that he did hear her say,

Made her own weapon do her finger bleed
To feel if pricking were so good indeed.

Within the brevity of the poem's perfectly turned *strambotto* form, the conceit of piercing is transferred neatly from the lover's heart, to the sampler, to her finger, to sexual penetration. Barbara Estrin has pointed out that the woman's needle arms her with the male penetrating and inscribing tool, both pen and penis, with which she fictively represents his pain on her sampler.[40] Within the fantasy of the poem, the male lover turns the woman's pricking instrument upon her own body, appropriating it for decidedly male uses. Of course, the very skilfulness of the balet reminds us that the narrating pen, the instrument of representation and power, has always been male because it is Wyatt's. The poem miniaturizes an obliquely implied virginal rape – 'pricking' makes the lady bleed. Such violence may seem to the modern reader out of all proportion to the demure silence of the lady whose expressive medium, her sewing of a sampler, is itself a mark of her propriety. The violence should, however, be understood in terms of deep-seated resentments and frustrations for which the woman and her decorous power are merely ciphers. The male speaker's initial, effeminate, vulnerability is aggressively transformed into sexual potency: the supposedly helpless object of a female script imagines himself as the controlling subject. Such retaliations are represented as mere justice within the perfectly turned form, a model of fashionable wit and sophistication (for a discussion of the *strambotto* form see Chapter 3, pp 83–6).

The desires and resentments which find expression in Wyatt's best-known poem, 'They flee from me' (Reb. lxxx), are more ambiguous – one reason, perhaps, for its perennial fascination. Who are 'they' (bird, deer or women?) who in the first stanza come 'stalking' in the poet's chamber, putting 'themself in danger / To take bread at my hand'? In the second stanza, 'they' becomes 'she' and the poet is

caught in her arms long and small,
Therewithal sweetly did me kiss,
And softly said, 'Dear heart, how like you this?'

In the final stanza, the speaker lies 'broad waking', the strange, dream-like images have vanished, and he is left abandoned, aggrieved and vengeful:

But all is turned thorough my gentleness
Into a strange fashion of forsaking,
And I have leave to go of her goodness
And she also to use newfangleness.
But since that I so kindly am served
I would fain know what she hath deserved.

Mason pointed out that behind Wyatt's poem lies a passage from Chaucer's *The Squire's Tale* in which a female falcon complains of the faithlessness of a noble tercelet:

Men loven of propre kinde newefangelnesse,
As briddes doon that men in cages fede.
For though thou night and day take of hem hede,
And strawe hir cage faire and softe as silk,
And yeve hem sugre, hony, breed and milk, *yeve: give*
Yet right anon as that his dore is uppe,
He with his feet wol spurne adoun his cuppe,
And to the wode he wole, and wormes ete;
So newefangel been they of hire mete, *so newfangled are they in their tastes*
And loven novelries of propre kinde;
No gentillesse of blood ne may hem binde.[41]

Many of the elements in 'They flee from me' are here: the word 'newefangelnesse', repeated as 'newefangel' in line 618, and the representation of fickle lovers as wild things whose nature it is to flee: they cannot be constrained by 'gentillesse'. However, Chaucer's female falcon complains of men, Wyatt's male lover complains of the faithlessness of women. Chaucer's falcon becomes a 'signe of trouthe that is in women sene' (l. 645), but Wyatt's wild woman/women are deceitful and fickle, and it is the male speaker who occupies the place of the truthful and weeping mate. This role seems a distinctly effeminate one. Reposing in his chamber, Wyatt's lover is 'stalked' by the wild creatures as, in the second stanza, he submits to the lady's sexual advances ('[his] will was [her] willes instrument' to adapt Chaucer's words (l. 569)), and it is he who is forsaken to complain of injustice when she departs. Wyatt's poem muddles traditional distinctions of gender: the fickle lady fulfils a misogynist stereotype, but she also usurps the active liberty of the male, while he occupies the passive, powerless, homebound place traditionally assigned to women.[42]

Something of the comedy and shame associated with the passive male is apparent in a balet, 'My darling dere, my daisy floure', published in 1527 by the poet John Skelton (1464?–1529), which may provide another subtext for Wyatt's poem. Skelton mocks an abandoned lover, soothed to sleep like a child in the lap of his lady who then abandons him for a more vigorous lover:

> He wanted wit her love to win:
> He trusted her payment and lost all his pray;
> She left him sleping and stale away.
> With hey lullay etc.[43]

The abandoned lover lies dreaming, rocked like a child by the poem's comic refrain, bereft, the words seem to suggest, of both potency and lady:

> Behold, thou lieste, luggard, alone!
> Well may thou sigh, well may thou grone,
> To dele with her so cowardly;
> I wis, powle hatchet, she blered thine I! *Certainly, you prick, she hoodwinked you*[44]

'They flee from me' does not allow the reader the simple, mocking viewpoint of Skelton's poem. We shift between the perspectives of a detached observer of the lover's humiliation and the pain of the lover's own point of view. Differences and distinctions are persistently confused and dissolved through the poem: male and female, wild and tame, natural and civil, outside and inside.[45] The lady's 'strange fashion' and 'newfangleness' translate the natural fickleness of wild things and women into the terminology of courtly modishness. By contrast, the 'gentleness' of the forsaken lover is both a euphemism for his passivity and also a sign of his old-fashioned, well-bred civility which has been violated by the 'newfangleness' of the lady ('gentle' as in 'gentleman'). The 'kindly' of the penultimate line points in opposite directions: it means 'naturally' (in the 'nature' of women and wild things), and also 'courteously' or 'considerately', a sign of 'gentle' behaviour.[46] In the latter sense, of course, it functions ironically (the lady's behaviour may be 'natural', but it is not 'gentle'). The language situates the lady at two opposite extremes which come to be interchangeable: she is both a wild, uncivil thing and the epitome of a new courtly mode of behaviour whose 'newfangled' immorality has superseded the old-fashioned, chivalrous codes of the lover.

If the lady represents those 'othernesses' which threaten the lover's values, what of the lover himself? Why does he feed the wild creatures in the first stanza – as a gesture of kindness or in order to entrap them? Is their wildness a sign of ingratitude, or simply natural to them? The lover blames the wild things of the first stanza for failing to 'remember', failing to remain loyal to the past, like the lady's 'newfangleness', but that past is filtered through the lover's memory in the second stanza in a strangely ambiguous moment of erotic gratification in which the lady is imagined both as seducer and as the object of a voyeuristic gaze, the 'thin array' of her 'loose gown' falling from her shoulders. The fantasy of passivity and abandonment which characterizes the lover's self-presentation in this poem co-exists with hints of something quite different, the lover as himself predatory, his gentleness/gentlemanliness masking possessive desire and vengefulness. In relation to these contradictory fantasies of maleness in the poem, the lady, figuring what is most desirable and what is most feared, occupies an impossible range of positions, fascinatingly wild and reprehensibly undomesticated, corrupt by nature and newfangled, under-civilized and over-civilized, seducer and object of seduction.

'They flee from me' reveals, with particular complexity and power, a pattern not unlike that of 'She sat and sewed', in which the woman is both desirable and blamed; she exerts a resented, but glamorous, charisma and control in the present, but the poet fantasizes about reasserting his own potency through victimizing her in the future. In such poems, traditional topoi of the cruel or faithless mistress and the rebellious lover who turns, or dreams of turning, the tables on his mistress may displace wider frustrations and resentments arising from the contradictions, for male courtiers, inherent in courting itself, an activity perceived in the Henrician period as glamorous and shameful, its rewards both desirable and unstable.[47]

The language ('favour', 'grace', 'deserving', 'trust') in which service to fickle women could image service on the 'slipper top' of courtly ambition and vice versa was readily to hand and the transference easy to make. Jonathan Kamholtz points out that when a number of Wyatt's poems were printed in *Tottel's Miscellany*, they were given titles which suggest that their theme is amorous dalliance even when it is not at all clear whether their context is political or amatory.[48] 'It may be good, like it who list' (Reb. lxxxv), for example, may well describe the uncertainties of political courting, although Tottel entitled it 'The lover taught, mistrusteth allurements'. Line 5, 'The windy words, the eyes' quaint game', is typical of the poem's ambiguous language, equally applicable to fickle women and untrustworthy courtiers. The proverbial phrase 'Woman's wordes they be but winde', and its like, often figure in contemporary balets.[49] On the other hand, Wyatt also used a version of the proverb in an explicitly political epigram:

Throughout the world, if it were sought,
Fair words enough a man shall find.
They be good cheap; they cost right nought;
Their substance is but only wind.[50]

Similarly, 'the eyes' quaint game' could encompass the meanings of 'quaint' = 'cunning, crafty, scheming' (*OED*, adj. I.1b), and also 'queynt' = "cunt" (*OED* 'quaint' sb.). The effect is to suggest that untrustworthiness and betrayal are synonymous with women's sexual organ, but it is impossible to decide in this case whether political or sexual deception is the primary object of blame.

If the lady embodied courtly glamour, exploitation and uncertainty, she could also figure Fortune herself, traditionally represented as a fickle goddess with a face as contradictory as that of a desired mistress, at one moment favourable, at the next cruel and indifferent.[51] The elision of the mistress's favour with that of Fortune is ubiquitous in poetry of the period and is, to a great extent, built into the traditional language of courtly love. One of Wyatt's balets, for example, entitled by Tottel 'The Lover waileth his changed joyes', may as readily refer to fickle Fortune:

For broken now are her behests
  And pleasant looks she gave;
And therefore now all my requests
  From peril cannot save.

(Reb. cxlviii, ll. 29–32)

Surrey draws on the same imagery when, having depicted love as 'A comon plage that bindes, / A travell [labour] without mede [reward]', he offers, in the voice of the abandoned lover, a stoic consolation against the turns of Love/Fortune's wheel:

Farewel, thou hast me tought
To thinke me not the furst
That love hath set aloft
And casten in the dust.

(Jones no. 19)

Here the favour of the mistress and Fortune are interchangeable; stoic indifference is the virtuous response to either.

One court lady very nearly did bring all Wyatt's wealth to woe: 'Brunet that set my wealth in such a roar' ('If waker care', Reb. xxviii). In Wyatt's own Egerton MS, this line originally read 'her that did set our country in a rore'. Wyatt may have revised the line because in its original form it was too clear a reference to Anne Boleyn, with whom Wyatt seems to have enjoyed some kind of amorous liaison in the early 1520s, leading to his arrest and imprisonment in May 1536.[52] Wyatt's revision to 'If waker care' has the effect of transferring Boleyn's disruptive effect on the macrocosm of the state to the microcosm of Wyatt's well-being, both emotional and financial ('wealth', *OED* 1 and 2). The poem looks back on a period of extreme political and personal insecurity and hopes for a new stability, figuring both states through women: false Brunet and stable Phyllis (see my discussion below, p 59).

A colourful anecdote told by Wyatt's grandson, which may derive from Anne Boleyn's maid, Anne Gainsford, tells of an exchange between Wyatt and Henry VIII which neatly illustrates the role and dilemma of the courtly lady.[53] Wyatt 'intertaininge talke with [Anne Boleyn] as she was earnest at worke, in sportinge wise caught from her a certain smale jewel hanginge by a lace out of her pocket . . . which he thrust into his bosome, neither with any earnest request could she obtaine it of him againe'. Aware of this, the king, a few days later, at a game of bowls, takes an occasion to display his own favour, Anne's ring on his finger:

> in his game takinge an occasion to affirme a cast to be his that plainly appeared to be otherwise . . . he [the King], pointinge with his finger whereon he ware her ringe . . . said, 'Wiat, I tel thee it is mine,' smilinge upon him withal. Sir Thomas at the leangth castinge his eye upon the King's finger, perceived that the Kinge ment the Lady whose ring that was, which he wel knew, and pausinge a littel, and findinge the Kinge bent to pleasure, after the words repeated againe by the Kinge, the Knight replied, 'And if it may like your Majestie to give me leave to measure it, I hope it will be mine'; and withal tooke from his necke the Lase where at honge the tablet, and therewith stooped to measure the cast, which the Kinge espiinge knew, and had seene her were, and therewithal sporn'd away the bowle, and saide, 'It may be so, but then I am deceived,' and so brake up the game.
>
> (*LL* p 18)

The anecdote, whether true or apocryphal, captures some of the characteristics of male courtly performance that we have already discussed in this chapter as a context for the verse. Successful male courtly behaviour is represented as a heady mixture of hubristic display and risky boldness played out through a symbolic language of amorous favours and the skilful exploitation of double meanings, while the woman negotiates a potentially dangerous feat of balance between graceful good humour and propriety. The incident begins with a jesting game of provocation between the sexes, but soon develops into a competitive vaunting between males. Although her favour is considered a mark of success, Anne Boleyn does not control the rewards in this system, any more than other courtly ladies did. The anecdote relegates her to the glamorous occasion for, on the one hand, a courtier's bid to make a daring gesture before his playful monarch, and on the other, a monarchical display of power in which the mistress's genuine preference, whatever it may have been, is neither here nor there.

'Whoso list to hunt' (Reb. xi) has often been related to Henry VIII's claiming of Anne Boleyn. The deer/dear of the poem may indeed refer to Anne Boleyn, but it also figures all courtly women in the system of male competition and reward which dictated their significance and limited their power:

> Whoso list to hunt, I know where is an hind,
> But as for me, helas, I may no more.
> The vain travail hath wearied me so sore,
> I am of them that farthest cometh behind.
> Yet may I by no means my wearied mind
> Draw from the deer, but as she fleeth afore
> Fainting I follow.
>
> (ll. 1–7)

Marguerite Waller, in a subtle analysis of the sonnet, has pointed out that its rhetoric excludes the woman reader. The speaker addresses other men in a hunt for a hind who is clearly a figure for a woman who is seen exclusively as prey. The exclusion of the woman as reader and potential hunter is matched by the 'non-identity' of the woman within the poem, who does not even speak the words that are engraved around her neck:

> And graven with diamonds in letters plain
> There is written her fair neck round about:
> '*Noli me tangere* for Caesar's I am,
> And wild for to hold though I seem tame.'
>
> (ll. 11–14)

Her structural function is as prize for the strongest of the 'fierce, insatiable appetites' which constitute male identity within the poem.[54] Waller's argument is not invalidated by the possibility that actual women in the early sixteenth century read the poem, inserting themselves into or, perhaps even then as now, contesting, the aggressively male construction. Nevertheless, as Waller points out, within the fiction of the poem, and the system of male courtship to which it belongs, 'the woman who makes the competitive male relationship, and hence the sovereign self, possible, is herself placed in a highly unstable, highly unflattering, perilous and powerful double bind. She is structurally required, only to be denied and despised, abused for her role in a dynamic not of her own choosing' (p 178).

Waller's powerful account nevertheless oversimplifies both the construction of the speaker's male ego within the poem and the significance of the woman. Hunting was one of the most manly of courtly recreations.[55] Its association with masculinity and virility is clearly illustrated by the hunting song in the King Henry VIII MS which I quoted above (p 46). In this context, the ambivalence of the speaker of 'Whoso list to hunt' reflects disparagingly on his own sexual potency. His identity is certainly male, but it is of a male who is failing in the hunt, fears his ability to 'tame' the lady, and suspects he is seeking to catch the wind in a net anyway (l.8). Even the winner gets a hind who, it is implied in the last line, will prove faithless and coltish. The misogyny constitutes a retaliatory masculine aggression, as in 'She sat and sewed', but the poem also speaks of weariness and distaste for an activity that shames the speaker, but which he cannot quit.[56]

Wyatt's sonnet changes the visionary and adorational theme of its Petrarchan source (*Rime* 190) into that of a sexual hunt. Patricia Thomson has shown that contemporary annotators of Petrarch's poems drew attention 'to the well-known Latin motto *Noli me tangere quia Caesaris sum*' (Do not touch me for I belong to Caesar), supposed to have been 'inscribed on the collars of Caesar's hinds', referred to in Petrarch's concluding lines:[57]

> 'Nessun me tocchi' al bel collo d'intorno
> scritto avea di diamanti e di topazi,
> 'libera farmi al mio Cesare parve'.
>
> (*Rime* 190)
>
> (Round its fair neck was written in diamonds and topazes: 'Let no man touch me, for Caesar's will is that I remain free'.)[58]

Wyatt's decision to render only the first part of the motto in Latin makes its coincidence with the Vulgate version of Christ's words to Mary Magdalene in the Garden of Gethsemane ('Noli me tangere') more apparent.[59] This biblical echo in the first half of the line alerts us to another biblical echo in the second half of the line, Christ's answer to those who asked whether it was lawful to pay tribute to Caesar: 'And he said unto them: whose is this image and superscription? They said unto him: Caesar's. Then said he unto them:

Give therefore to Caesar, that which is Caesar's: and give unto God, that which is God's' (Tyndale's translation of Matthew 22.20–1).[60] The two biblical echoes seem to point in contradictory directions: the echo of Christ's words in the Garden of Gethsemane associates the lady with his untouchable charisma, while the second reduces her, like the coins, to a sign of wealth, irredeemably of this world, in opposition to the things of God. One biblical echo invokes a spiritualizing and idealizing rhetoric of woman as saint or goddess, only to expose her, through the second biblical echo, as dependent on wealth and power. Her double identity in the courtly system is strung round her neck as a necklace or a collar, a vaunt or a warning to others and a sign of her own servitude.

The hind/lady of this poem is fleeting and fickle, bejewelled and desirable, tantalizingly out of reach and on offer. The kind of slippage which we have been tracing in this chapter, both in Wyatt's poetry and more generally in the rhetoric which he inherited and used, between women, fortune and worldly success, makes it impossible to decide whether the 'her' of this poem is a particular woman (Anne Boleyn), any woman as prize ('fetishized woman', in Waller's phrase) or woman as a figure for worldly favour, especially the rewards of court service. The object of the 'vain travail' of 'Whoso list' is not unlike that worldly success which, at the moment of seeming possession, 'irketh straight and by itself doth fade . . . / And yet the thing that most is your desire / Ye do mis-seek with more travail and care', against which Wyatt warned John Poyntz in the satire 'My mother's maids' (Reb. cl ll. 83 and 90–1).

'HAPPY DAMES' AND 'GOOD LADIES'

R. Howard Bloch in his study of medieval misogyny has argued that it is closely related to an idealizing language of courtly love: 'The two medieval discourses on women are not contraries but intermingling zones of a common conception of gender. Antifeminism and the idealization of the feminine are mirror images of each other.'[61] If glamorous and fickle women embodied and displaced frustrations and attractions attendant on courtly service for many of the young male poets of the 1520s and 1530s, a different kind of woman became associated, in the poetry of Wyatt and particularly in that of Surrey, with an alternative, domestic bliss, nurturing and stable, although frequently as distant and ungraspable as her fleeting and unstable cousin. We have already seen how Wyatt's sonnet 'If waker care' (Reb. xxviii) contrasts Brunet 'that set my wealth in such a roar' with Phyllis whose 'unfeigned cheer' provides comfort and security:

> She from myself now hath me in her grace.
> She hath in hand my wit, my will, and all.
> My heart alone well worthy she doth stay
> Without whose help scant do I live a day.
>
> (ll. 11–14)

It is probable that to those in Wyatt's circle, among whom this sonnet would have circulated, Phyllis was identifiable as Elizabeth Darrell, an attendant on Katherine of Aragon and later in the household of the former queen's supporter and sympathizer, the Marquis of Exeter. When Wyatt was arrested in January 1541, his house and goods were sequestered by government officials who reported that Darrell, heavily pregnant, had been living with him at Allington (*LL* pp 84–5, 177). Wyatt's representation of Phyllis suggests, however, that he attributes to her a significance and a role that is in part defined by its opposition to Brunet. Where Brunet causes uproar whether in the country at large or to her lover's 'wealth', Phyllis is 'unfayned' [true] and 'stays', supporting and nurturing him.

Two poems, written by Wyatt in Spain in 1538/9, deal with similar desires and fears through the figure of a nurturing woman. 'So feeble is the thread' (Reb. lxxvi), entitled in the Egerton MS 'In Spaine', is a translation of a *canzone* by Petrarch.[62] The speaker describes his self-division, his body in Spain, his thoughts and soul fleeing towards England and his mistress:

> when I think upon the distance and the space
> That doth so far divide me from my dear desired face,
> I know not how t'attain the wings that I require
> To lift my weight that it might fly to follow my desire.
>
> (ll. 23–6)

Spain is a place of uncertainties, of not knowing when he might return, whether his mistress is still faithful, how his 'wealth doth bate' (l. 42), what, in sum, is going on at home. In lines added to the Petrarchan original, he writes: 'Thus am I driven to hear and hearken after news; / My comfort scant, my large desire in doubtful trust renews' (ll. 79–80). Erotic longing becomes inextricably intermingled, and identified, with a longing for certainty and stability:

> I fear and yet I trust to see that I require:
> The resting place of love where virtue lives and grows,
> Where I desire my weary life also may take repose . . .
> Then tell her that I come; she shall me shortly see;
> If that for weight the body fail, this soul shall to her flee.
>
> (ll. 92–4, 99–100)

The mistress occupies 'that pleasant place' (l. 95) of reward and protection; she is the perfect patron, to whom the poet sends his lines of humble petition.

H. A. Mason pointed out how closely the concluding lines (99–100) of this poem are echoed in the final lines of one of the most powerful of Wyatt's poems, 'Tagus, farewell' (Reb. lx), in which the poet anticipated his imminent return from Spain to London in June 1539: it is 'possible that the love, the mighty love, of *Tagus, farewell*, besides the tribute to his loyalty and patriotism, was also a mask for his love for his mistress'.[63] Conversely, as we have seen, love for a mistress could figure political service. In such poems as 'So feeble is the thread', 'Tagus, farewell' and 'Of Carthage he' (see Chapter 1, pp 30–31), the themes of erotic longing, self-division, geographical distance and political desires and vulnerabilities are inextricably entangled together. 'Tagus, farewell' figures the Thames as female, 'her wealthy pride' suggesting a fertility more promising than the golden sands of the Spanish Tagus:

> With spur and sail for I go seek the Thames,
> Gainward the sun that shew'th her wealthy pride — *gainward: towards* (eastward)
> And, to the town which Brutus sought by dreams,
> Like bended moon doth lend her lusty side.
> My king, my country, alone for whom I live,
> Of mighty love the wings for this me give.
>
> (ll. 3–8)

The Thames curves around London; she is both London's sexual partner and also its mother, carrying the town in the curve of her body (the moon was patroness of childbirth). The image seems to excite yet further the speaking voice which has moved from farewell to the urgent but physical seeking, 'with spur and sail', of a lover, following, as Brutus did, his dreams. The voice now seeks wings to fly. There is a complete identification here of an idealized England and royal service ('My king, my country') with an idealized woman who is both complacent partner and protective mother, a figment of dreams. That such an identification was not peculiar to Wyatt alone is indicated by a letter written to Henry

VIII by Cardinal Wolsey, the powerful chief minister of the earlier part of the reign, when returning from a continental mission in 1527: 'there was never lover more desirous of the sight of his lady, than I am of your most noble and royal person'.[64] In 1541, Wyatt's king and country were to prove, as Wolsey had discovered in 1529, as fickle and ungrateful as any mistress.

Wyatt imagines an idealized woman who holds 'me from myself' in a place of assurance and security. The 'pleasant place' in which he imagines her is England, London, perhaps a fantasized court, or 'home', a place where the rewards for service come without the vicious insecurities of the court. Like Wyatt, Surrey also found the image of the chaste and faithful woman offering, like Penelope, a haven of rest and stability for her wandering husband a potent means to express his own fears and anxieties. In two poems, 'O happy dames' and 'Good ladies, you that have your pleasure in exile' (Jones nos. 23 and 24), Surrey adopts the voice of the faithful wife, lamenting the absence of her husband on the seas.

The first of these is the poem by Surrey copied by his sister into the Devonshire MS (see p 45 above). Although it is normally interpreted as being in the voice of Surrey's wife, and connected with Surrey's requests, when on military service in France in 1545/6, for leave to have his wife join him there, its context in the Devonshire MS may suggest appropriation by some of the women connected with the manuscript for their own purposes.[65] Baron suggests that the poem may have been copied into the manuscript in 1544 by the Duchess of Richmond 'as a gesture of celebration, commiseration, and valediction' to her friend Margaret Douglas, who was due to leave court after her marriage that June and whose new husband, the Duke of Lennox, departed on a military campaign to Scotland the following month.[66] Such adaptability may have been written into the poem, for in the spring of 1544, many of Surrey's and the duchess's Norfolk acquaintances had to part with lovers and husbands as the English army left for France. With it went Mary Shelton's lover, Thomas Clere, her brother, John Shelton, whose wife, Magaret Parker, was a relative of the Howards, and her brother-in-law, Sir Edmund Knyvet, some of whose poems are copied into the Devonshire MS.[67]

'O happy dames' may have been written with some or all of these wives, lovers and absent husbands in mind, but both this and 'Good ladies, you that have your pleasure in exile', on a similar theme but more specifically related to Surrey's own biography (the little son is called 'Thomas', l. 22, as was Surrey's own son), point to preoccupations beyond the immediate circumstances of actual separation in 1544 or 1545/6. In both poems the faithful lady who speaks is imagined in specifically female company: in that of other happy wives in 'O happy dames', and specifically faithful ones in 'Good ladies', where they are contrasted with other, faithless, wives, 'suche as by their lords do sett but litle price, / Lett them sitt still, it skills them not what chaunce come on the dice' (Jones no. 24 ll. 3–7). The poet imagines his faithful Penelope standing at a window at night ('O happy dames', l. 25) or rushing to the nursery where she dreams her returned husband may be, playing with his 'litle sonne' ('Good ladies', l. 22). This specifically female homeliness is contrasted with that of the absent man who, interestingly, is not imagined, as might be expected, facing danger on the battlefield, but always tossed by waves and driven by wind on the high seas:

> And in grene waves when the salt flood
> Doth rise by rage of wind,
> A thousand fansies in that mood
> Assaile my restlesse mind.
>
> (Jones no. 23 ll. 29–32)

While Surrey and those who went to France with him in 1544 had undoubtedly to cross the Channel, a more perilous journey then than now, the prominence given to the sea and its dangers in these poems seeems to owe more to its traditional associations with instability, loss of control and the fickleness of fortune than to the 1544 or 1545/6 campaigns. In Surrey's poems, as in Wyatt's, the faithful mistress, modelled on Penelope waiting for her wandering Ulysses, powerfully embodies a fondly imagined, but always absent, alternative to the uncertainties and insecurities of the male world, dominated by the fickle favours of a monarch, the political machinations of others, or the fortunes of war on the battlefield.

Ventriloquizing a female voice allowed Surrey to personify a version of femininity very different from, but closely related to, aggressively misogynist representations.[68] Both the idealization of a Penelope figure in the poems of Wyatt and Surrey, and the flood of anti-feminist poems characteristic of courtly poetry of the period, can be explained, I suggest, by the male courtier's experience of courtly service, subjected to intense and shifting social and political pressures at the Henrician court. A female voice may also have allowed Surrey to give expression to aspects of his own experience not easily articulated by a male voice in the cultural codes of his time. The woman's experience as represented in Surrey's female-voiced poems is one of marginality and passivity. She sits at home, or on the sidelines, hoping for good fortune or the intervention of a beneficent providence to resolve her anxieties. The sense of helplessness and dependency, imaged in the male lover's case by his position in a ship 'amidd the foming floodds, at pleasure of the windes' (Jones no. 24 l. 12), can be distanced from, and disowned by, the poet even as it is articulated, if the persona is female. As I suggested in Chapter 1, attraction to the expressive possibilities of a female voice to articulate vulnerability and helplessness may again be apparent in Surrey's translation of Book 4 of *The Aeneid*, in which Dido is left on the shore, deprived of all power of action except that of self-sacrifice, while her lover, spurred on by destiny, sails away to action and triumph, displacing his own fickleness onto the woman he abandons: 'Come of, have done, set all delay aside, / For full of change these women be alway' (ll. 761–2). Action, when available, did not surely lead to triumph for Henry's poet courtiers. The place of women in their poetry, as goddesses and whores, sustaining mothers and *alter egos*, testifies to the tensions of their experience and the complexity with which their ephemeral verse could 'tune in temper just and meet / The rage' (Reb. lxxvi l. 86) that often threatened to disrupt it.

NOTES

1. The quoted words are from the correspondence of John Husee, court agent for Lord Lisle, quoted by Miller, H. (1986) *Henry VIII and the English Nobility*. Oxford: Basil Blackwell, p 29. For the association of courts and women, see my quotation from Bryan's translation of Guevara, Ch 1 pp 13–14 above.
2. Bates, C. (1992) *The Rhetoric of Courtship in Elizabethan Language and Literature*. Cambridge: Cambridge University Press, ch 2, discusses the shifting significance of the term in this period. See also Elias, N. (1978) *The Civilizing Process*, trans. Edmund Jephcott. 2 vols, Oxford: Basil Blackwell, vol 1 *The History of Manners*, esp. pp 102–4.
3. Osborne, J. M., ed. (1962) *The Autobiography of Thomas Whythorne: Modern Spelling Edition*. Oxford: Clarendon Press, p 24.
4. Castiglione, B. (1976) *The Book of the Courtier*, trans. George Bull (2nd edn). Harmondsworth: Penguin, pp 90, 94. References to this translation and edition are given in parentheses in the text in the following discussion.
5. Lull, R. (1926) *The Book of the Ordre of Chyvalry*, trans. William Caxton. Early English Text Society, OS 168, ed. T.P. Bayles. London: Oxford University Press, pp 57–8. For the association of courtly verse and effeminacy, see Wall, W. (1993) *The Imprint of Gender: Authorship and Publication in the Renaissance*. Ithaca: Cornell University Press, esp. pp 50–1.

6. *LP* x 798. The full conversation is transcribed from the Constable's report, which was partly burned in a later fire, by Thomson, P. (1964) *Sir Thomas Wyatt and His Background*. London: Routledge & Kegan Paul, p 38. See also *LL* p 29. George Boleyn, Earl of Rochford, Anne's brother, was executed as one of her lovers. Wyatt was also imprisoned in the Tower at this time, but was never accused.
7. Jones, A. R. (1987) 'Nets and bridles: early modern conduct books and sixteenth-century women's lyrics'. In *The Ideology of Conduct: Essays on Literature and the History of Sexuality*, eds N. Armstrong and L. Tennenhouse. London: Methuen, pp 39–72 (p 43).
8. Castiglione (1976) p 212, quoted by Jones (1987) p 45.
9. I follow the account in Ives, E. W. (1986) *Anne Boleyn*. Oxford: Basil Blackwell, p 367. Smeaton was one of those accused of adultery with Anne Boleyn. For other examples of Anne Boleyn's attempts to recall possibly incriminating moments of dalliance, see ibid pp 365–6.
10. Stevens, J. (1961) *Music and Poetry in the Early Tudor Court*. London: Methuen, p 207, and Mason, H. A. (1959) *Humanism and Poetry in the Early Tudor Period: An Essay*. London: Routledge & Kegan Paul, p 171. While Stevens follows Mason's valuation of courtly balets, he nevertheless provides an invaluable discussion of the tradition and social contexts of Tudor courtly verse, and particularly its relation to music. Mason claims that he could 'compose a dictionary' of the conventional phrases Wyatt uses. He helpfully cites many such phrases in his 1986 edition of a selection of Wyatt's poems (see Bibliography).
11. Mason (1959) pp 168, 171. For an alternative view which stresses the social nature and manuscript culture in which courtly balets were written, see Marotti, A. (1995) *Manuscript, Print and the English Renaissance Lyric*. Ithaca, NY, and London: Cornell University Press, esp. pp 2–10, 40, 135–47.
12. See, for example, Foxwell, A. (1911) *A Study of Sir Thomas Wyatt's Poems*. London: Hodder & Stoughton for University of London Press, appendix A; Southall, R. (1964) *The Courtly Maker: An Essay on the Poetry of Wyatt and his Contemporaries*. Oxford: Basil Blackwell, ch 2 and appendix B, and the discussion of the Devonshire MS in Harrier, R. (1975) *The Canon of Sir Thomas Wyatt's Poetry*. Cambridge, Mass.: Harvard University Press, pp 23–54.
13. The most authoritative account is by Baron, H. (1994) 'Mary (Howard) Fitzroy's hand in the Devonshire Manuscript'. *Review of English Studies* n.s. 45: 318–35. See also Heale, E. (1995) 'Women and the courtly love lyric: the Devonshire MS (BL Additional 17492)'. *Modern Language Review* 90: 296–313.
14. Baron (1994) p 326. Baron points out that no independent examples of Lord Thomas's handwriting are known to exist, and it is possible that the poems were copied into the manuscript after Lord Thomas's death by someone close to Lady Margaret. The relevance of the affair to the manuscript was first pointed out by Bond, E. A. (1871) 'Wyatt's poems'. *The Athenaeum* 2274: 654–5.

15. At least one other poem in her hand, in the form of a will, on fol. 88^r, may also be by Margaret: see Heale (1995) pp 308–9.

16. In quoting from the manuscript in this discussion, I shall use my own transcriptions and follow my usual practice of normalizing 'u'/'v','i'/'j', 'y'/'i', and expanding contractions. Most of the poems in the manuscript have been printed, with no indication of their sequence, either in M&T, or in Muir, K. (1947) 'Unpublished poems in the Devonshire MS'. *Proceedings of the Leeds Philosophical Society: Literary and Historical Section* 6: 253–82. Reb. also prints a number of the poems in his edition of Wyatt's poems. I shall refer readers to one of these published sources in parentheses in my text. This poem is printed by Muir (1947) no. 12.

17. For information on Mary Shelton, see Heale (1995) pp 299–300, and Warnicke, R. (1991) *The Rise and Fall of Anne Boleyn: Family Politics at the Court of Henry VIII.* Cambridge: Cambridge University Press, pp 46, 171. Both Harrier (1975) p 26 and Ives (1986) pp 242, 246 seem to confuse Mary Shelton with her sister-in-law, Margaret Shelton. See also Remley, P. G. (1994) 'Mary Shelton and her Tudor literary milieu'. In *Rethinking the Henrician Era: Essays on Early Tudor Texts and Contexts*, ed. P. C. Herman. Urbana and Chicago: University of Illinois Press, pp 40–77, who discusses Mary Shelton in relation to the Devonshire MS. His attribution of Mary Shelton's hand in the manuscript differs significantly from that of Baron (1994) and Heale (1995).

18. E.g. Muir (1947) nos. 37, 38 and 34 (the final stanza and a half constitute a separate entry in the manuscript).

19. Rollins 1 p 161 and 2 pp 22–9. Rollins collates the three versions of the poem: 2 pp 281–2.

20. The Knyvet poem copied by Mary Shelton is on fol. 60^r (Muir (1947) no. 32). Sir Edmund Knyvet was married to Mary Shelton's sister Anne.

21. Seaton, E. (1956) 'The Devonshire Manuscript and its medieval fragments'. *Review of English Studies* n.s. 7: 55–6. In fact, some of the stanzas are by a woman, the fifteenth-century Christine of Pisan whose 'L'Epitre au Dieu d'Amours' was translated by Hoccleve as 'Letter of Cupid' and printed as Chaucer's in Thynne's *Workes.*

22. The handwriting, which is the same as that of the poems apparently exchanged between Lady Margaret Douglas and Lord Thomas Howard, has not been identified. Baron (1994) p 326 and her Table 1 (hand TH 2) follows Bond in tentatively ascribing it to Lord Thomas Howard.

23. On the need for caution in assuming that women-voiced lyrics were necessarily composed by women, see Boffey, J. (1993) 'Women authors and women's literacy'. In *Women and Literature in Britain, 1150–1500*, ed. C. M. Meale. Cambridge: Cambridge University Press, pp 159–82 (p 169). Apart from the final medieval stanzas, approximately eleven other poems in the manuscript are, or appear to be, in a woman's voice. Of these, four are copied by one or other of the women associated with the manuscript.

24. For other evidence about women's writing in late fifteenth-century and early

sixteenth-century manuscripts, see Barratt, A. (1992) *Women's Writing in Middle English*. London: Longman, pp 262–300, and Boffey (1993). Boffey refers to the Devonshire MS on pp 173–4 but, unfortunately, bases her remarks on Southall's inaccurate description. She also views sceptically the claim by Hanson-Smith, E. (1979) 'A woman's view of courtly love: the Findern Anthology: Cambridge University Library MS Ff.16'. *Journal of Women's Studies in Literature* 1: 179–94, that the fifteenth-century Findern Anthology contains poems both composed and copied by a 'circle of women friends in Derbyshire'.

25. Kelly, J. (1984) *Women, History, and Theory*. Chicago: University of Chicago Press, p 23.

26. Bloch, H. R. (1991) *Medieval Misogyny and the Invention of Western Romantic Love*. Chicago: University of Chicago Press, p 160, defines misogynism as a tendency to characterize women as 'fickle, sexually rapacious, and terminally untrustworthy'.

27. Utley, F. L. (1970) *The Crooked Rib. An Analytical Index to the Arguments about Women in English and Scots Literature to the End of the Year 1563* (2nd edn). New York: Octagon Press, p 62; Salomon, L. B. (1961) *The Devil Take Her! A Study of the Rebellious Lover in English Poetry* (2nd edn). New York: Barnes & Co. Inc., p 70.

28 Utley (1970) p 201. On a different social level, Edward Gosynhill claimed in his anti-feminist *Scole house of women* (1542) that he wrote 'that the masculine, might hereby / Have somme what to [j]est, with the feminy', cited by Woodbridge, L. (1984) *Women and the English Renaissance: Literature and the Nature of Womankind, 1540–1620*. Hassocks, Sussex: Harvester Press, p 30.

29. Utley (1970) p 186.

30. The poem is collected in the 'Henry VIII MS' (BL Add. 31922), which contains a number of Henry VIII's own poetic and musical compositions, and printed by Stevens, J., ed. (1962) *Music at the Court of Henry VIII*. Musica Britannica xviii. London: Stainer & Bell Ltd, no. 35. See also nos. 62, 65 and 109, which describes an attempt on a dairymaid. Utley (1970) p 47 discusses hunter poems as part of a misogynist tradition.

31. Hall, E. (1965) *Chronicle, Containing the History of England* (reprint of the 1809 edn). New York: AMS Press Inc., p 515.

32. Castiglione (1976) pp 199–200.

33. Quoted by Freccero, C. (1992) 'Politics and aesthetics in Castiglione's *Il Cortegiano*: Book III and the Discourse on Women'. In *Creative Imitation: New Essays on Renaissance Literature in Honor of Thomas M. Greene*, eds D. Quint, M. W. Ferguson, G. W. Pigman III and W. Rebhorn. Binghampton, NY: Medieval and Renaissance Texts and Studies, pp 259–79 (p 262). Freccero's argument about the function of the court lady as a displacement of some of the anxieties and frustrations of the male courtier in Italian courts is complementary to mine.

34. Miller (1986) pp 34–5. For the increasing demand for education by the gentry, see Caspari, F. (1954) *Humanism and the Social Order in Tudor England*.

Chicago: University of Chicago Press, ch vi, and Dowling, M. (1986) *Humanism in the Age of Henry VIII*. London: Croom Helm.

35. For an account of the career and skills of an Henrician courtier who loved riding, but who was also required to read and speak French and sing with the king, see Vowell, J. (1840) 'The life of Sir Peter Carewe of Mohun Ottery, Co. Devon'. *Archaeologia* 28: 91–151.
36. My argument that the language of courtly love may act as a displacement of, or a coded language for, political frustration is particularly indebted to Kamholtz, J. Z. (1979) 'Thomas Wyatt's poetry: the politics of love'. *Criticism* 20: 349–65, and Marotti, A. F. (1982) ' "Love is not love": Elizabethan sonnet sequences and the social order'. *English Literary History* 49: 396–428.
37. Bloch (1991) p 52.
38. I quote from Thomson (1964) p 40. My description of the manuscript is indebted to Thomson's discussion on pp 39–41. See also Dowling (1986) p 199.
39. Thomson (1964) p 41. Cazeaux, I. (1975) *French Music in the Fifteenth and Sixteenth Centuries*. Oxford: Basil Blackwell, p 71, notes that Anne de Pisseleu's name was rendered as 'l'âne' (ass, donkey) in a satirical song at the court of Francis I in France.
40. I am indebted to the discussion of this poem by Estrin, B. L. (1994a) *Laura: Uncovering Gender and Genre in Wyatt, Donne, and Marvell*. Durham and London: Duke University Press, pp 98–123, and also to MacFie, P. R. (1987) 'Sewing in Ottava Rima: Wyatt's assimilation and critique of a feminist poetic'. *Renaissance Papers*: 25–37.
41. Chaucer, G. (1974) *The Works*, ed. F. N. Robinson. Oxford: Oxford University Press, ll. 610–20. Mason (1986) p 127 points out the similarity of Chaucer's passage to Wyatt's poem.
42. See Estrin (1994a) pp 93–122, and idem (1994b) 'Wyatt's unlikely likenesses: or, has the lady read Petrarch'. In *Rethinking the Henrician Era: Essays on Early Tudor Texts and Contexts*, ed. P. C. Herman. Urbana and Chicago: University of Illinois Press, pp 219–39 (esp. 220–3), for helpful discussions of female power in the poem and its destabilizing effect on the male speaker.
43. The poem is the first of Skelton's *Divers Balettes and Dities Solacious* (1527). Quoted from Skelton, J. (1983) *The Complete English Poems*, ed. J. Scattergood. New Haven, Conn.: Yale University Press, pp 41–2. See my discussion in Ch 3 p 74 below.
44. Scattergood explains 'powle Hatchet' as 'a soldier who uses a pole-axe': Skelton (1983) p 394 n 28. Presumably there is an obscene implication.
45. Greene, T. M. (1982) *The Light in Troy: Imitation and Discovery in Renaissance Poetry*. New Haven, Conn.: Yale University Press, p 258, comments on this poem: 'signifiers keep trading in meanings for new, often uglier ones', but his reading of the poem takes a male point of view, seeing the poem as defining 'the plight of the nobleman . . . [who discovers] that the games are dirtier than he realized'.

46. The Egerton MS has 'kindely' but the Devonshire MS version of this poem has 'gentillie' in the last line. Ferry, A. (1983) *The "Inward" Language: Sonnets of Wyatt, Sidney, Shakespeare, Donne*. Chicago: University of Chicago Press, p 101, discusses the implications of 'kindely' and 'gentilnes'.
47. For examples of the topoi of the cruel mistress and the rebellious lover, see Utley (1970) and Salomon (1961).
48. Kamholtz (1979).
49. The quoted example is from Jansen, S. L. and Jordan, K. H., eds (1991) *The Welles Anthology. MS Rawlinson C.813*. Binghampton, NY: Medieval and Renaissance Texts and Studies, no. 57 l. 35. For other examples, see Reb. xl and cciii. For the proverb, see Tilley, M. P. (1950) *A Dictionary of Proverbs in England in the Sixteenth and Seventeenth Centuries*. Ann Arbor: University of Michigan Press, W833.
50. Reb. lxx, and see cli l. 36.
51. Patch, H. R. (1927) *The Goddess Fortuna in Medieval Literature*. Cambridge, Mass.: Harvard University Press, pp 42–60.
52. The best account of these events is by Ives (1986) ch 5.
53. George Wyatt's 'Some particulars of the Life of Queen Anne Boleigne' is reprinted in *LL* p 17. It was first printed as an appendix to Singer, S. W., ed. (1825) *The Life of Cardinal Wolsey by George Cavendish*. 2 vols, Chiswick, London: Harding, Triphook and Lepard, who identified George Wyatt's source, 'a lady that first attended on her [Anne Boleyn] both before and after she was queen', as Anne Gainsford, a relative of the Wyatts (2 p 180). Ives (1986) pp 97–8 discusses the anecdote.
54. Waller, M. (1989), 'The empire's new clothes: refashioning the Renaissance'. In *Seeking the Woman in Late Medieval and Renaissance Writings: Essays in Feminist Contextual Criticism*, eds S. Fisher and J. E. Halley. Knoxville: University of Tennessee Press, pp 160–83, at p 179. See also Ferry (1983) pp 112–13, on the poem's ambiguities.
55. Castiglione describes hunting as, after war, the most important of the 'manly exertions' appropriate for courtiers: Castiglione (1976) p 63.
56. Compare Reb. lxxxv, 'It may be good', especially the conclusion: 'And yet my life thus do I waste'. See Crewe, J. (1991) *Trials of Authorship: Anterior Forms and Poetic Reconstruction from Wyatt to Shakespeare*. Berkeley and Los Angeles: University of California Press, pp 37–45 for a particularly stimulating discussion of 'Whoso list'.
57. M&T p 267.
58. The translation is by Mason (1986) p 135. In Petrarch's poem Caesar is clearly a figure for God.
59. John 20.17: 'Noli me tangere, nondum enim ascendi ad Patrem meum.' Tyndale translates the words 'Touch me not, for I am not yet ascended unto my father.' Quoted from Tyndale, W. (1989) *New Testament: A modern-spelling edition*, ed. D. Daniell. New Haven, Conn.: Yale University Press.
60. See M&T p 267 and Reb. pp 343–4.

61. Bloch (1991) p 160. For a similar point, see Utley (1970) p 31.
62. M&T pp 335–7 give Petrarch's text.
63. Mason (1986) p 222. On p 220 Mason describes the poem as 'the most passionate single utterance Wyatt has left us'. See the discussion by Fox, A. (1989) *Politics and Literature in the Reigns of Henry VII and Henry VIII*. Oxford: Basil Blackwell, pp 274–5.
64. Scarisbrick, J. J. (1968) *Henry VIII*. London: Eyre & Spottiswoode, p 203.
65. For Surrey's requests that his wife be allowed to join him, see Casady, E. (1938) *Henry Howard, Earl of Surrey*. New York: The Modern Language Association of America, p 163.
66. Baron (1994) pp 320, 329. On pp 314–15 she provides a transcription of the Devonshire MS version of the poem.
67. Heale (1995) p 309.
68. For theoretical problems raised by male writers' use of a female voice, see Harvey, E. D. (1992) *Ventriloquized Voices: Feminist Theory and English Renaissance Texts*. London: Routledge, pp 15–24.

Chapter 3

The New 'Italian Poesie'

When George Puttenham, in *The Arte of English Poesie* (1589), hailed Wyatt and Surrey as 'the two chieftaines' of 'a new company of courtly makers', he saw 'the sweete and stately measures and stile of the Italian Poesie' which they introduced into English as marking a decisive break away from the 'first age' of medieval English poetry.[1] There is never an absolute break with the past; as Thomas Greene has written, 'the past is formative: visibly or obscurely, it shapes us, filling our names with content and setting the conditions of our freeedom'.[2] Much of what seems new in the balets of the 1520s and 1530s can be seen as a continuation and revitalizing of traditions of verse going back to the fifteenth century and earlier. Petrarch was, after all, in many respects a medieval poet, and one of his sonnets had already been reworked in Troilus's voice in Chaucer's *Troilus and Criseyde.*[3] Indeed, Chaucer's verse could seem modern enough in the 1530s to be borrowed by Lord Thomas Howard and Lady Margaret Douglas to express their devotion to one another in the Devonshire MS. One of Chaucer's ballades even found its way into *Tottel's Miscellany*, where it was printed as the work of one of the 'Uncertain Authors'.[4]

Thomas Greene also reminds us that in the sixteenth century imitators were eclectic, synthesizing sources in order to find voices and forms appropriate for a new age and new conditions.[5] The changing conditions of courtiership and service in the early modern court, which we have touched on in Chapters 1 and 2, demanded new or modified fictions, altered cultural forms and languages through which courtiers could shape and glamorize their experience. In this chapter, I shall first try to define the kind of courtly style against which the new poets reacted, and then turn to the influence of three new Italian forms upon them, the frottola, the strambotto and the sonnet.

CHANGING TASTES AT COURT: FROM HAWES TO WYATT

In the Proheme to his 1526 edition of *The Canterbury Tales*, Pynson praised Chaucer, who 'by his labour / embelished / ornated / and made faire our englisshe'.[6] Such praise shares a view of the best poetic style which prevailed among the courtly, and those who aspired to be courtly, at the end of the fifteenth century and into the first decade or so of the sixteenth. The admired 'aureate' poetic style, for which the work of John Lydgate (*c.*1385–1449/50) was the prestigious model, was polished and ornate, garnished with the 'flowers' or 'jewels' (figures and tropes) which the poets learned from their medieval education in the arts of rhetoric. These ornaments were transferred from Latin to vernacular writing in a massive effort to bring English, regarded as rude and barbarous in its natural state, up to an international ideal of courtliness.[7]

A highly elaborate example of such poetry which reveals its social assumptions with particular clarity is Stephen Hawes's *Pastime of Pleasure*, dedicated to Henry VII and printed in 1509. The poem is a kind of manifesto for the arts of language, and its stanzas were plundered by manuscript collectors for ready-made courtly lyrics.[8] Hawes tells of the quest of a courtly lover, Grand Amour, for the favour of La Bel Pucelle who represents both the desired mistress and the promised social reward for his pains. These pains are largely grammatical and rhetorical. Grand Amour is sent to the Tower of Doctrine to be instructed in arts about which, to judge by his address to Rhetoric, he has little left to learn:

> o sterre / of famous eloquence
> O gilted goddesse / of the high renowne
> Enspired / with the hevenly influence
> Of the doulcet well / of complacence *doulcet: sweet*
> Upon my minde / with dewe aromatike
> Distill adowne / thy lusty Rhetorike[9]

Rhetoric banishes coarseness of speech with 'the aromatike fume' of eloquence (l. 923), and scorns it in those who for 'lacke of conninge [knowledge]' cannot penetrate her 'ryall arte' (ll. 898, 903). Rhetoric's art is royal both because it is fit for the education of a prince, and because it is firmly hierarchical in its allegiances. Indeed, it is presented to the king as an effective instrument of social control:[10]

> rethoricians / founde Justice doubtles — *founde: invented, established*
> Ordeninge kinges / of righte hie dignite
> Of all comyns / to have the soverainte — *comyns: the commons, common people*
>
> (ll. 876–82)

The poem projects an idealized image of courtly behaviour and the high calling of the poet. On a couple of occasions, it condemns the 'vainfull vanite' of 'balades / of fervent amite' (ll. 1390–1), and punishes those who use their 'sugred mouthes' to seduce by hanging them upside down over holly bushes, while the 'folisshe maidens' they have betrayed lash them with knotted whips (ll. 4219–37). Hawes provides his readers with an approved model of a courtly ballade (one of the medieval fixed forms for short poems) on the theme of idealized virtuous love:

> Farewell all Joye / and all perfite pleasure
> Fare well my lust / and my likinge
> For wo is comen with me to endure
> Now must I lede / my life in morninge
> I maye not lute / or yet daunce / or singe
> O la bel pucell / my lad [sic] glorious — *O lovely young girl, my lady glorious*
> You are the cause / that I am so dolorous
>
> (ll. 1625–31)[11]

The purity of the idealized lover and the lady's desirability are predicated upon, and justify, self-denial and aspiration.

Occasionally a very different voice intrudes into Hawes's poem, that of the 'other' of the idealized courtly lover, the gross, hideous but comic outsider Godfrey Godbylyve, who speaks his cynicism and barbarous misogynism without the help of golden rhetoric:

> They be not stedfast but chaunge as the mone
> Whan one is gone they love another sone
> Who that is single and will have a wife
> Right out of Joye he shall be brought in strife
>
> (ll. 4112–15)

As a punishment for his rudeness Godfrey is imprisoned with false rhetoricians in the rather grimly realist Tower of Correction where a lady scrapes 'His furde tonge that he cried like an ape', a punishment akin to that Spenser metes out to the ill-speaking poet at the Court of Mercilla, whose tongue is nailed to the Screen of the Hall.[12]

Hawes's ornate eloquence is a 'ryall arte'; its polished and bejewelled style is a version of the court's wealth, and serves as an instrument of social control through its power of demonizing outsiders and idealizing a courtly standard. But it also, everywhere, announces itself as 'clerkly', a product of the schools and of lengthy training. Grand Amour, the poem's hero, who scorns the rude, ignorant commons, is himself a parvenu, without 'grete land / treasure and riches' (l. 1854) with which to win his noble lady. His qualifications, in spite of the trappings of chivalry later on in the poem, appear to be largely those of a mastery of language and fidelity to the courtly ideals of virtue and loyalty. Hawes's fantasy of the meritorious success of Grand Amour may reflect his own class aspirations. If he was, as he claims, a groom of the king's chamber, he would have belonged to a group whom Starkey describes as 'hardly even' gentlemen.[13]

A more maverick and transitional contemporary of Hawes, John Skelton, veers between a number of styles. If for Hawes the voice of a Godfrey Godbylyve represented all that was rude and disorderly, for Skelton a similar style could be used to express a plain-speaking integrity directed against the vices of the courtly:

> take no disdaine
> At my style rude and plaine,
> For I rebuke no man
> That vertuous is.[14]

In different circumstances, Skelton could adopt more elevated registers. *The Garland or Chaplet of Laurell*, published in 1523 (no. XXI), although probably drawing on material written much earlier, is an elaborate and only partially playful account of Skelton's claims to the laurel crown.[15] In spite of his own impressive poetic achievements, the crown can be gained only if he composes 'some goodly conseit [witty poem]' in praise of the courtly ladies who weave his crown. Skelton's delicately implied contempt for such a task does not prevent him from writing courtly verses in an appropriately elevated diction not unlike that used by Hawes, although handled with a much lighter touch:

> Of Margarite
> Perle orient,
> Lodesterre of light,
> Moche relucent;
> Madame regent
> I may you call
> Of vertuows all.
>
> (ll. 947–53)

The vitality of, and public appetite for, the more demotic anti-idealist style of Godfrey Godbylyve is more evident in Skelton's *Divers Balettes and Dities Solacious* (Scattergood no. IV) which was printed in 1527, making it the 'earliest surviving printed collection of secular lyrics in English'.[16] In this volume Skelton felt himself at liberty to mix registers. One of the balets contained in the volume is 'My darling dere, my daisy floure' (see Chapter 2, p 52) with its cynical view of women's faith and its colloquial diction. Another, 'The auncient acquaintance, madam', seems at first to speak the idiom of aureate courtly praise:

> Of all your feturs favorable to make tru discripcion, — *feturs: features*
> I am insufficient to make such enterprise,

only to descend vertiginously into lewd misogynism in the third stanza:

> With bound and rebound, bounsingly take up
> His jentill curtoil, and set nowght by small nagges!
> Spur up at the hinder girth with, 'Gup,
> morell, gup!' — *gup . . . jaist: exclamations used to a horse*
> With, 'Jaist ye, Jenet of Spaine, for your taill
> wagges,' — *jenet: a kind of horse*
> Ye cast all your corage uppon such courtly hagges!
>
> (IV ii. ll. 15–19)

Scattergood's notes tell us that 'curtoil' is a pun meaning both 'a horse with a docked tail' and 'a tunic', while 'nagges' means both 'small horses' and 'testicles'.[17] Here the lewdly sexualized body of the woman and a scandalously 'country' vocabulary provide Skelton with the fertile means to collide a courtly, idealizing discourse with its cynical opposite.

Further evidence of a growing taste in the early decades of the sixteenth century for anti-idealist balets, often using or imitating popular forms and deploying a plain, demotic vocabulary, is apparent in a courtly manuscript collection of balets which appears to belong to the 1520s or early 1530s, known as the Welles Anthology (Bodleian MS Rawlinson C.813).[18] Although the compiler copies stanzas from Hawes, and, indeed, Chaucer, to form courtly balets, the manuscript as a whole suggests that Hawes's idealizing and aureate style was becoming out of date. Much fun could evidently be derived, as in Skelton's *Divers Balettes*, from colliding aureate and 'popular' registers. 'When that brydes [birds] be brought to rest' (no. 51), for example, juxtaposes the conventionally idealizing voice of the plaintive male lover with the unromantic plain-speaking of his mistress. In the following lines, the man speaks the first stanza and the second is the lady's answer:

> My ladie as freshe as floures in may
> meke your hard harte and Rewe on me
> or ellis I die long be fore my daie
> Swete harte all is for your love perde
>
> Me thinketh Soo by your coloure
> that ye be full weike and feble of corage
> your legges be small be nethe the kne
> your bryde shall never hoppe in my cage
>
> (ll. 9–16)

The balet continues in this vein for eight stanzas until the woman's capitulation: 'and in a place of privite / your bryde shall hoppe in my cage'. The woman's voice in this balet speaks a very different idiom from that of Hawes's lovers, La Bel Pucelle and Grand Amour, with their elaborate courtesies, but the Welles Anthology poem is no popular street ballad; its parody of the idealizing idiom of the male lover is too sophisticated. Like other balets in the anthology it may well adapt the words, or be written to fit the tune of, some well-known song circulating at court in the 1520s and early 1530s.[19]

The editors of the Welles Anthology quote R. H. Robbins on a trend in lyric poetry at the end of the fifteenth and beginning of the sixteenth centuries: 'Those writing in the courtly style were turning to forms which had hitherto been typical of popular origin (that is, not primarily for upper-class interest).'[20] In the new courtly poetry of the 1520s and 1530s, it is not only the forms associated with popular song, like the quatrain and rhyming refrains, that are becoming fashionable, but their anti-idealist, often explicitly lewd, themes and idioms. Such a taste is apparent in the Henry VIII manuscript (BL Add. 31922) which preserves songs composed and sung in the most intimate circles around the king, and which contains, as we have seen, the rollicking balet 'Blow thy horne hunter' with its lewd innuendos (see Chapter 2, p 46). The manuscript also includes aureate lyrics expressing such high sentiments as 'Love maintain'th all noble courage; / Who love disdain'th is all of the village.'[21] A number of the balets in this manuscript, as in the Welles and Devonshire manuscripts, appear to be courtly adaptations of, or provide new words for, pre-existing carols or songs.[22]

The plain and 'popular' style of the more demotic balets, as unlike as possible the stiff aureation of Hawes, or the more ornate courtly songs which the Henry VIII MS also contains, suited the display of rude male vigour and fresh informality cultivated by the new generation of courtiers surrounding the young king. Henry himself clearly took pride in 'singing, daunsing . . . setting of songes, making of balettes'.[23] A courtier, Sir Peter Carewe, records that, even towards the end of his life, the king 'havinge a pleasaunte voice . . . woulde very often use hime to singe with hime certeine songes they called *fremen* songs, as namely "By the bancke as I lay" and "As I walked the wode so wilde", &c.'[24] Such balets were designed for improvisation and performance by the aristocratic amateur rather than by the well-trained professional. They belonged to gatherings after the hunt, or accompanied boisterous pastimes – they were part of a display of privileged male lustiness.

The courtly verse of Wyatt and many of his contemporaries clearly draws on the elite use of 'popular' song styles with their simple stanza forms and diction, and their often blunt and assertive themes. In much of their verse, however, the counterbalancing note of idealism which characterized many of the poems in the Welles Anthology and in the Henry VIII MS largely disappears. In addition, the wanton, sexually active woman is no longer a country maid, an object of comedy and a trophy of male libido, but the courtly mistress herself. In this new representation of the relationship of powerful lady and servant lover, the lady is fickle and libidinous while the male lover occupies the previously female role of victim and dupe. The characteristic strategy of such balets, as we saw in the last chapter, is one of turning the tables on the mistress through misogynist insult. Simple metres and plain diction are used to add a mocking down-to-earthness, as in the case of 'Ah Robin, / Jolly Robin' (Reb. cxxxix), a reworking by Wyatt of an already existing song, in which the plaintive tone of the old opening:

'Ah Robin,
Jolly Robin,
Tell me how thy leman doth — *leman: sweetheart*
And thou shall know of mine.'

'My lady is unkind, perdie!'
'Alack, why is she so?'
'She loveth another better than me
And yet she will say no.'

is usurped by a new cynicism:

Résponse
But if thou wilt avoid thy harm
  Learn this lesson of me:
At others' fires thy self to warm
  And let them warm with thee.

(ll.1–8, 25–8)

In another example, 'I have sought long with stedfastnes' (Reb. cx), Wyatt follows the strategy of Skelton's 'The auncient acquaintance' and 'When that brydes be brought to rest' of the Welles Anthology. The opening complaint, expressed in polished polysyllables, quickly shifts into a different idiom:

I have sought long with stedfastness
To have had some ease of my great smart,
But nought availleth faithfulness
To grave within your stony heart . . .

For fancy ruleth though right say nay,
Even as the good man kissed his cow:
None other reason can ye lay
But as who sayeth, 'I reck not how.'

(ll. 1–4, 21–4)[25]

Such poems turn a language of idealizing service and a subject position of aspiring dependence into its comic opposite, rude self-assertion and the gestures of a 'manly' independence. Wyatt's poems, as do many of the balets of the period, restrain their fantasies of rebellion and retaliation within the light, deceptively simple and unserious idioms of popular-seeming song.

This deceptively artless style suits a class strategy which Frank Whigham has argued was designed, in a time of threatening upward mobility, to mark the behaviour of successful courtiers as innate, natural, impervious to penetration by outsiders:

> there arose a basic governing principle of the display of *effortlessness*, Castiglione's *sprezzatura*, designed to imply the natural or given status of one's social identity and to deny earned character, any labor or arrival from a social elsewhere . . . This means that useful effort *can* be expended, if it is hidden . . . Theoretically speaking, then, if rank cannot be grasped voluntarily, its fundamental manifestations will be seen as unchosen, simply self-expressive, not aimed to transmit information or to persuade a witness: in short, as not rhetorical.[26]

This is a strategy quite different from, though no less rhetorical than, Hawes's valuing of conspicuous effort, in the form of labour, training, polishing and embellishing, as a sign of worthiness at court. The sophisticated appropriation of popular song styles could mark Wyatt and his fellow courtly makers as gentlemanly insiders, nonchalant amateurs, belonging to the court, yet adopting an idiom and a stance which pretended a sardonic detachment from it.[27]

THE *FROTTOLA* AND THE COURTLY SONG

The question of how much English courtly verse was, or was intended to be, sung, and in what manner, is a vexed and to some extent an unanswerable one. C. S. Lewis probably overstated the case when he wrote that 'most, perhaps all, the lyric poetry of that age is to be regarded as words for music'.[28] The fullest study of the rather thin evidence is by John Stevens, who concluded that very few of the balets of the period were written to be set, professionally, to music. Henry VIII's own songs were an exception, being set to music, sometimes of his own making, and settings survive for more elaborate, 'aureate' courtly poems in vogue earlier in the century.[29] There are no contemporary settings for Wyatt's poems with the exception of ' "Ah Robin, / Jolly Robin" ' a balet which, as we have seen, may well have pre-existed Wyatt's version.[30] The earliest lute settings for Wyatt's and Surrey's poems date from no earlier than the 1550s.[31]

Nevertheless, there is evidence that many of the verses we now read as printed poems were informally fitted and sung to well-known tunes associated with popular dances or existing songs.[32] Notes occasionally added at the end of manuscript copies of balets seem to refer to well-known tunes to which the verses could be fitted and sung.[33] On one occasion, an annotator of the Devonshire MS, probably Lady Margaret Douglas, wrote 'lerne but to sing it' against verses that begin 'Now all of change / Must be my song' (Reb. cclvi), and other poems in the manuscript are marked, possibly for memorization and singing.[34]

A newly fashionable genre, or style of song, which similarly mixed the courtly and the seemingly popular was the *frottola*, which developed under the patronage of Isabella d'Este at Mantua at the end of the fifteenth century and became associated with a new Italianate courtly culture and taste distinct from the more ornate styles and the complex contrapuntal music dominant in the more formal courtly cultures of northern Europe: 'the *frottola* makes light of all ceremonials and avoids all affectation. A new world opens before us.'[35] The word *frottola* was used both for a type of stanzaic song with a refrain, and as the generic term for a kind of singing which included settings for such forms as the *strambotto*, the *barzalletta*, *canzone* and even sonnets. In a way that we have seen was becoming typical of much courtly poetry and song favoured by Henry and his court in England, the *frottola*, while thoroughly courtly, used popular forms and idioms, incorporating snatches of street songs, proverbs and popular sayings.[36]

Frottole and, to some extent, their distinctive, declamatory style of performance, sometimes, although not necessarily, performed solo to the lute, had been known at the English court since 1515 when Nicolo Sagudino, secretary to the Venetian ambassadors to Henry, wrote home urgently for 'qualche *frottola* nova' to amuse his English hosts.[37] Castiglione picks out the style for particular praise in *The Courtier*, as 'especially pleasurable . . . giv[ing] the words a really marvellous charm and effectiveness'.[38]

The most typical verse form of the *frottola* has a recurring, often mocking, refrain. An example from the Devonshire MS, 'Tangled I was in love's snare' (Reb. cciii), is modelled, though freely, on a song by Serafino de'Ciminelli dall'Aquila (1446–1500), who had become famous for performing his own songs to the accompaniment of a lute at the Mantuan court. The Devonshire poem is either by Wyatt himself or by someone who uses similar themes and shares a fondness for some of the same proverbs.[39] Serafino's 'Viddi casa altiera e illustra', on which it is based, is not in fact a love poem, but expresses 'a personal grudge against his master Cardinal Ascanio', developing the theme of Serafino's bitter disillusionment with patronage and its deceptive entrapments.[40] Each stanza concludes with the refrain 'Ha ha ha men rido tanto' [Ha, ha, ha, I laugh it (or him) to scorn]. The third stanza of the English version particularly picks up Serafino's themes:

> Everything that fair doth show,
> When proof is made it proveth not so.
> But turneth mirth to bitter woe
> Which in this case full well I see.
> But ha, ha, ha, full well is me
> For I am now at liberty.

It complains, however, of the faithlessness of women rather than of an unscrupulous patron:

> With feigned words which were but wind
> Too long delays I was assigned.

> Her wily looks my wits did blind;
> Thus as she would I did agree.
> But ha, ha, ha, etc.

The facility with which the English version can adapt the themes of Serafino's criticism of a patron for a poem about the faithlessness of women demonstrates with particular clarity the easy interchangeability of the two discourses of sexual favour and courtly success.

For Wyatt, writing in the 1520s and 1530s, the forms and themes of the *frottola*, witty and concise, sophisticated and sceptical, offered a charismatic model. Serafino's verse was first published after his death in 1502, and by the middle of the sixteenth century more than forty editions had appeared, far in excess of any other Italian vernacular writer in those years.[41] Wyatt may well first have come across it in Italy in 1527 (see Chapter 1, p 12). Equally he may have already heard of Serafino and experienced his style of performance during his brief diplomatic visit to the French court in the previous year. There, the courtly Mellin de St Gelais famously performed his own compositions to the lute as Serafino had done, in an apparently improvisatory manner.[42] Mellin's early twentieth-century biographer, Molinier, rather disapprovingly attributed the tendency towards libertarianism and cynicism in the poetry of Mellin and his more eminent contemporary Clement Marot to the influence of Serafino and the Italian *strambottisti*.[43]

Wyatt on a number of occasions develops images and conceits from Serafino's verse into *frottola*-like poems (e.g. Reb. c and ci). Even when translating Serafino's eminent compatriot, the fourteenth-century poet Francesco Petrarca, Wyatt sometimes gives his august model a lighter, more sardonic voice. For example, in Wyatt's version of a Petrachan *canzone*, in 'Perdie, I said it not' (Reb. lxxvii), the subtle and flexible metrical form of the original 'S'i'l dissi mai' (*Rime* ccvi) is transformed into the strongly accented, vigorous rhythms typical of the *frottola*. I. L. Mumford points out that Wyatt may have known a setting of this Petrarchan *canzone* by Bartolomeo Tromboncino, a well-known *frottola* composer.[44] The robust rhythms add a mocking edge to the lover's protestations which, in lines 35–40 (not in the original), unsentimentally challenge the mistress to make good the harm she has done:

> Then is this thing but sought
> To turn me to more pain.
> Then that that ye have wrought
> Ye must it now redress.

Of right therfore ye ought
Such rigour to repress.

In a number of poems, Wyatt represents the lover as performing his own complaint to the accompaniment of a lute in an informal, apparently improvisatory manner typical of the *frottola.* In 'My lute, awake!' (Reb. cix), the lover's song is imagined as lasting only as long as the lute vibrates:[45]

Now is this song both sung and past.
My lute, be still, for I have done.

(ll. 39–40)

The sound of the lute figures the frailty and pathos of the lover's complaint. Part of the poem's success is that it represents itself as the quintessential courtly balet of the period, seemingly spontaneous, ephemeral, graceful and plangent, mere vibrating air. The fragility of the song and its singer are, however, carefully contrasted with the lady's impenetrable hardness; she is imaged as 'marbill stone' and rock. When the lover's song is done his melodious voice evaporates, or so runs the conceit; in fact it has left, on the manuscript page, a powerful and indelible retaliation:

May chance thee lie withered and old
The winter nights that are so cold,
Plaining in vain unto the moon.
Thy wishes then dare not be told.
Care then who list for I have done.

(ll. 26–30)

The apparently artless spontaneity of the lover's song, wrung from his heart and both accompanied on, and figured by, the quivering lute strings, masks the careful and retaliatory craft with which the poem recycles the *carpe diem* trope of the disdainful virgin who misses her chance.[46]

Similarly in Wyatt's 'Blame not my lute, for he must sound / Of this or that as liketh me' (Reb. xciv), the initial conceit of the lover spontaneously performing his own song on the lute gives way to the conceit of the lover as himself a stringed instrument (depending on a pun on the Latin term for a heart, *cor, cordis*, with the Latin *chorda*, gut, or the 'strings' of an instrument or a heart), whose songs are produced by the lady who scorns him:

Blame but thy self that hast misdone
And well deserved to have blame.
Change thou thy way so evil begun
And then my lute shall sound that same.
But if till then my fingers play
By thy desert their wonted way
Blame not my lute.

(ll. 29–35)

Blame not my lute, and blame not me. As the lady touches the strings of the poet/lover's heart, so he touches the strings of his lute. Both, it turns out, are the innocent instruments of the lady's cruelty, and both are vulnerable to the lady's aggression. But instrument and lover escape in the last stanza with a display of just such faithlessness and spite as he accuses the lady of showing: 'Yet have I found out for thy sake / Strings for to string my lute again.' The poet may ascribe the lute's notes to the lady as she plays on the lover's heart, but the song in fact articulates only the lover/poet's words of 'blame'. Under the guise of a graceful, lamenting spontaneity and insubstantiality appropriate to courtly song, the poet aggressively reasserts a threatened masculinity.

There is no evidence that Wyatt himself could perform on the lute, and no contemporary lute settings of these balets have survived if they ever existed.[47] Poems such as 'My lute, awake' or 'Blame not my lute', with their refrain-like repeated variants on the last line of each stanza and their cynical view of a woman's love, may well deliberately invoke the Italianate style of performance associated with the *frottola*, known by reputation, or through performances by professional Italian lutenists at Henry's court. Wyatt probably knew the description of Serafino's passionate ('tanto ardente') performance of his songs to the lute in the biography prefixed to early editions of the poetry. He would also have known Serafino's own affecting lament to his 'cethra' (Grk. a stringed instrument/lyre) in a *strambotto*: 'E tu mia cethra sconsolata e mesta / Fida compagna à miei nocturni passi' [And you my disconsolate and melancholy lyre, faithful companion of my nocturnal steps]. The instrument will not record his last sigh, for he will break it on the stones first.[48] Very similar in spirit to the elegant chauvinism of 'My lute, awake' is Serafino's lamenting song, 'Moro, abruscio, & non me pente', whose refrain, 'Voglio prima aprirte el core / E da poi moro contento' [I wish first to disclose my heart to you, and then I shall die content], lends an ironic twist to the final stanza:

Tu serai chiamata acerba
Da ciascun che tama, ò vede,
Falsa, ingrata, aspra, e superba
Inimica di mercede,
Che sé io mor per troppa fede
Di me lasso eterno honore
  Voglio prima aprirte el core
  E da poi moro contento.

(You will be called sour by everyone who loves, or sees you; false, ungrateful, harsh and proud, enemy of grace. Thus if I die for my excessive faithfulness, I shall have eternal honour for my poor self. I wish first, etc . . . .)[49]

The themes and style of the Italian *frottola* had much to recommend them to Wyatt and his courtly contemporaries, bringing a fashionable Italianate sophistication to the 'popular' balet styles inherited from the medieval vernacular tradition. Their often colloquial diction and strong, cheerful rhythms and refrains contrast ironically with the poems' content, suggesting a playful artifice, a sophisticated detachment of singer from song.[50] They mimic a spontaneous, plain-speaking voice that contrasts with an ostentatiously aureate discourse of deference and flattery, but their song-like effect, capable of repeated performance, also renders their speaking voice anonymous and timeless, 'moving the poetry away from any sense that it expresses an individual's unique feelings'.[51] In such a form individual discontent may be assuaged and recast as amorous complaint, and bitterness rendered, at least in appearance, less dangerous by being presented as a witty and fashionable pastime.

THE *STRAMBOTTO*

Serafino's influence on English court poetry of the 1520s and 1530s was not confined to the stanzaic *frottola*. His most commonly used form is the eight-line *strambotto*, rhyming ab,ab,ab,cc, a form which Wyatt particularly made his own. Serafino uses the *strambotto* as an abbreviated sonnet, reducing Petrarchan complexity to focus on a single conceit or antithesis which is developed with a sardonic wit. Wyatt imitates this effect with success in, for example, 'She sat and sewed' (Reb. xli; see Chapter 2, pp 49–50). In 'What nedeth these threnning words' (Reb. xl), Wyatt translates, 'A che minacci' by Serafino, in which the motif of a stolen glove, developed by Petrarch over three sonnets (*Rime* cxcix, cc and cci), is reduced to a witty comparison between the lady's glove and the lover's heart.

Patricia Thomson remarks of this and another of Wyatt's translations from Serafino: 'these strambotti breathe the air of the court, its sophisticated amours and frivolous gallantries . . . Unimportant feminine tantrums are seen from the view-point of the worldly male',[52] revealingly identifying courtly superficiality with 'feminine' behaviour, an equation which the *strambotto* encourages:

> What nedeth these threnning words and wasted wind? *threnning: lamenting*
> All this cannot make me restore my prey.
> To rob your good, iwis, is not my mind, *iwis: certainly*
> Nor causeless your fair hand did I display.
> Let love be judge or else whom next we meet
> That may both hear what you and I can say:
> 'She took from me an heart and I a glove from her.
> Let us see now if th'one be worth th'other.'[53]

The lover complains of the lady's words, but his own, fluent, amused, wittily insulting, display him securely as a man of the world, at ease in the idiom of courtly pastime yet detached from it, a mocking practitioner.

In 'My heart I gave thee, not to do it pain' (Reb. xiv), Wyatt combined two of Serafino's *strambotti* to fit them to the form of another Italian innovation, the fourteen-line sonnet, in a thoroughly unPetrarchan spirit. The first, 'El cor ti diedi non che el tormentassi', is a 'rebellious lover' piece in which the lover, meeting only ingratitude from the lady, quits her service. Wyatt fits the eight lines of the *strambotto* into the first two quatrains of the sonnet, following the original closely. The compression of the second *strambotto*, 'La donna di natura mai si satia' [Women are, by nature, never satisfied], into the sestet leads to more originality.[54] Where Serafino accused the lady of vindictiveness and arrogance, Wyatt insinuates corrupt desires and craft:

> Unsatiate of my woe and thy desire,
> Assured by craft to excuse thy fault.
> But since it please thee to feign a default,
> Farewell, I say, parting from the fire:
> For he that believeth bearing in hand,
> Plougheth in water and soweth in the sand.
>
> (ll. 9–14)

The English version of the Italian proverb 'Zappa nel acqua & nell haren semina', which Wyatt uses in his final line, was already current, and its idiomatic harshness is increased by the colloquial 'bearing in hand' of the previous line.[55] In the context of the poem, 'plougheth' and 'soweth' add a sexual insult, exploited later by Shakespeare for Agrippa's comment on Caesar and Cleopatra: 'he plough'd her, and she cropp'd' (*Antony and Cleopatra* II.2.232). The *strambotto* form ends with a couplet, lending itself to a sharp turn or summation of the poem in its conclusion, an effect Wyatt exploits in his own innovation of a couplet at the end of the sonnet (for this point, see p 87 below). His original sonnet, 'Farewell, Love' (Reb. xxxi), whose anti-Petrarchan rebellious lover theme may itself owe something to Serafino's example, ends with a couplet whose final line is a deflating proverb, 'Me lusteth no longer rotten boughs to climb', a conclusion very much in the spirit of Serafino's *strambotti.*

On lightly amorous topics, the *strambotto* used the antitheses and witty conceits of Petrarchan poetry far more simply and to more ironic effect. On the other hand, the form's compression could be used to produce considerable emotional drama, even violence. An anonymous *strambotto* in the Blage MS, for example, condenses into eight lines and two sentences a passionate and bitter self-defence in the voice of Dido ('Dido am I', Reb. clxxi).[56] Wyatt himself translated the grotesque antitheses of an anonymous Italian *strambotto,* in the voice of a mother who in time of famine eats her own child, 'In doubtful breast whilst motherly pity' (Reb. xlv). Another *strambotto*, by Serafino, comparing the lover's frustration to an exploding cannon, is similarly baroque in its emotional effects. Wyatt translates it as 'The furious gun in his raging ire' (Reb. xliii), its drama deriving in part from its brevity:

> The furious gun in his raging ire,
> When that the ball is rammed in too sore
> And that the flame cannot part from the fire,
> Cracketh in sunder, and in the air doeth roar
> The shivered pieces. Right so doth my desire
> Whose flame increaseth from more to more;
> Which to let out I dare not look nor speak,
> So inward force my heart doth all to-break.

The single image of the exploding gun structures the eight lines, the actual explosion occurring in the middle two lines, its violent climax marked by a caesura in line five, after which the image is applied to the lover's own state. In Serafino's version the poem ends with stasis and a final comment by the lover: 'Sel taccio imor, sel dico altrui molesto. / Sospeso vivo, amor me dá tal sorte [If I am silent, I die, if I speak I harm others / I live suspended. This is the fate love gives me].'[57] In Wyatt's version, however, the drama rebuilds as the lover's growing emotion ('more and more') in the last three and a half lines imitates the cannon's growing crisis in the poem's first four lines.

Although Serafino habitually used the *strambotto* as a form for witty play on Petrarchan conceits, and as a text for singing, Wyatt's use of it in 'The furious gun' produces an energy and ferocity of effect at odds with the song-like graceful nonchalance for which the courtly balet seemed to strive, suggesting that he saw the form's brief structure as a suitable shape for the emotional power, or satiric force, of the classical epigram.[58] In 'Tagus, farewell' (Reb. lx), the emotional violence of the speaker's longing for home is not made explicit until the last line, but its force can be felt through the accumulating speed of the concentrated form (see my discussion in Chapter 2, p 60). Characteristically, Wyatt uses a final vivid image, intensified by the couplet, to disrupt any sense of closure at the end of his brief poems, as in the *strambotto* 'Sometime I fled the fire that me brent' (Reb. lv):

> Lo, how desire is both sprung and spent!
> And he may see that whilom was so blind,
> And all his labour now he laugh to scorn,
> Meshed in the briers that erst was all to-torn.
>
> (ll. 5–8)

This sense of energy or passion, scarcely contained within the concentrated form, differentiates the potential effect of the *strambotto* from that of the courtly balet, and brings us closer to the angry truth speakers of the moral poems, or the more complex subject position of the sonnet.

THE SONNET

The sonnet provided discourses as sensitive to the social and political strains of the Henrician court as did the more mocking balets and witty *strambotti*, but its strategies were different. The form was particularly associated with Petrarch's *Rime*, a sequence of sonnets and songs (*canzone*) addressed to Laura which had acquired classic status in Italy by the early sixteenth century and had begun to be imitated by vernacular poets throughout Europe.[59] The form was first introduced into England by Wyatt and Surrey who characteristically use it for very different effects. For both, its association with the culturally glamorous cities of northern Italy and with one of the giants of the humanist Renaissance must have been attractions. The brevity of the form seems particularly to have appealed to Wyatt. We have already seen that he was attracted to the eight-line *strambotto* and used two *strambotti* linked together to create a sonnet (see above). It is probable that Wyatt's modification of the Petrarchan sonnet rhyme scheme (typically abba abba, plus a sestet rhyming cde cde or cdcdcd), by introducing a concluding couplet, derives from the *strambotto*, typically rhymed abababcc.[60] For Wyatt, the sonnet combined the *strambotto*'s witty condensation with a complexity of thought and structure that went far beyond its limits.

In the sonnet, the lover's tortured consciousness becomes the main focus of attention, an aspect that seems particularly to have appealed to Surrey. Sonnets are not necessarily any more confessional or biographical than balets, but their fictions give fuller space and status to a voice defined by privacy and inwardness. They create fictions in which alienation and failure can be analysed and re-represented as refinement and suffering, so that lack of success becomes almost a mark of virtue, revealing the quality of the inner man. Fictions of privacy should not, however, be confused with private poems. The differences between the *frottola* or the *strambotto* and the sonnet do not depend on social performance or audience. All were written for manuscript circulation and copying in exactly the same way. Indeed, many of Petrarch's sonnets, which we now think of as exclusively for reading, were set to music in Italy and France in the early decades of the sixteenth century.[61] Seductive as a voice of inwardness and confession may be, it is no more the 'real' voice of the poet than any other.

In the following sections, I shall examine first Surrey's use of the form to dramatize a voice and dilemma characteristic of much of his other poetry. I shall then turn to Wyatt's less coherent, but often dazzling, experimentation with the form.

'To live and lacke the thing should ridde my paine': Surrey's use of the sonnet

The mocking tone and misogynism typical of Wyatt's balets is rarely in evidence in Surrey's work. Characteristically, Surrey constructs little narratives, or implied narratives, of faithfulness and loss, in which the speaking subject represents a point of stillness and integrity in a world of change and forgetfulness. But Surrey is also an innovative poet, intent on finding new forms to reshape old ideals. In longer poems such as 'The sonne hath twise brought forthe the tender grene', 'Good ladies, you' or 'If care do cause men cry' (Jones nos. 11, 24, 17), Surrey developed a new genre in English in the form of an extended dramatic soliloquy, usually 30–50 lines long and implying a larger narrative of loss and suffering. The genre looks to Chaucerian, Petrarchan and Virgilian paradigms to construct an idealized figure, a passionate hero, like Troilus, or Dido, or the Petrarch of the *Rime*, defined by a tragic steadfastness in an unkind or unjust world. If these poems were set to music, as it seems probable some were, the effect for which Surrey strove may have been closer to the 'plaintive sweetness' to which 'our souls . . . respond with great delight and emotion', that Castiglione attributed to the singing and playing of Marchetto Cara, than to the more mocking *frottola* performance implied by many of Wyatt's balets.[62]

The sonnet form with its Petrarchan themes of suffering and idealization particularly suited Surrey. Petrarch interspersed his own love sonnets and songs with elegaic sonnets lamenting the death of noble friends, for example Colonna (*Rime* 269) or the poet Cino da Pistoia (*Rime* 92), as well as satirical sonnets which scourge the corruption of the Avignon papacy (*Rime* 114 and 136–138). These different uses are not as unrelated as they at first appear. In Petrarch's sequence the death of the poet's friend Colonna at the same time as Laura marks a major shift in the sequence, intensifying the poet/lover's isolation, but also lending a spiritual quality to both his love and its objects. In the satirical sonnets, on the other hand, the materialistic papal court is imagined as feminine, a corrupt whore ('putta sfacciata'). The whore's viciousness, together with that of her followers, is implicitly compared to the chastity of Laura, and to all 'Anime belle e di virtute amiche' [noble souls, friends of virtue] whose present isolation, death or defeat will be transformed in an imagined future when such as they will inherit the earth after the destruction of the whore, returning it to the old virtuous pattern (*Rime* 137).[63]

Surrey was attracted by Petrarch's use of the sonnet for elegaic and satirical themes as well as amatory ones, and similarly cultivates fictions of the private integrity of 'anime belle', noble souls, in opposition to a public world of corruption and change. In his elegaic sonnet on Wyatt, 'Divers thy death doo diverslie bemone' (Jones no. 29), the dead poet, Wyatt, is feminized as Thisbe:

> But I that knowe what harbourd in that hedd,
> What vertues rare were tempred in that brest,

Honour the place that such a jewell bredd,
And kisse the ground where as thy coorse doth rest
 With vaporde eyes; from whence such streames availe
 As Pyramus did on Thisbes brest bewaile.

(ll. 9–14)

Like the dead Laura, mourned by Petrarch in the second part of the *Rime*, Wyatt is transformed into a figure of spiritualized faithfulness, lost to the passionate lover. Surrey may have had in mind Petrarch's elegaic sonnet on the dead poet Cino da Pistoia, for whom Petrarch imagines lovers, and Love himself, mourning (*Rime* 92). In Surrey's sonnet, as in Petrarch's, love, poetry, nobility of soul and civic virtue are linked together and set in opposition to the vulgar degeneracy of the political enemy, the 'cittadin perversi' [wicked citizens] in Petrarch's sonnet, or those 'whose brestes envie with hate had sowne' in Surrey's.

Another model for Surrey's sonnets on Wyatt may be Petrarch's double elegy for Colonna and Laura, 'Rotta è l'alta colonna e 'l verde lauro' ['Broken is the high column and the green laurel'] (*Rime* 269). This sonnet of Petrarch's seems to have had a powerful significance for Surrey. Wyatt had used it for a sonnet which probably mourns the execution of his patron Cromwell, 'The pillar perished is whereto I leant' (Reb. xxix).[64] Surrey had also used the image of the broken column for the sumptuous portrait of himself, commissioned in 1546, in which he leans on a broken column on whose base are painted the words 'Sat Super Est' [enough survives].[65] The iconography of the broken column seems to refer to Surrey's dead friend and potential political patron, Henry Fitzroy, Duke of Richmond, who had died in 1536. Surrey represents himself set apart from the darkened, ruinous landscape of the present, peopled no doubt by those who cravenly 'yield Cesars teres uppon Pompeius hedd' (Jones no. 29). Surrey's elegaic sonnets aspire to the inscriptional brevity of an epitaph, like the image of the broken column, surviving monuments against an eroding sea of time. At the same time, however, Surrey represents them as fragile, vulnerable, and private gestures offered instead of those 'temples' and 'rich arke' (Jones nos. 30 and 31) that monumentalized the virtuous heroes of worthier ages.

Although the tone and the occasion seem so different, Surrey's amatory sonnets similarly construct implied narratives of alienation and personal faithfulness, in which the first-person speakers figure as passionate and steadfast heroes. In 'Set me wheras the sonne doth perche the grene' (Jones no. 3), for example, the lover's unchanging integrity is defined in opposition to a series of fluctuating alternatives:

> Set me in earthe, in heaven, or yet in hell,
> In hill, in dale, or in the fowming floode;
> Thrawle, or at large, alive whersoo I dwell,
> Sike, or in healthe, in ill fame or in good:
> Yours will I be, and with that onely thought
> Comfort my self when that my hape is nowght.
>
> (ll. 9–14)

Petrarch often uses repeated antitheses to suggest a divided and tormented mind, but Surrey has chosen to translate one sonnet (*Rime* 145) in which, more rarely, they are used to emphasize the fixedness of the lover's mind.[66] Intriguingly in line 8 Surrey jettisons the antithesis of Petrarch's line, 'a la matura etate od a l'acerba [in maturity or youth]', for a line which situates the lover's own age between '*loste* yowthe, or when my heares be grey' (my italics). By adding 'loste' Surrey gives us the lover's own perspective from which youth is looked at nostalgically; it is past, it is no longer an alternative. A change in line 11 also contributes a distinctively personal touch to this translation: instead of the figurative binding of the spirit to the body of Petrarch's line, 'libero spirto od a' suoi membri affisso [the spirit unfettered or chained to the body]', Surrey substitutes the literal imprisonment of the speaker, 'thrawle, or at large'. It may be that Surrey, for those in the know, is evoking an aspect of his own biography. Surrey had been imprisoned probably in 1537, and certainly in 1542 and 1543. The sonnet may thus invite us to see Surrey himself, or a Surrey-like figure, as its passionate hero.

Surrey's boldest change to his Petrarchan model comes in the final couplet. Where Petrarch juxtaposes the alternating oppositions of his first twelve lines with an assertion of his own unchanging state ('sarò qual fui [I shall be what I was]') and the permanence of his sighs which will not alter whatever his fortune, Surrey gives himself up: 'Yours will I be', and in so doing achieves peace of mind in misfortune: 'Comfort my self when that my hape is nowght.' Although superficially the strategy is similar, the effect is quite different.

Petrarch suggests that even in good fortune the lover will remain the same sadly sighing figure he has been for fifteen years ('continuando il mio sospir trilustre'). Desire continues to be, as it is throughout the *Rime*, a source of pain. In Surrey's sonnet, on the contrary, desire turns out to be the source of comfort and firmness even in the midst of misfortune. Indeed, in Surrey's sonnet there is a sense that all the antithetical states of life listed throughout the poem are equivalent, 'thrawle, or at large'. His 'onely thought' of comfort is his love. The poem's argument, that the lover's inward affections and faith are the sole source of happiness in an uncertain world, makes of love an equivalent to that inner virtue which stoic philosophy advised wise men to cultivate as a remedy to the ills of fortune.

The source of Petrarch's sonnet is a well-known ode by Horace, 'Integer vitae scelerisque purus (He who is upright in his way of life and unstained by guilt)', in which Horace playfully attributes his carefree peace of mind both to his virtuousness, and to his undying love for Lalage (*Odes* 1.22).[67] Sessions suggested that Surrey translated Petrarch with Horace's poem by him.[68] Like Horace, though less playfully, love and virtue are rendered equivalent in Surrey's poem. Paradoxically, integrity of life, inner certitude, will be found in an imagined erotic self-giving ('Yours will I be'). Virtue lies in giving up, but also in a private faithfulness, located in the heart and mind in opposition to the fortunes of the public world. For all its paradoxes, Surrey's closing couplet brings the sonnet to a conclusion with a triumphant affirmation of private, affective value.

A sonnet which similarly depends on juxtaposing the lover with a series of accumulating images of the world's changes is 'Alas, so all thinges nowe doe holde their peace' (Jones no. 7), another adaptation from a Petrarchan sonnet (*Rime* 164). Our sense of the lover's steadfastness is reinforced by the virtuoso use of only two rhymes alternating to line 12; only the couplet changes the pattern. The main turn comes in line 6, which establishes the lover's difference from 'all thinges':

> Alas, so all thinges nowe doe holde their peace,
> Heaven and earth disturbed in nothing;
> The beasts, the ayer, the birdes their song doe cease;
> The nightes chare the starres aboute doth bring.
> Calme is the sea, the waves worke lesse and lesse;
> So am not I, whom love alas doth wring . . .
>
> (ll. 1–6)

Surrey has expanded the first quatrain of his Petrarchan model by adding another line, the all-embracing first, and where Petrarch's sea lies motionless in its bed ('e nel suo letto il mar senz'onda giace'), Surrey's moves slowly towards stasis: 'the waves worke lesse and lesse'. The effect of Surrey's version is to prolong the gradually expanding sense of rest with which the lover's state contrasts; the value-laden words 'peace' and 'calm' are introduced by Surrey into the description. As in another sonnet, 'The soote season' (Jones no. 2), the lover and the landscape define each other by what they are not: if the rest of the world moves towards nocturnal entropy, the lover suffers 'the great encrease / of my desires'; if the only movement in the outer world is the diurnal path of the stars and the slowing lap of the waves, the lover's mind jumps fretfully between sweet and stinging thoughts. As in 'The soote season', the lover's present life is experienced as lack and disruption while the natural world seems to continue its ancient, unreflecting continuities. The 'cause of my disease' (l. 11) is neither located clearly in the object of his love (as in Petrarch) nor in himself. No fault, no disillusion, seems to adulterate the speaker's elegaic account of the age-old rhythms of nature from which his faithful love excludes him. The sonnet with its antithetical structure seems to offer to Surrey a form and a language in which the experience of alienation and loss is given coherent form. The lover's isolation is aestheticized within the sonnet's polished form and balanced oppositions.

In the sonnets by Surrey that we have so far considered, the lady is almost completely absent, a mere pretext for the love that constructs the speaker as a passionate, tragic hero; the sexual vigour and harmony of the natural world represent a social order from which the lady's absence or denial cuts off the lover. Indeed, his very identity as a desiring and steadfast subject depends on her absence and his isolation. In an essay on the construction of the subject position of the lover in the Petrarchan sonnet, Nancy J. Vickers, citing previous work on Petrarch's use of the veil as a kind of idolatry, a substitution for the absent body of Laura, suggests that 'the speaker's "self" (his text, his "corpus")' depends for its unity on such absence, such a reduction of Laura to her symbolic parts.[69] In an interesting variation on the theme, Surrey's sonnet, 'I never saw youe, madam, laye aparte / Your cornet black' (Jones no. 6), a Petrarchan *ballata* (*Rime* 11) is remodelled as a sonnet which substitutes for the veil a long, pointed hood ('your cornet black') which covers the lady's hair and, Surrey suggests, also her face:

> But since ye knew I did youe love and serve
> Your golden treese was clad alway in blacke,
> Your smiling lokes were hid thus evermore,
> All that withdrawne that I did crave so sore.
> So doth this cornet governe me alacke
>
> (ll. 8–12)

This veiling has come about, as in the Petrarchan original, because the lover revealed his desire. As Vickers has argued, 'it is in fact the loss, at the fictional level, of Laura's body that constitutes the intolerable absence, creates a reason to speak, and permits a poetic "corpus" '.[70] Surrey's lover, like Petrarch's, establishes his identity on the basis of loss and absence.

However, by substituting the 'cornet black' for Petrarch's veil, Surrey significantly alters the connotations of his absent lady. The 'cornet' was the long, pointed hood, usually made of black material, which, in women's fashions of the Henrician period, hung down behind a frame of cloth around the face. It would hide the hair and, looped up onto the frame, might shade the face, but it was not a veil and was not worn across the face.[71] Surrey's 'cornet' brings his sonnet up to date, but its main motive may well be literary. The word 'cornet' (little horn), with its potential phallic symbolism, may recall such commonplace fifteenth-century attacks on 'unnatural' horned head-dresses as Lydgate's 'Of god and kinde / procedith al bewte':

arche wives egre in their violence	*arche wives egre: ruling wives eager*
ffers as *Tigre* for to make affray	
They have despit / and agein conscience	*they are spiteful, and against their consciences,*
List nat of pride / ther hornes cast away.[72]	*do not wish for pride, to cast . . .*

Surrey's reference to the lady's 'cornet' transforms the ever-absent but ever-desirable lady into something more threatening. Her black head-dress associates her with phallic power and with courtly fashion. She punishes, denies and 'governs' the lover by means of a headgear implicitly linking courtly modes with male emasculation and feminine usurpation. The lover's paradoxical position is that his passion and faithfulness, that which renders him noble, is a function of the lady's denial and absence, but she is an ambiguous object of worship, both desirable and resented, and even, given the tradition represented by Lydgate's poem, scorned. The sonnet's confrontation between a male voice of passionate nobility and the symbols of a fashionable effeminate power shares some features in common with Surrey's poem 'Eche beeste can chuse his fere' (Padelford no. 34; see my discussion in Chapter 1, p 23), in which the noble first-person speaker, endowed with details of Surrey's own biography, is denied by, and in turn scorns, a lady who is associated with a craven courtly power.

Surrey's passionate hero, defined by his truth and his inner steadfastness in the face of absence, denial and even unworthiness, is implicated in this sonnet in the same slippage between amorous and courtly service as, in Chapter 2, I argued was the case with many of the balets of Wyatt and other courtly poets of the 1530s. Surrey's fictions of the subject's noble integrity and passive suffering are, however, quite different from the characteristic aggression and cynicism mobilized by Wyatt. The very different strategies through which each poet's work deflects and mythologizes the challenging force of ambitious desire can be neatly compared through a consideration of their versions of Petrarch's sonnet 'Amor, che nel penser mio vive e regna' (*Rime* 140).[73]

In Surrey's version, love figures as a chivalric king reigning over the subjected body of the lover:

> Love that doth raine and live within my thought,
> And built his seat within my captive brest,
> Clad in the armes wherin with me he fowght
> Oft in my face he doth his banner rest.
>
> (Jones no. 4 ll. 1–4)[74]

Surrey goes further than Petrarch in stressing the captive, conquered subjection of the lover, defeated, the third line suggests, in knightly combat with Love. Within the terms of this miniature chivalric narrative, the personified Love is thus the lover's rightful lord.[75] However, the lover's desire, authorized and emblazoned by his feudal lord, is answered by the lady's veiling of her 'smiling grace' in aggressive wrath. Before this female power, Love flees:

> And cowarde love than to the hert apace
> Taketh his flight where he doth lorke and plaine
> His purpose lost, and dare not show his face.
> For my lordes gilt thus fawtless bide I paine; *gilt: guilt*
> Yet from my lorde shall not my foote remove.
> Sweet is the death that taketh end by love.
>
> (ll. 9–14)

Surrey's lover, faithfully serving Love as his chivalric lord, emerges as ennobled, loyal to his lord in spite of everything, even his lord's cowardice and the certainty of death. The heroism and innocence of the first-person speaker is the creation of the allegorical narrative which puts a nobly romantic gloss on the emotional narrative it figures, in which the lover's desire has overstepped allowed limits. The lady's denial of the lover's 'hote desire' establishes her as the governing authority in opposition to the bold and chivalric Love to whom the lover owes a tragic faithful service. Within the fiction of the sonnet, Surrey has created a miniature scenario of tragic nobility which transforms, for a moment, its little narrative of disruptive self-assertion and illicit aspiration.

Wyatt's version of Petrarch's sonnet precipitates us into a quite different world from Surrey's. Instead of smoothly alternating stresses, traditional personification and sonorous chivalric terms, we find ourselves amid rhythmic shifts from iambs to trochees, instances of double stress in adjacent syllables, caesurae and feminine rhymes, all producing a sense of a troubled, emphatic speaking voice:

> The long love, that in my thought doth harbour
> And in mine heart doth keep his residence
> Into my face presseth with bold pretence
> And therein campeth, spreading his banner.
>
> (Reb. x ll. 1–4)

Surrey's conceit depended on the separation of Love ('my lorde') and the innocent lover (Love's conquered subject), but Wyatt's opening at once confuses that clear distinction.[76] When the shift to personification occurs at the end of Wyatt's second line, love is a rebel and usurper, harboured, that is, sheltered, by the lover's thoughts, from which he sorties out 'with bold pretence' (*OED* 1. putting forth a claim, 2. ostentation or display, and possibly 4. a pretext or a cloak). The 'pretence' may be the usurpation of the lover (closer to Surrey) or directed against the lady (closer to Petrarch) or both.

In Wyatt's version, love, only half-personified, is a rebel, licensed, it is implied, by 'lust's negligence', a failure of self-rule:

> She that me learneth to love and suffer
> And will that my trust and lust's negligence
> Be reined by reason, shame, and reverence,
> With his hardiness taketh displeasure.
>
> (ll. 5–8)

In the face of her displeasure, Love retreats to the 'heart's forest' (l. 9), a striking phrase with complex implications (Petrarch simply says Love flees to the heart, 'fugge al core'). Forests were, in the sixteenth century, the special domain of the monarch, subject to laws which protected the deer (hart/heart) for royal use. They were also wild places, although not necessarily entirely wooded, the refuge of the outlaw, not easily accessible, within the fiction of this sonnet, to the lady's or reason's authority.[77] If Love's 'residence' is the poet's 'heart's forest', is Love the monarch whose royal domain is the forest of the heart? Or is he an outlaw taking refuge in the fastness of the forest? Does his 'residence' there associate him with the hunted animal, the hart, or with the hunter? Is he a creature of the forest, belonging on the margins of civilized society, or an aristocratic predator? Where Surrey's lover owed a simple chivalric allegiance to his lord Love, whatever the consequences, Wyatt's lover occupies a much more ambiguous position, owing a duty of trust to the lady, yet occupied by a love which is both rebel and monarch, a thing of nature and a natural lord.

The ambiguity about love's nature brings into focus the lover's dilemma. To whom does he owe allegiance? Is love his 'natural' lord, resident in his 'heart's forest', with all its beast-like connotations? Or is love a usurper whose rights over the lover are a 'bold pretence'? Should the lover more properly serve the lady whose reign/rein is 'reason, shame, and reverence' and whose laws and trust he has violated? If his capitulation to love is 'lust's negligence', it scarcely warrants the grandiose claim of the last lines:

> What may I do when my master feareth,
> But in the field with him to live and die?
> For good is the life ending faithfully.
>
> (ll. 12–14)

In the context of Love's flight, 'field' suggests less the noble field of battle than the open countryside where the outlaw will eek out a starvation existence. Wyatt's lover occupies a place of perplexing loyalties in which the bases of legitimate feeling and action are far from clear. From the point of view of the lady and the culture of restraint she represents, the lover's rude desires banish him from the confines of courtly civility, but at the same time the poem covertly asserts, though it also mocks, an alternative authority, seated in 'nature' and the manly–aristocratic domain of hunting, through which male desire is rendered natural and, in that wilder arena, legitimate.

Both sonnet translations are skilful poems which transform the original in quite different and independent ways. Surrey's changes and developments show a thorough understanding of the form and wittily create a miniature narrative which for a moment transforms an account of frustrated sexuality into one of tragic nobility. Wyatt's version, quite differently, threatens to burst the sonnet structure apart with its emphatic rhythms, its surprising verbal juxtapositions, and its development of the tensions between love, lover and lady. Where Surrey's version establishes the coherence of the first-person speaker and his virtuous and tragic steadfastness in opposition to the problematic authorities of repressive lady or doomed chivalric codes, Wyatt's complex drama, fraught with contradictions and ironies, exposes the incoherence of his 'I' speaker, undermined by the very language he uses. Where Surrey found in the resources of the sonnet a highly usable voice of ennobled complaint, Wyatt, on the contrary, exploited the form for its antitheses and dense verbal texture, constructing first-person speakers whose subject positions are always relative and often playfully undercut. The Wyatt we detect through the sonnets is crafty and evasive, the professional diplomat whose skills as a negotiator of the king's and his own business depended on a sense of the flexibility of meaning and the dangers of fixed positions.[78] It is surely no mere coincidence that the sonnet form's inventor, Giacomo de Lentino (*c*.1210 – after 1240), was, like Wyatt, 'a courtier academically trained for diplomatic service, writing for and in a group of courtiers' for whom the form seems 'to have offered a kind of courtierly utterance safely below the level of political action'.[79]

'All my thoughts are dashed into dust': Wyatt's use of the sonnet[80]

Where Surrey's sonnets tend to simplify Petrarch's antitheses, Wyatt's characteristically complicate the play of oppositions, creating a network of echoes and repetitions within which meaning seems to circulate without any final resolution. Thus the relationships between the lover, his love/lust and the lady in 'The long love' are constructed via a series of contradictory terms which are never resolved within the poem: the lady is tyrannical and virtuous; love/lust is beast-like but bold and the lord of the heart's forest; the lover's desire is both 'natural' and 'lust's negligence', both dutiful and rebellious. The 'inward' conflicts of the first-person speaker are vividly dramatized, but his identity is also undercut and mocked. We as readers are drawn into the subjective perspectives of the lover, but also distanced from them by contradiction and irony.

Characteristically, Wyatt's sonnets create what might be called a 'fertile semiosis', a rich range of meanings, produced to some extent by Wyatt's intensification of antitheses within the condensed form of the sonnet. Because such circulating meanings tend to subvert rather than reinforce a single subject position within the sonnet, it is impossible to know how deliberate Wyatt's alterations to the original are, or to what extent they are the result of accidental touches or mistranslations. Nevertheless, as Anne Ferry and Thomas

Greene have argued, Wyatt's sonnets consistently exploit the form for irony, innuendo and ambiguity.[81] Some of the problems, as well as some of the striking successes, of Wyatt's translations from Petrarch are evident in his sonnet 'Love and Fortune and my mind, rememb'rer' (Reb. xxii), a translation of *Rime* 124. The poem starts clumsily but grows in strength:

> Love and Fortune and my mind, rememb'rer
> Of that that is nowe with that that hath been,
> Do torment me so that I very often
> Envy them beyond all measure.
> Love slayeth mine heart. Fortune is depriver
> Of all my comfort. The foolish mind then
> Burneth and plaineth as one that seldom
> Liveth in rest, still in displeasure.
> My pleasant days, they fleet away and pass,
> But daily yet the ill doth change into the worse,
> And more than the half is run of my course.
> Alas, not of steel but of brickle glass
> I see that from mine hand falleth my trust,
> And all my thoughts are dashed into dust.

The word 'rememb'rer' at the end of line 1 is highly appropriate for the sense of dismemberment and fragmentation which runs throughout the poem.[82] The shatterings, of past from present, of heart from mind, of the divided mind itself, of inner aspiration and outer success, these are themselves painful, but the 'remembering', with its sense of an attempt to bring severed limbs back together, not in the original Italian, adds a Frankenstein-like effort to the 'torment'.

As in 'The long love', Wyatt seems deliberately to avoid metrical or verbal smoothness. Line 2 is almost ostentatiously 'unpoetic' in its repetitive clumsiness, 'that that is now with that that hath been', suggesting to the reader a distinctive, dramatic speaking voice, engrossed in the matter and indifferent to the art of his utterance. The repetition of 'that', with a strong central pause, also draws our attention to the antithetical structures of the poem, amongst which any subjective coherence is fragmented. The first-person voice battles all through the poem with the tropes of self-division. Antitheses, more even than Petrarch provides, shape the second quatrain: love, produced by the heart, kills it; fortune 'deprives' the lover of what she gave; the mind 'burneth and plaineth'; and Wyatt's addition, 'seldom / Liveth in *rest*', is set wittily against '*still* in displeasure' (my italics).

The most striking success of the translation occurs in the final three lines. Petrarch's image had been of diamond and of glass which breaks in the middle:

> Lasso, non di diamante, ma d'un vetro
> veggio di man cadermi ogni speranza,
> e tutt'i miei pensier romper nel mezzo.
>
> (*Rime* 124)

> (Alas! not made of diamond, but of glass, I see every hope fall from my hand, and all my thoughts break in half.)

Wyatt changes this into images of steel and of 'brickle glass . . . dashed into dust'. Steel, unlike the ideal brilliance of diamond, suits the dramatization of the plain-speaking voice of Wyatt's sonnet, as does the use of the word 'trust', suggesting loyalty or faith, to translate the more aspiring 'speranza' (hope).[83] But 'steel' also introduces the imagery of mirrors which were made of both polished steel and silvered glass in this period.[84] Thus the lover's trust falls and is shattered, but, like a mirror, that trust when kept intact reflected the lover's self-image, his sense of his own wholeness; thus shattered, he is dismembered. The speaker's trust has functioned as a delusory mirror, generating an image of wholeness, but now, finding no object, no response from a stable, desirable other, it fragments the speaker and his thoughts, 'dashed into dust'. The 'dust' points to worthlessness, to the final death and physical disintegration of the body, and to the sands run out through a shattered hour-glass. Wyatt's development of the complex oppositions and juxtapositions inherent in the patterned brevity of the sonnet here produces an explosive mixture as shattering to the fragile fiction of the sonnet persona as the fallen glass.

The final shattering of illusory identity at the end of this sonnet has to be held in tension with the dramatic sense of presence created throughout the sonnet by the speaker's distinctive speaking voice. Wyatt's use of a plain English vocabulary helps to dramatize an honest and artless speaking voice, one who speaks in terms of 'steel' rather than Petrarch's diamonds, of an honest 'trust', and the Middle-English mouthful of 'brickle glass'. In fact for this speaker, glass, the Venetian glass of luxury mirrors, reverses the relative preciousness of the Petrarchan original.[85] Petrarch's contrast between diamond and glass compares the preciousness of the first to the fake imitation of the second. Wyatt's speaker has foolishly trusted that a luxury object, fashionable glass, its fragility emphasized by 'brickle', would be as tough as the homely material, steel. At the same time as we register the shattered, fragmented identity of the speaker, we are also invited to imagine him complete and identifiable, a fustian down-to-earth character gulled and disillusioned by love (and the evasive lady), Fortune, and the fashionable fragile objects that epitomize their courtly world.

Even as this plain man speaks in his native vernacular, Wyatt shapes his gutturals and monosyllables into a graceful Petrarchan sonnet, creating a new fashion for a courtly world. Wyatt has followed closely the grammatical articulation of his model: the final word of the first line, 'rememb'rer', hangs unresolved, while the verbs that make sense of the quatrain are delayed until the beginning of the third and fourth lines. The sense within the quatrain flows uncompleted until its close, giving a sense of a 'natural' pause, and thus of an artless fit of form and content – an effect achieved only, of course, by careful craft. In fact, as we have seen, Wyatt's control at this point is less smooth than Petrarch's due to the oddness of 'rememb'rer' ('remembre' in old spelling) and the uncertain identity of 'them' in the fourth line, although even these moments of verbal confusion may be read as mimicking the confusion of the speaker's thoughts. The final three lines sum up the whole with the new image of delusory glass and broken thoughts, in which the witty and innovative form belies the ostensible fragmentation of the speaking voice.

Such antithetical tropes as the oxymoron, beloved of the Petrarchan sonnet, and the subdivided structure typical of the form contribute to the sense of complexity and paradox that characterize Wyatt's Petrarchan translations. Within the brief, dense form, words and their connotations easily accumulate significance, even augmented on occasion by apparent clumsiness of syntax or mistranslation. In Wyatt's own original sonnets, brevity, antitheses and flexibility of syntax and punctuation similarly work to undermine and question the coherent identity of the speaking voice. Typical are the sonnets 'Each man telleth I change most my device' (Reb. xxx), which centres around the mirroring doubleness of the subject and other(s), or 'Farewell, Love' (Reb. xxxi), in which the speaker's motives for renouncing love shift and turn as the sonnet develops. Is it the 'lore' of 'Senec and Plato' that teaches him wisdom, or the sore pricking of love? Is he too old for love now, or is he peeved because he has been unsuccessful? And what does the last unpunctuated line – 'Me lusteth no longer rotten boughs to climb' – mean? Are the 'rotten boughs' women? If so, are all women rotten boughs, or is he only renouncing the 'rotten' or unrewarding women?[86] Perhaps most typical of Wyatt's exploitation of circulating meaning through the dense antithetical structure of the sonnet is the bewildering 'There was never file half so well filed / To file a file for every smith's intent' (Reb. xxxii), in which all is unstable and trustless, the speaking subject, others, and language itself:

> Then guile beguiled plained should be never
> And the reward little trust forever.[87]

Wyatt's use of the sonnet form both to dramatize a sense of psychic and emotional intensity and also to subvert any coherent perspective on that drama is perhaps most strikingly illustrated by 'Unstable dream, according to the place' (Reb. xxvii). Like 'They flee from me', this sonnet draws on the erotic dream motif. It has been suggested that Wyatt is imitating a *strambotto* by the Italian poet Filosseno, although M&T's and Rebholz's editorial notes point out that he may as easily have got the idea from Petrarch himself or a number of other Italian poets. In fact, Wyatt might also have drawn upon examples already existing in English.[88] What Wyatt undoubtedly has learned from Italian models is his form with its emphasis on brevity, its structural complexity, and its conventions of emotional self-analysis.

In Wyatt's sonnet, the lover addresses his dream, a potentially absurd scenario, rendered more so by the witty illogic of expecting a dream, flitting by its very nature, to be stable and steadfast:

> Unstable dream, according to the place,
> Be steadfast once or else at least be true.
> By tasted sweetness make me not to rue
> The sudden loss of thy false feigned grace.
> By good respect in such a dangerous case
> Thou brought'st not her into this tossing mew
> But madest my sprite live my care to renew,
> My body in tempest her succour to embrace.
>
> (ll. 1–8)

The dream is blamed in terms that Wyatt, and the tradition of misogyny, reserve for women, 'unstable . . . / Be steadfast once or else at least be true'. Like a fickle mistress, it has shown him 'false feigned grace'. In lines 5 and 6 the dream's falseness is comically reinterpreted as its sense of propriety: the dream has done well to keep 'her', the lover's mistress, from his 'tossing mew' (a cage for a moulting hawk, *OED* 1; a breeding cage, *OED* 2b; a secret place, a den, *OED* 3b). In 'such a dangerous case', the dream has provided him instead with an imaginary erotic object.

The sestet is characteristically ambivalent. On one reading, the lines look back with nostalgia to his dreaming happiness:

> The body dead, the spright had his desire;
> Painless was th'one, th'other in delight.
> Why then, alas, did it not keep it right,
> Returning to leap into the fire,
> And where it was at wish it could not remain?
>
> (ll. 9–13)

Since the spirit's (the mind's) delight has been an erotic dream, the deadness and thus insensitivity of the lover's body are comically inappropriate, as is the lover's irritation with his waking body ('it' in line 11) which could not remain happily dead (asleep). But the 'spright' may also be the masculine animal spirits, expelled in the semen (cf. Shakespeare's sonnet 129, 'Th' expense of *spirit* in a waste of shame'), and the dead and painless body that of the imaginary form of his mistress brought to him in his dream.[89] On this reading there is a disconcerting suggestion of necrophilia, of lust as the merest self-gratification on the inert form of the desired. The two 'it's of line 11 compound or sustain the uncertainty: the first 'it' might be the lover's body which could not keep 'itself' still and shattered the dream, or 'it' might refer to the dream which was, as the first quatrain asserted, unstable, and 'could not remain' at the wish of the lover. In either case, the word 'right' acquires considerable moral tension: in what sense would the body or the dream have been 'right' to preserve a fantasy of erotic gratification?

Wyatt throughout exploits the antithetical structuring which he learned from the Petrarchan sonnet. The juxtaposition of line 2, 'Be steadfast once or else at least be true', differentiates steadfastness and truth, and neatly plays on a double possibility of 'true', meaning 'faithful' (be true to me/come when I want you even if you don't last) and 'veracious' (bring me the woman herself rather than a false image of her). This is not at all the way Surrey used the concepts of steadfastness and truth. The antitheses of 'spright' and 'body' which organize lines 7–10 shift disconcertingly, as we have seen, from an apparent opposition between the speaker's body and his dreaming mind (spirit), to the opposite possibility of his bodily semen ('spright') and her dreamed image ('the body dead'). The final line neatly concludes the sonnet by turning the direct voice of address used throughout the sonnet to a more experienced voice of commentary: 'Such mocks of dreams they turn to deadly pain.' Here too, however, antitheses focus the attention on possible ambiguities.

The dreams have been 'mocking', deliberately derisive (*OED* sb.1), with, perhaps, the suggestion of being counterfeit (*OED* sb.3), investing the dream, which the lover has addressed throughout, with a deliberate malice. More subversively, 'mocks' may be gulls, objects of scorn (*OED* sb. 2), self-deluding lovers like this one. The final line displays the lover as dupe and fool, mocked by the dream which produces a fantasy of the lady he had thought to master. But in its final phrase, 'deadly pain', it also suggests the bitterness of that experience. The poem represents the lover ambiguously as a conventional amorous dreamer, and exposes him as a gull; it dramatizes an intense moment of desire and frustration, but also shares a rude joke with the reader about the nature of that desire, and the kind of (wet) dream that is being described. Even while Wyatt develops the potential of the sonnet form to explore a moment of intense inwardness, his use of its antithetical structure, and the play of meaning it produces, fragments any sense of coherence and integrity in the speaking voice.

The sonnet form, with its subdivisions and its antitheses, offers Wyatt opportunities beyond the reach of the witty or dramatic *strambotto*. But while acknowledging, with Nicholas Bielby, that Wyatt and Surrey 'learned the art of compression, of writing personal and complex short poems' from Italian models, care must be taken against confounding the 'personal' with the autobiographical.[90] The development of a 'personal', apparently private voice of self-analysis is a rhetorical effect of the sonnets, part of the Petrarchan genre. What is 'personal' is the way that, in the hands of Surrey and Wyatt, the genre produces quite different fictions of the individual lover's distinction from and relationship to an imagined outer world and the objects of his desires. In the work of Surrey, as we have seen, the lover's private feelings are invested with coherence and nobility in opposition to an outer world marked by change and loss. It is characteristic of Surrey's subject position in his love poems, that in his complaint, 'The sonne hath twise brought forth the tender grene' (Jones no. 11), Surrey's lover wishes for night to 'withdrawe from everie haunted place' where 'with my mind I measure paas by paas / To seke that place where I my self hadd lost' (ll. 32, 34–5). In a place of privacy, he tries to find an idealized version of self, rather than weave a perplexing web of erotic fantasies as Wyatt's lover does in 'Unstable dream'. In Wyatt's sonnets, the meditative voice of the lover threatens continually to fragment among the ambiguities and ironies of the sonnet's production of meaning, from which neither the desirable objects, nor the lover himself, emerge intact and unproblematic. Lisa Klein has suggested that the cruel mistress in Wyatt's poetry 'is an image of contradiction and doubleness, symbolizing the poet's desires, yet forbidding their fulfilment', and that 'the Petrarchan language of contradiction expresses the poet's moral paralysis and the impossibility of achieving virtuous action in a fallen world'.[91] But even while Wyatt's sonnets often construct such a fiction of personal victimization and the doubleness of others, the innovative and glamorous artfulness of the sonnet form displays the poet, the courtier Wyatt, as an ambitious and successful performer of courtly arts, an innovator in the latest, elite, Italianate forms, and an exceptionally subtle manipulator of words.

The evidence of contemporary manuscripts and of *Tottel's Miscellany* suggests that the sonnet form was not immediately very popular among courtly poets.[92] Part of the reason for this may have been the extraordinary demands the form makes on the writer. At a time when courtly poets seem to have increasingly favoured less formal kinds in which artfulness was disguised, the sonnet's intricate structure and its Petrarchan idealizing themes and rhetoric may have seemed too formal. In addition, the very distinctiveness of Petrarch's tropes and topics may have made assimilation and adaptation of the form a challenge of huge proportions at a time when English was often felt to be short on vocabulary and cumbersome in syntax. For many mid-Tudor poets, such as Nicholas Grimald (*c.*1519–*c.*1562), the form is assimilated to that of the epigram and used, as Surrey sometimes used it, for elegant panegyric, or for epitaphs.[93] A rare, but revealing, example of a love sonnet by one of the anonymous contributors to *Tottel's Miscellany* demonstrates a quite different use of the Petrarchan model from Wyatt and Surrey's cultivation of a psychic and private inwardness, although it seems to owe some verbal debts to the work of both poets:

> With Petrarch to compare there may no wight,
> Nor yet attain unto so high a stile,
> But yet I wote full well where is a file, *wote: know*
> To frame a learned man to praise aright:
> Of stature meane of semely forme and shap,
> Eche line of just proportion to her height:
> Her colour freshe and mingled with such sleight:
> As though the rose sate in the lilies lap.
> In wit and tong to shew what may be sed,
> To every dede she joines a parfit grace,
> If lawra livde she would her clene deface. *Laura, Petrarch's sonnet mistress*

For I dare say and lay my life to wed
That Momus could not if he downe discended,
Once justly say lo this may be amended.[94]

Here Petrarch's style is straightforwardly admired as 'high', 'filed' (with none of the problematical associations of that word with deceptive smoothness that we find in Wyatt), appropriate for 'learned' men and for a poetry of fulsome praise, although the poem benefits from the paring down of aureate diction and the command of a fluent and brief articulacy, developed by Wyatt and his generation of Tudor poets. This sonnet works so neatly because the praise of the lady in the second quatrain and the first three lines of the sestet acts as a little emblem of the sonnet itself and its own style: of middling stature, exactly proportioned, with just the right touch of colouring, decorously erotic ('as though the rose sate in the lilies lap'), witty and elegant.[95]

Wyatt and Surrey and their contemporaries and imitators could learn from Petrarch and his Italian imitators useful and sophisticated verbal arts: a compression akin to that of the epigram, and often used for epigrammatic effects; the development of a semi-dramatized 'I' speaker; and a dense and complex verbal and metaphorical texture which could, especially in the sonnets of Wyatt, set off a complex semiosis in which a scenario of contradictory or subversive desires could be articulated. The sonnet provides a glamorously Italianate model of a kind of poetry whose art depends not on the conspicuous display of rhetorical ornament, but on an understated wit and control that could evoke an articulate and sensitive private voice. It creates a tiny 'private' space in which, while bewailing its own powerlessness, the speaking voice can assert its superiority of judgement and feeling, its integrity, or at least its ironic self-knowledge in a faithless and unsympathetic world. In Wyatt's sonnets, the suggestive brevity of the form, its capacity for innuendo and multiple interpretative possibilities, produce a complex effect, both voicing and undermining a subject position of frustrated desire. In Surrey's work, the sonnet is used as a condensed complaint, giving elegant and up-to-date voice to a nostalgic, medievalizing, chivalric virtue. Such voices, flexible, plaintive, vengeful and assertive, could provide powerfully enabling fictions for the highly cultivated, but socially and politically insecure, denizens of Henry's court, even while the sonnet form itself displayed its writer as sophisticated, masterful and articulate.

NOTES

1. Puttenham, G. (1968) *The Arte of English Poesie (1589)*. Menston, Yorks: The Scolar Press Ltd, p 48. See my Introduction, p 1.
2. Greene, T. M. (1982) *The Light in Troy: Imitation and Discovery in Renaissance Poetry*. New Haven, Conn.: Yale University Press, p 10.
3. *Troilus and Criseyde* Bk 1 ll. 400–20.
4. Rollins 1 no. 238. For the use of Chaucer in the Devonshire MS, see Ch 2 pp 44–45 above.
5. Greene (1982) pp 30ff.
6. Quoted by Jones, R. F. (1953) *The Triumph of the English Language: A Survey of Opinions Concerning the Vernacular from the Introduction of Printing to the Restoration*. Oxford: Oxford University Press, p 26.
7. Atkins, J. W. H. (1968) *English Literary Criticism: The Renascence* (2nd edn). London: Methuen & Co. Ltd, pp 163–81; Vickers, B. (1970) *Classical Rhetoric in English Poetry*. London: Macmillan, pp 30–3. For this aspect of Lydgate's style, see Spearing, A. C. (1985) *Medieval to Renaissance in English Poetry*. Cambridge: Cambridge University Press, pp 63, 76–82, and Pearsall, D. (1979) *John Lydgate*. London: Routledge & Kegan Paul, pp 268–74.
8. Boffey, J. (1985) *Manuscripts of English Courtly Love Lyrics in the Later Middle Ages*. Woodbridge, Suffolk: D. S. Brewer, pp 27, 69.
9. Hawes, S. (1928) *The Pastime of Pleasure*, ed. W. E. Mead. Early English Text Society OS 173. Oxford: Oxford University Press, ll. 668–75, 681–6. Line references to this edition will be given in parentheses in the text in the following discussion.
10. See the discussion of the connection between rhetoric and political order in *The Pastime* in Parker, P. (1987) *Literary Fat Ladies: Rhetoric, Gender, Property*. London: Methuen, p 114.
11. This stanza appears, among others borrowed from Hawes, in a courtly poem in the Welles Anthology: see Jansen, S. L. and Jordan, K. H., eds (1991) *The Welles Anthology: MS Rawlinson C.813*. Binghampton, NY: Medieval and Renaissance Texts and Studies, p 129. See my discussion on p 74 above.
12. *The Faerie Queene* V ix 25.
13. Starkey, D. (1987) 'Intimacy and innovation: the rise of the Privy Chamber, 1485–1547'. In *The English Court: From the Wars of the Roses to the Civil War*, ed. D. Starkey. London: Longman, pp 71–118 (p 74). J. Frank, in his introduction to Hawes, S. (1975) *The Works*. Delmar, NY: Scolar's Facsimiles & Reprints, p x, notes that 'the tone of *The Conversion of Swearers* . . . suggests that Hawes was associated with the domestic circle rather than the social or political circles round the King'. Loades, D. (1992) *The Tudor Court* (2nd edn). Bangor: Headstart History, p 46, suggests some grooms had diplomatic as well as domestic duties. Fox, A. (1989) *Politics and Literature in the Reigns of Henry VII and Henry VIII*. Oxford: Basil Blackwell, pp 56–72, identifies Grand Amour with Hawes himself.

14. Skelton, J. (1983) *The Complete English Poems*, ed. J. Scattergood. New Haven, Conn.: Yale University Press, no. XIX ll. 1081–90. Numbering of Skelton's poems in the text will refer to this edition. Walker, G. (1988) *John Skelton and the Politics of the 1520s*. Cambridge: Cambridge University Press, pp 100–2, 126, discusses Skelton's adaptation of a 'popular' oppositional style in the anti-Wolsey satires. See also Heiserman, A. R. (1961) *Skelton and Satire*. Chicago: University of Chicago Press, pp 213–29, for an account of the stylistic traditions Skelton follows.
15. For the dating of this poem, see Walker (1988) pp 16–21.
16. Boffey (1985) p 30.
17. Skelton (1983) p 394. Cf. Skelton's use of a similar idiom in 'Manerly Margery Milk and Ale' (no. II), which was set to music by the court musician William Cornish and is copied into the courtly Fairfax MS, described by Stevens, J. (1961) *Music and Poetry in the Early Tudor Court*. London: Methuen, p 379.
18. The anthology is edited by Jansen and Jordan (1991) as *The Welles Anthology*. Future references to the Welles Anthology will be to this edition and will refer to its numbering of individual poems.
19. For the suggestion that some of the texts are those of well-known songs, see Boffey (1985) p 27. Jansen and Jordan (1991) pp 26–7 comment on the closeness to Wyatt, in tone and attitude, of a number of the poems in the Welles Anthology.
20. Jansen and Jordan (1991) p 17, quoting from Robbins, R. H. (1954) 'A late fifteenth-century love lyric'. *Modern Language Notes* 69: 158. The question of what is genuinely 'popular' and what is written in an ostensibly 'popular' idiom (i.e. made for a broad audience beyond the courtly one, or in the manner of such widespread songs) is a fraught one. Both Greene, R. L., ed. (1977) *Early English Carols*. Oxford: Clarendon Press, pp cxviii, cxxxiii, and Stevens (1961) p 41 warn about the ambiguity of the word.
21. Quoted from the modern-spelling version by Stevens (1961) Appendix A no. 51. Quotations from this manuscript will be followed by Stevens's numbering in parenthesis in my text.
22. For example, Stevens (1961) nos. 25, 31, 33, 35, 41, 50, 101. And for discussions of adaptations of current songs, see ibid pp 53–4, 123–5. For Stevens's suggestion that Wyatt and his contemporaries may have written words that would fit pre-existing well-known tunes, see pp 127–32. For the same suggestion in relation to carols, see Greene (1977) p cxxxvii.
23. Hall, E. (1965) *Chronicle, Containing the History of England* (reprint of the 1809 edn). New York: AMS Press Inc., p 515.
24. Stevens (1961) p 286.
25. For a discussion of the part proverbs play in this poem, see Ross, D. M. (1987) 'Sir Thomas Wyatt: proverbs and the poetics of scorn'. *The Sixteenth Century Journal* 18(2): 201–12 (p 204).
26. Whigham, F. (1984) *Ambition and Privilege: The Social Tropes of Elizabethan Courtesy Theory*. Berkeley: University of California Press, pp 33–4 and 93–5,

for a fuller discussion of the concept of *sprezzatura.* See also Javitch, D. (1978) *Poetry and Courtliness in Renaissance England.* Princeton, NJ: Princeton University Press, pp 55–7.

27. Surrey's social position, and the themes of his poems, are rather different, and I shall pay more attention to his amorous verse later in this chapter.
28. Lewis, C. S. (1954) *English Literature in the Sixteenth Century Excluding Drama.* Oxford History of Literature. Oxford: Oxford University Press, p 222.
29. Stevens (1961) esp. Pt. 1 chs 6, 7.
30. Thomas Whythorne, a professional musician apprenticed to the musician and interlude writer John Heywood in 1545, notes that he copied 'divers songs and sonnets' including some of Wyatt's: see Osborne, J. (1962) *The Autobiography of Thomas Whythorne. Modern Spelling Edition.* Oxford: Clarendon Press, p 6. The context suggests that they may have been set to music. Whythorne's settings would postdate Wyatt's death, and may be evidence of a growing taste for lute music in the middle of the century, but his task also suggests an assumption that some courtly verse should be sung. On the question of the singing and performance of medieval courtly love lyrics up to the end of the fifteenth century, see Boffey (1985) pp 93–112.
31. See Stevens (1961) pp 135–7, and Mumford, I. L. (1957) 'Musical settings to the poems of Henry Howard, Earl of Surrey'. *English Miscellany* 8: 9–20, who has found that five of Surrey's poems were set to music in the sixteenth century. For the probable dating of the manuscript in which a number of the earliest lute settings are found, see Ward, J. (1960) 'The lute music of MS Royal Appendix 58'. *Journal of the American Musicological Society* 13: 117–25. For the probability that a number of Surrey's 'poulter's measure' poems were written to be sung, see also Woods, S. (1984) *Natural Emphasis: English Versification from Chaucer to Dryden.* San Marino, Ca.: The Huntington Library, p 70.
32. For fuller discussion, see Stevens (1961) pp 127–32 and Maynard, W. (1965) 'The lyrics of Wyatt: poems or songs?' *Review of English Studies* n.s.16: 1–13 (pt 1) and 245–57 (pt 2).
33. For example, Reed, E. B. (1910) 'The sixteenth-century lyrics in Add. MS 18,752'. *Anglia* 33: 344–69 (p 361), and the Devonshire MS fol. 16^{r}.
34. See Heale, E. (1995) 'Women and the courtly love lyric: the Devonshire MS (BL Additional 17492)'. *Modern Language Review* 90: 296–313, p 302. Harrier, R. (1975) *The Canon of Sir Thomas Wyatt's Poetry.* Cambridge, Mass.: Harvard University Press, p 53, does not think 'Now all of change' is by Wyatt. A version of this balet appears to have the name of a song tune written below it in a contemporary manuscript: see Reb. note on p 537, and Stevens (1961) p 124.
35. Einstein, A. (1949) *The Italian Madrigal*, trans. Alexander H. Krappe, Roger H. Sessions and Oliver Strunk. 3 vols, Princeton: Princeton University Press, 1 p 75. For the *frottola*, see also Reese, G. (1954) *Music in the Renaissance.* London: Dent, pp 156–65; Prizer, W. F. (1989) 'North Italian courts'. In *The Renaissance*, ed. I. Fenlon. Man and Music Series. Englewood Cliffs, NJ:

Prentice Hall, pp 133–55; and Winn, J. A. (1981) *Unsuspected Eloquence: A History of the Relations between Poetry and Music*. New Haven, Conn.: Yale University Press, esp. pp 137–40.

36. Einstein (1949) p 83 and Reese (1954) p 159.
37. Mumford, I. L. (1971) 'Petrarchism and Italian music at the court of Henry VIII'. *Italian Studies* 26: 49–67 (pp 52–3).
38. Castiglione (1976) p 120. Reese (1954) p160 n 49 suggests the instrument Castiglione referred to was the 'viola da mano (i.e. the vihuela or the lute)'. He notes that all the sixteenth-century translations of Castiglione into English, including that by Sir Thomas Hoby, refer to the instrument as a lute or vihuela.
39. The poem is copied on fols. 79^{v} and 80^{r} of the Devonshire MS. Harrier (1975) pp 53–4 does not consider the group of poems in which this one occurs to be by Wyatt. Among the proverbs in this poem also used by Wyatt are 'words are wind' (l. 25; see my discussion in Ch 2 p 53 above) and 'climbing rotten boughs' (l. 33; cf. Reb. xxxi l. 14).
40. Serafino (1516) *Opere*. Firenze: Philippo di Giunta, sigs. 202^{v}–204^{r}. The description is that of Mumford, I. L. (1963) 'Sir Thomas Wyatt's verse and Italian musical sources'. *English Miscellany* 14: 9–26 (p 11). Unless otherwise indicated, all the translations from the Italian are mine.
41. Rosso, A. (1980) *Serafino Aquilano e la Poesia Cortigiana*. Brescia: Morcelliana, p 11.
42. Mellin's influence on French court culture seems to have been considerable, through his own compositions and performance, through his influence on, and his instruction of, both Francis I himself and the royal children, and through the publications of Piere Attaignant, royal music printer, in whose many publications, beginning in 1527, settings of Mellin's poems, along with those of Jean's son, Clement Marot, 'lead all others in frequency'. See Molinier, H.-J. (1910) *Mellin de Saint-Gelays (1490?–1558): Etude sur sa Vie et sur ses Oeuvres*. Rodez: Imprimerie Carrère, pp 93, 102, and Heartz, D. (1964) 'Les gouts réunis or the worlds of the madrigal and the chanson confronted'. In *Chanson and Madrigal, 1480–1530*, ed. J. Haar. Cambridge, Mass.: Harvard University Press, pp 88–138.
43. For a poem by Wyatt in this spirit which translates an Italian madrigal which was also translated by Mellin, and for which there is an analogue by Clement Marot, see Newman, J. (1957) 'An Italian source for Wyatt's "Madame, withouten many wordes" '. *Renaissance News* 10: 13–15. The poems of Mellin and Marot are quoted and briefly discussed in relation to Wyatt's version in Richmond, H. (1981) *Puritans and Libertines: Anglo-French Literary Relations in the Reformation*. Berkeley: University of California Press, p 121.
44. Mumford (1963) p 20. Maynard (1965) p 11 suggests that Wyatt's version may have been sung to a dance tune currently popular at the Henrician court.
45. For an earlier version of my argument, see Heale, E. M. (1996) 'Lute and harp in Wyatt's poetry'. In *Sacred and Profane: Secular and Devotional Interplay in Early Modern British Literature*, eds H. Wilcox, R. Todd and A. MacDonald.

Amsterdam: VU University Press, pp 3–15. See also Hollander, J. (1961) *The Untuning of the Sky: Ideas of Music in English Poetry, 1500–1700*. Princeton, NJ: Princeton University Press, pp 128–31, on the lute in Wyatt's poems as a metaphor for poetry itself. Maynard (1965) p 250, on the other hand, is convinced the poems were meant to be performed to the lute.

46. For Wyatt's strategies of retaliation and revenge, see Estrin, B. L. (1994a) *Laura: Uncovering Gender and Genre in Wyatt, Donne, and Marvell*. Durham, NC, and London: Duke University Press, pp 96–7.
47. Stevens (1961) pp 136–8 and 278–89. Interestingly, Stevens p 288 cites the father of Wyatt's son's wife, Sir William Hawte, a Kentish neighbour of the Wyatts, as one of the very few gentlemanly amateurs who is known to have been able to compose music. For Hawte and Wyatt, see *LL* pp 37, 38, 55.
48. Serafino (1516) sig. 137^{v}.
49. Ibid sigs. 200^{v}–201^{v}. Professor Rosi Colombo from the University of Rome kindly assisted me with the translation of these lines. Richmond (1981) pp 165–6 cites a poem by St Gelais which plays on the conceit of lute strings/heart strings.
50. Einstein (1949) 1 p 82; Winn (1981) p 139.
51. Hunter, G. K. (1970) 'Drab and golden lyrics of the Renaissance'. In *Forms of Lyric: Selected Papers from the English Institute*, ed. R. A. Brower. New York: Columbia University Press, pp 1–18 (p 5).
52. Thomson, P. (1964) *Sir Thomas Wyatt and his Background*. London: Routledge & Kegan Paul, p 232.
53. Reb. capitalizes 'Love' in l. 5.
54. Serafino (1516) sigs. $151^{r–v}$. The Italian texts are printed in M&T pp 279–80.
55. M&T p 280. For 'bearing in hand', see Whiting, B. J. and Whiting, H. W., eds (1968) *Proverbs, Sentences, and Proverbial Phrases from English Writings Mainly Before 1500*. Cambridge, Mass.: Harvard University Press, H 65.
56. The manuscript has been edited with an introduction by O'Keefe, S. (1986) 'T.C.D.MS.160: a Tudor miscellany' (unpublished M.Litt. thesis, Trinity College, Dublin). For debate about its ownership, see also Baron, H. (1989) 'The "Blage" manuscript: the original compiler identified'. *English Manuscript Studies* 1: 85–119.
57. Full Italian text in M&T p 312.
58. Wyatt may have known some of Clement Marot's epigrams which sometimes used an eight-line form, though not normally ending with a couplet: see Reb. p 364.
59. For a full discussion of the form and its history, see Spiller, M. R. G. (1992) *The Development of the Sonnet: An Introduction*. London: Routledge. For the extraordinary popularity, indeed institutionalization, of Petrarch in Italy in the early years of the sixteenth century, see Thomson (1964) pp 166–8 and 190–200 (on Wyatt's possible use of early annotated editions of Petrarch).
60. See Spiller (1992) p 51 for an account of Petrarch's rhyme schemes, and pp 85 and 96 for an account of the relationship of the *strambotto* and the sonnet, and

Wyatt's and Surrey's characteristic innovations to the sonnet's rhyming structure.

61. For musical settings of Petrarchan sonnets in Italy, see the articles by Mumford (1963) pp 18–19 and (1971) p 62, and in France, see Cazeaux, I. (1975) *French Music in the Fifteenth and Sixteenth Centuries*. Oxford: Basil Blackwell, p 201.
62. Castiglione (1976) p 82.
63. I discuss Petrarch's anti-papal sonnets in relation to Surrey's poetry further in Ch 4 pp 141–42 below.
64. For the probable circumstances to which the sonnet refers, see Mason, H. A. (1959) *Humanism and Poetry in the Early Tudor Period: An Essay*. London: Routledge & Kegan Paul, p 197.
65. For the painting and discussions of its dating and the circumstances of its painting, see Ch 1 n 55 above. I am indebted to a paper on the painting and the symbolism of the pillar, given by William Sessions at the 1995 Reading Early Modern History and English Conference.
66. Thomson (1964) pp 201–3 gives the Italian (*Rime* 145) and discusses Surrey's translation.
67. The quotation and translation are from Horace (1988) *The Odes and Epodes*, trans. C. E. Bennett. The Loeb Classical Library. London: William Heinemann Ltd, p 65.
68. Sessions, W. A. (1986) *Henry Howard, Earl of Surrey*. Twayne English Authors Series. Boston: G. K. Hall, pp 47–50.
69. Vickers, N. J. (1982) 'Diana described: scattered woman and scattered rhyme'. In *Writing and Sexual Difference*, ed. E. Abel. Brighton: Harvester Press, pp 101–2.
70. Ibid pp 106–7.
71. For the 'cornet', see Boucher, F. (1967) *A History of Costume in the West*. London: Thames and Hudson, pp 235, 428.
72. Hammond, E. P., ed. (1927) *English Verse between Chaucer and Surrey*. Durham, NC: Duke University Press, p 112. In her introduction to the poem, Hammond cites other French and English examples of attacks on women's horned headgear. See also Brown, C. and Robbins, R. H. (1943) *The Index of Middle English Verse*. New York: Columbia University Press, nos. 811, 3698, 4093.
73. For previous comparisons between the two poems, see Smith, H. (1946) 'The art of Sir Thomas Wyatt'. *Huntington Library Quarterly* 9: 323–55; Thompson (1964) pp 172–4. See also Estrin (1994a) pp 134–6; Ferry, A. (1983) *The "Inward" Language: Sonnets of Wyatt, Sidney, Shakespeare, Donne*. Chicago: University of Chicago Press, pp 114–16; and Greene (1982) pp 252–3.
74. For Petrarch's version, see Jones p 105, or M&T p 265.
75. Sessions (1986) p 45 describes the sonnet as turning the relationships of the Petrarchan original 'into a narrative, weaving them, on a reduced scale' into a tapestry-like design.

76. Ferry (1983) p 115 makes this point.

77. I am indebted to the discussion of this phrase in Holohan, M. (1993) 'Wyatt, the heart's forest, and the ancient savings'. *English Literary Renaissance* 23: 46–80, esp. pp. 62–3. My conclusion is quite different from Holohan's suggestion that the sonnet is Wyatt's 'assurance to the King, of a good life that will end in faithfulness' (p 47). See also Estrin (1994a) p 135.

78. My discussion of Wyatt's sonnets, and his poetry more generally, is particularly indebted to the chapter on 'Wyatt's craft' in Crewe, J. (1991) *Trials of Authorship: Anterior Forms and Poetic Reconstruction from Wyatt to Shakespeare.* Berkeley and Los Angeles: University of California Press.

79. Spiller (1992) pp 14, 84–5.

80. Among the very fine discussions of Wyatt's debts to Petrarch, I am particularly indebted to Ferry (1983); Greene (1982) ch 12, who discusses Wyatt's successful development of an 'idiolect' based on a sense of moral, as well as emotional, crisis; and Klein, L. M. (1992) 'The Petrarchism of Sir Thomas Wyatt reconsidered'. In *The Work of Dissimilitude: Essays from the Sixth Citadel Conference on Medieval and Renaissance Literature*, eds D. G. Allen and R. A. White. Newark: University of Delaware Press, pp 131–47, who discusses Wyatt's use of Petrarch as a model to explore doubleness and conflict.

81. For example, Ferry (1983) esp. pp 83–91, and Greene (1982) esp. pp 253–4. Klein (1992) p 138 sympathetically, but perhaps too schematically, has suggested that for Wyatt 'the irreconcilable extremes of the oxymoron parallel the equally unacceptable alternatives of retirement from and participation in a corrupt society'.

82. The word 'rememb'rer' is an editorial suggestion based on the spelling 'remembre' in both manuscript versions and in *Tottel's Miscellany*.

83. For the significance of the word 'trust' in Wyatt's sonnets, see Ferry (1983) pp 86–7.

84. Steel mirrors seem to have been more common than glass ones even in Italy in the early sixteenth century. Venice became the main centre for the production of glass mirrors during the course of the century. See Thornton, P. (1991) *The Italian Renaissance Interior.* New York: Harry N. Abrams, Inc., p 235, and Canning, M. (1936) *Costume in the Drama of Shakespeare and His Contemporaries.* Oxford: Clarendon Press, p 273.

85. George Gascoigne used the opposition between steel and glass mirrors to similar effect in his satire 'The Steele Glas' (1576), in which the satirist claims to have bequeathed 'a glasse of trustie steele' which shows things as they are, while 'the christall glasse' was given 'To such as love to seme but not to be'. See Gascoigne, G. (1907–10) *The Complete Works*, ed. J. W. Cunliffe. 2 vols, Cambridge: Cambridge University Press 2 pp 148–9.

86. For a discussion of the ambiguous punctuation of the last line of this sonnet, see Ferry (1983) p 84.

87. Daalder, J., ed. (1975) *Sir Thomas Wyatt: Collected Poems.* Oxford: Oxford University Press, p 18, notes that 'file' (verb) can mean '1 to polish, 2 deceive,

3 defile'. For the word 'file' and its connotations in Wyatt's sonnet, see Ferry (1983) pp 88–90, and Greene (1982) p 256.

88. The Welles Anthology has three examples altogether, nos. 36, 37 and 46: Jansen and Jordan (1991). See their introduction, pp 27–8, and for the theme, Frankis, P. J. (1956) 'The erotic dream in Middle English lyrics'. *Neuphilologische Mitteilungen* 57: 228–37.

89. In this sense 'spirit' is usually in the plural, *OED* sb. IV 2.

90. Bielby, N., ed. (1976) *Three Early Tudor Poets: A Selection from Skelton, Wyatt and Surrey*. Wheaton, Exeter: Wheaton Studies in Literature, p 16.

91. Klein (1992) p 132.

92. Rollins 2 p 108 makes this point.

93. See Merrill, L. R., ed. (1969) *Nicholas Grimald: The Life and Poems* (2nd edn) Archon Books, nos. 10 'Concerning Virgils Eneids', 19 'To m[istress] D[amascene] A[udley]', and 29 'An epitaph of Sir James Wilford knight'.

94. Rollins 1 no. 219. The sonnet echoes especially ll. 3–4 of Wyatt's 'There was never file half so well filed' in its ll. 3–4, and ll. 13–14 and 17 of Surrey's elegy on Wyatt in l. 9.

95. For an exploration of the use of the female body as a figure for sixteenth-century love poetry, particularly the sonnet, see Wall, W. (1993) *The Imprint of Gender: Authorship and Publication in the Renaissance*. Ithaca, NY: Cornell University Press, pp 60–70.

Chapter 4

The Arts of Plain Speaking

> The real deceiver is the plain stylist who pretends to put all his cards on the table. Clarity, then, is a cheat, an illusion. To rhetorical man at least, the world *is* not clear, it is *made* clear. The clear stylist does it with a conjuring trick.[1]

'A DIEPE DISCURSING HEAD'

In Sir Thomas Elyot's 'merry treatise', *Pasquil The Playne*, published in 1533, one of the characters, a courtier named Gnatho, appears in a contradictory garb, with the ostrich feathers of a dandy and the long gown of a sober counsellor. The sardonic Pasquil comments:

> What have we here? a cappefull of aglettes & bottons / this longe estrige[ostrich] fether doeth wonderly wel . . . but this longe gowne and straite sleves is a non sequitur.

Gnatho holds in his hand a book, labelled the *Novum Testamentum*, which is found to conceal a copy of Chaucer's amorous romance *Troilus and Criseyde*:

> Lord what discord is bitwene these two bokes? yet a great dele more is there in thin[e] aparail. And yet most of al betwene the boke in thy hande & thy condicions. As god helpe me, as moche as betwene trouth & lesing [flattery].[2]

Gnatho tries to perform both as a courtier and a counsellor, a double role which Elyot satirizes as potentially a mere matter of style, as superficial as clothing, or the kind of text one quotes.

Elsewhere, in *The Book Named The Governor* (1531), Elyot is more willing to countenance a virtuous combination of some courtly arts with moral seriousness, cautiously advising the young man being groomed for high office, even while dancing 'base dances, bargenettes, pavions, turgions and rounds', to understand and express 'in his motion and countenance fortitude and magnanimity . . . [and] a pleasant connection of fortitude and temperence'.[3] The ideal of the royal servant in whom moral weight is balanced by courtly accomplishment was pithily summed up in the epitaph for Sir Philip Hoby, a fellow diplomat of Wyatt's:

> A diepe discursing head, a noble brest:
> A courtier passing, and a curteis knight.[4]

In spite of such ideals, the roles of sage and good companion pulled potentially in opposite directions. When Castiglione's courtiers discuss the matter in Book 4 of *The Courtier*, the sardonic Gaspare mocks their ideal with the comment, 'I'm not yet certain that I believe that Aristotle and Plato ever danced or made music at any time during their lives, or performed any acts of chivalry'.[5] Even so, for the aspiring courtier a mastery of the discourses of moral weightiness could be as advantageous as the ability to compose and perform balets at moments of courtly pastime.

The discourses of sagacity could, to a large extent, be learned. Thomas Wilson, humanist and future principal secretary to Elizabeth I, exploited the fact in *The Art of Rhetoric*, written in the early 1550s to advise an ambitious, upwardly mobile readership on the art of acquiring a sober but graceful style. Appropriate for men aspiring to public office was a carefully honed plainness, clearly differentiated, for example, from the 'effeminate' speech of the 'fine courtier':

> some will be so fine and so poetical withal, that to their seeming there shall not stand one hair amiss, and yet everybody else shall think them meeter for a lady's chamber than for an earnest matter in any open assembly.[6]

On the other hand, a plainness that borders on rudeness (the speech of Godfrey Godbylyve, or Skelton's Colin Clout) is, for Wilson, socially disastrous. Adopting, like Elyot, a sartorial metaphor, Wilson describes men who should know better but who take no care to refine their speech as

> like some rich snudges having great wealth, [who] go with their hose out at heels, their shoes out at toes, and their coats out at both elbows. For who can tell if such men are worth a groat, when their apparel is so homely, and all their behavior so base?
>
> (pp 187–8)

For Wilson, the ideal is a judicious semi-invisibility of style, avoiding affectation above all, 'using our speech as most men do, and ordering our wits as the fewest have done' (p 188). The adage displays Wilson practising what he preaches, using a witty rhetorical embellishment, a proverb, from an impeccably learned source (Aristotle), to suggest a pithy but idiomatic everyday English.[7]

Wilson's graceful plainness is a carefully chosen and mastered style, but it aspires to invisibility; it should appear plain and familiar, but reveal to the attentive listener a rare wit and discretion. Having described the goal, Wilson is coy about how it is to be achieved:

> Now a wise man that hath good experience . . . will not be bound to any precise rules nor keep any one order, but such only as by reason he shall think best to use, being master over art rather than art should be master over him, rather making art by wit than confounding wit by art . . . For what mattereth whether we follow our book or no, if we follow wit and appoint ourself an order such as may declare the truth more plainly?
>
> (p 185)

Somehow those who aspire to this art must already know how to do it before they can do it well – or rather, the art lies in hiding all signs of its own acquisition. That 'basic governing principle of the display of *effortlessness*', Castiglione's *sprezzatura,* which we discussed in relation to the courtly use of simpler styles in the love lyric, can also be seen at work in Wilson's *Art of Rhetoric.*[8] The art was to acquire the skills of social success in the Tudor polity, the exact inflections of manners or speech that distinguished graceful and able insiders from well-born lightweights or gross outsiders. Wilson's experienced 'wise man . . . rather making art by wit than confounding wit by art' creates just such an impression of naturally accomplished 'effortlessness' even while he is presented to us as a model for painful imitation; the aim is to appear, if not born, then naturally endowed, to be a member of a social and moral elite. Like the long gown with straight sleeves of Elyot's Gnatho, the deployment of appropriate styles could work transformational wonders.

Cultivated plainness was a carefully acquired and deployed style whose aim was transparency. It purported to give unmediated access to truth and the integrity of the speaker. As such it proved a powerful medium. Ben Jonson, a later exponent of the style, had such carefully honed transparency in mind when he noted:

> Language most shews a man: speak that I may see thee . . . No glass renders a man's form, or likeness, so true as his speech. Nay, it is likened to a man: and as we consider feature, and composition in a man; so words in language: in the greatness, aptness, sound, structure, and harmony of it.[9]

Such a manly 'glass' is far removed from effeminate artfulness which obscures 'nature', 'as if no face were fair that were not powdered or painted . . . All must be as affected, and preposterous as our gallants' clothes, sweet bags, and night dressings: in which you would think our men lay in, like ladies: it is so curious'.[10]

The humanist ideal of a morally weighty plain style has its origins in classical thought and was associated particularly with the 'Attic' orator, most influentially described by Cicero (106 BC–43 BC):

> He is restrained and plain, he follows the ordinary usage, really differing more than is supposed from those who are not eloquent at all . . . noticeable ornament, pearls as it were, will be excluded; not even curling-irons will be used; all cosmetics, artificial white and red, will be rejected; only elegance and neatness will remain. The language will be pure Latin, plain and clear.[11]

Cicero recognized that within the broad category of the style a range of kinds of plainness is possible: 'some were adroit and unpolished and intentionally resembled untrained and unskilful speakers; others had the same dryness of style, but were neater, elegant, even brilliant and to a slight degree ornate. Between these two there is a mean and I may say a tempered style, which . . . keeps the proverbial "even tenor of its way" '.[12]

To men like Sir Thomas Wyatt whose advancement lay through the court and who aspired to weighty office and to a reputation as serious men of affairs, an English style which might approximate the virtues of the admired Latin plain styles, the 'Attic' style, or the more relaxed *sermo*, imitating the philosophical conversation of serious men, could clearly be advantageous.[13] Such a language could construct its users as 'diepe discursing heads' (from the epitaph on Sir Philip Hoby), thoughtful and educated men, formed in the Roman mould. Vernacular English was increasingly taking over from Latin and French as the language of government business both at home and in diplomatic negotiation.[14] As I suggested in my discussions in Chapter 1 of Wyatt's letter to Henry reporting on the Brancestor incident, and his 'Defence' written in 1541, Wyatt's career, and possibly his life, depended, more than once, on his ability to represent himself as an honest, bluff, loyal servant, in an English prose that had to appear plain, but in fact had to be flexible, effective and, when necessary, devious (see Chapter 1, pp 14–19).

The Reformation gave new status to the vernacular. The translation of the Bible into English, and the importance for Reformers of disseminating God's word and reliable doctrine to a wide audience, was leading to a defence of a clear, plain English contrasted by Reformist propaganda with the deceptive 'rhetorical' Latin of Roman Catholicism.[15] To some extent, the Reformers' stylistic ideal could draw on the already existing medieval tradition of plain speaking represented, for example, by Skelton's Colin Clout whose 'style rude and plaine' was used to voice home truths.[16] A more overtly cultivated example of a vernacular plain style tradition, which demonstrates its characteristic association with proverbial terseness and claims to truth-speaking, is a ballade by Chaucer, variously called 'Of Truthe' or 'Of Good Counsel':

> Flee from the prese, and dwell with sothfastnes,
> Suffis to thee thy good though it be small,
> For horde hath hate and climing ticklenesse
> Praise hath envy, and weall is blinde in all.[17]

The popularity of such a style and its sentiments in the mid-sixteenth century is attested by the fact that this poem was included among the works of 'Uncertain authors' in *Tottel's Miscellany*, under the heading 'To leade a vertuous and honest life'.

A skilful command of English written style was an increasingly powerful instrument in the hands of the educated classes from the 1530s on, and much work was done on the language and its supply of words to try to make it sufficiently well-stored and flexible to serve the purposes to which it was to be put, whether for administration, political persuasion, the formulation of a popular but dignified idiom for the Bible and worship, the dissemination of Reformed polemic, or the translation and imitation of prestigious classical or modern European texts. Wyatt and Surrey and the generation of English writers in the second quarter of the sixteenth century were able both to use a sophisticated range of kinds of English, and to contribute, more than many other generations, to the expansion and potential of the vernacular.[18] If, as so many metaphors of the period indicate, style was like a garment which, nevertheless, revealed all about the speaker, then an adept user of the language had at his/her disposal a varied and flexible wardrobe of costumes and *dramatis personae*. In this chapter I shall be investigating some of the uses and connotations of 'plain' styles in the poetry of Wyatt and Surrey.

WISE COUNSELS AND PITHY ADVICE

The standard methods in the Renaissance of acquiring and developing verbal readiness and tailoring a wardrobe of styles was by studying, translating, paraphrasing and imitating approved classical writers. Wyatt's early *The Quyete of Mynde*, published in 1528, translates, via a Latin version by Guillaume Budé (*De Tranquillitate et Securitate Animi*), a philosophical treatise by the Greek writer Plutarch (AD 50 – *c.*120). The translation is dedicated to Queen Katherine of Aragon who had originally suggested that he translate a moral text in Latin prose by Petrarch. Her proposal in 1527 – the year in which Wyatt visited Italy – may imply that Wyatt had already begun to translate Petrarch's sonnets, and that the serious-minded queen wished to divert his talents to better purpose.

Wyatt chose to translate Plutarch instead. He justified this flouting of his patron's wishes in two prefaces, 'To the reader' and to Katherine herself, by attacking Petrarch's prolixity and aligning himself with Plutarch's plainness and brevity: Wyatt claims to seek 'rather the profite of the sentence than the nature of the wordes', and tells his readers, 'As for the shortnesse advise it well and it shall be the pleasanter, when thou understandest it'.[19] The style of Plutarch's treatise was described by its Elizabethan translator, Sir Thomas North, as 'sharpe, learned and short', at the brief end of the Attic plain style.[20] A. N. Brilliant has shown that the brevity of Plutarch's style had been rendered even more succinct and idiomatic by the Latin translation by Budé which Wyatt used.[21] Wyatt seems to have particularly enjoyed the opportunities the text gave him for striking and colloquial English phrases. Achilles, for example, is described as blaming himself for sitting idly 'like a dead lump of earth' (p 443 l. 17), and 'slipper riches' are described as 'not nailed with six penny nail, as they say' (p 457 l. 29). The proverb is derived from Budé, but Wyatt adds the sixpenny to give the phrase added colloquial vigour.[22]

Plutarch's treatise not only offers Wyatt and his readers a model of style, but also of thought. The wise counsels approved by Plu tarch's speakers combine advice for the high-flying with moral sentences on eschewing ambition. Plutarch attacks false counsellors who advocate withdrawal from public life to enjoy a life of ease, 'as it were with this word: lie still wretch in thy bed' (p 442 ll. 32–3). 'Sluggardy and slothfulness', whether mental or physical, are no part of Plutarch's programme. Such idleness is associated with the life of women, into whose heads creep so many 'diseases of the mind . . .

whereof no man can attain the number' (p 443 ll. 1–4). On the contrary, the wise man should use his abilities and skill (his 'craft') to make the best of the chances that are offered him, not wasting time on vain pity (p 447) or on envying others: 'fordo the unevenness of a starting or glittering heart'(p 457 ll. 40–1). Plutarch's counsellor, following the central plain style rhetorical device of endorsing tradition with experience, provides with his manly style and conformist discourse a highly usable model for the rising courtier or administrator of the Tudor period. Like Gnatho's long gown, although not necessarily with the deliberate hypocrisy attributed to Gnatho by Elyot, such a discourse might profitably be 'assumed' by Tudor courtiers to project an idealized version of the royal servant, able and willing to be active and to make the best of his gifts, but above envying others, and reassuringly patient when faced with demotion or disfavour. The translation displays the young Wyatt (he was probably twenty-four in 1527) as an able linguist, using the approved method of translation to digest and turn into nourishment for himself and others a sinewy and moral classical model.

The kind of pithy, aphoristic style to be found in Plutarch enjoyed a considerable vogue in the early to middle decades of the sixteenth century. Schoolchildren and scholars were taught to read ancient writers, pen in hand, ready to mark succinct and morally approved sentences for memorization, or for copying later into their own 'common place book'.[23] In turn the writings, or the speech, of adults who wished to display their well-schooled minds was often loaded or, as Erasmus would prefer, 'sprinkled' with memorable *sententiae* and apt adages. A 'dominant feature' of the Attic stylist as defined by Cicero was that 'he will employ an abundance of apposite maxims dug out from every conceivable hiding place'.[24]

Such a proverbial or aphoristic style is particularly appropriate for the epigram. Indeed, the classical epigrammatist Martial (AD 40 – *c.*104) defined his style as 'the license I use in calling a spade a spade'.[25] Both Wyatt and Surrey showed considerable interest in the witty terseness of the form. Wyatt's seven-line epigram, 'Right true it is' (Reb. lii), for example, strings proverbs together in a blunt, sometimes colloquial, vernacular which implicitly differentiates the honest speaker from the oleaginous smoothness of the flattering friend, the object of his attack:

> Right true it is, and said full yore ago,
> 'Take heed of him that by the back thee claweth,'
> For none is worse than is a friendly foe.
> Though they seem good, all thing that thee delighteth,

Yet know it well that in thy bosom creepeth:
For many a man such fire oft kindleth
That with the blaze his beard singeth.[26]

The epigram clearly illustrates the style and self-validating logic of such wise counsel. The authoritative didacticism of the speaker is supported by the proverbial wisdom he cites – the pithy distillation of previous men's experience. In turn the proverbial phrases, whether explicitly quoted or simply worked into the discourse, stamp the speaker's personal experience as true, and implicitly include him in a diachronic community of the wise and well-informed.

Surrey used the form and the style for a number of brief, epigrammatic verse letters to real or supposed friends. That addressed to Thomas Radcliffe, third earl of Sussex, adapts biblical proverbs, and refers to the authority of the (probably) dead Wyatt:

My Ratclif, when thy rechlesse youth offendes,
Receve thy scourge by others chastisement;
For such calling, when it workes none amendes,
Then plages are sent without advertisement.
  Yet Salomon said, the wronged shall recure;
  But Wiat said true, the skarre doth aye endure.

(Jones no. 34)

The poem's instruction and warning to the young Radcliffe echoes Solomon's repeated advice in the Book of Proverbs: 'Herken unto me, O ye children . . . O geve eare unto nurtoure, be wise, and refuse it not.'[27] The first two lines also draw on a familiar commonplace, that wise men learn from the punishment of others.[28] The unadvertised plagues that are the consequence of not learning echo Solomon's warning against the wicked: 'their destruccion shall come sodenly, & who knoweth the adversite that may come' (Proverbs 24 (v. 23)). Surrey's penultimate line draws on Ecclesiasticus 27 (v. 21): 'As for woundes, they maye be bounde up againe . . . but who so bewrayeth the secretes of a frende, there is no more hope to be had unto him.'[29] The adage attributed to Wyatt concludes by both endorsing and modifying Solomon's wisdom. Scars from sudden 'plages' may be borne by the good, it seems, and the speaker (surely to be identified as Surrey himself in this poem to a first cousin) implies that he speaks from experience. His punishment, leaving unhealable scars, should serve as a warning to Radcliffe, but in the speaker's case, as in that of Wyatt, they are the scars of the wronged. In Henrician England the innocent too might be punished, and although saved by their righteousness, permanently 'scarred'. The lesson gives a grim political warning.

Surrey draws for this poem not only on biblical wisdom and Wyatt's life, but on a *strambotto* addressed by Wyatt, apparently from prison, to Sir Francis Bryan. The proverb which Surrey quotes is used by Wyatt to give a final, terse, epigrammatic authority to his own experience:

> Sighs are my food, drink are my tears;
> Clinking of fetters such music would crave.
> Stink and close air away my life wears.
> Innocency is all the hope I have.
> Rain, wind, or weather I judge by mine ears.
> Malice assaulted that righteousness should save.
> Sure I am, Bryan, this wound shall heal again,
> But yet, alas, the scar shall still remain.
>
> (Reb. lxii)

Here the pared down poetry of statement, grounded in experience, seems to guarantee the grim integrity of the first-person speaker. He is, however, recycling the aphorisms of others. As Surrey borrowed Wyatt's last two lines, so Wyatt may well be borrowing lines from a poem by Bryan himself, 'The Proverbes of Salmon do plainly declare', which strings together twenty-three stanzas of proverbs including 'The wounde oft renewed is longe in the healinge'.[30] Thus a series of intertextual allusions links the three men and their poems: Wyatt addresses Bryan and cites proverbial wisdom, perhaps a proverb that Bryan himself had recycled, and Surrey in turn addresses Radcliffe and quotes Wyatt and Solomon. The style, the epigrammatic form and the topoi effectively dramatize a virtuous, intellectual community of wise but unfortunate men of affairs, each drawing on the experiences of themselves and others, and grounding their wisdom on the authority of biblical precepts and time-honoured aphorisms.

If the courts of princes were dangerous places, then the fortitude of a virtuous mind and the liberty of a middling estate in the country were recommended as assuaging comforts. This was the counsel of Plutarch in *The Quyete of Mynde*: 'if we hear any man say that our fortune is bare & wretched for that we have neither the consulship nor other mastership, we may say unto him that our fortune is fair and goodly and that . . . among porters and bearers we weary us not with burdens nor like flatterers are constrained to be as parasites to princes' (p 451 ll. 26–32).[31] The peace of mind of those in a middling estate was a favourite topic of the plain style genres and enjoyed, on the evidence of *Tottel's Miscellany*, huge popularity in the second quarter of the sixteenth century. Surrey may have helped set the fashion when he turned one of the subsequently oft-repeated models, Horace's ode on 'the golden mean' (Odes Bk 2.10), into a long epigram, 'Of thy life, Thomas, this compasse well marke' (Jones no. 39). It has often been suggested that the 'Thomas' Surrey addressed in this translation was his son, but if so, the advice to follow the mean estate seems strikingly inappropriate, especially from a father who built the splendid palace of Mount Surrey and was so sensitive to any aspersions on his own high estate. A more fitting candidate might be Sir Thomas Wyatt the younger, a client and companion of Surrey's on such escapades as the window-breaking episode in 1543, and in the trench warfare of Boulogne. If so, it is an instance of Surrey's sense of the decorum of matching style and theme to the rank of the addressee, also apparent in the elegy on the elder Wyatt, where the sober restraint of the style and voice complement Surrey's version of the man (see Chapter 1, pp 19–21).

If Surrey's 'Thomas' was the younger Wyatt, then the choice of genre and topic for the poem addressed to him may also be an indirect compliment to the elder Wyatt's particular success with both. A translation by Wyatt of part of a chorus from Seneca's play *Thyestes*, entitled by Tottel in his *Miscellany* 'Of the meane and sure estate', sets the 'slipper top / Of court's estates' against the quiet 'here' of the reflective speaker, who, unlike the victim of courtly ambition, claims to know himself. Wyatt's translation concentrates its dramatic source into a powerful epigram:

> Stand whoso list upon the slipper top
> Of court's estates, and let me here rejoice
> And use me quiet without let or stop,
> Unknown in court that hath such brackish joys.
> In hidden place so let my days forth pass
> That when my years be done withouten noise,
> I may die aged after the common trace.
> For him death grip'th right hard by the crop
> That is much known of other, and of himself, alas,
> Doth die unknown, dazed, with dreadful face.
>
> (Reb. xlix)

The even pace and prose-like syntax of the first seven lines shift in line 8, which departs most dramatically from the Latin model into a different gear.[32] The stoic truisms of the poem are suddenly energized by the aural intensity and the brutality of this line, an effect repeated in the poem's concluding stark image. The last three lines suggest the testimony of shocking personal experience. Wyatt undoubtedly saw public executions, and personal experience may well lie behind the success of this translation, but its effects are rhetorically produced and conform to the characteristic devices of the plain style in which ancient wisdom is given new force through an appeal to personal experience.

Wyatt follows a similar strategy in another poem, not an epigram this time, based on a Senecan original. In this case, the appearance of the poem in the Blage MS (which contains the only copy) explicitly draws on Wyatt's known history to authenticate the lessons it teaches. The poem's heading, which may not necessarily have been by Wyatt himself, sets his name in the middle of a defensive encirclement of virtues:

> *V. Innocentia*
> *Veritas Viat Fides*
> *Circumdederunt me inimici mei*
>
> (Reb. cxxiii)

Wyatt ('*Viat*' – 'w' is rendered as 'v' in Latin) is surrounded by the three virtues, Innocence, Truth and Faith, while below, a line from Psalm 17, 'my enemies surround me', speaks as though in the poet's own voice.

The poem itself begins with a series of generalized *sententiae* derived from a chorus in Seneca's tragedy *Phaedra* (or *Hippolytus*), from which the Latin refrain is also taken: '*circa Regna tonat* (around the throne of kings it thunders)'. This idea is a commonplace, close kin to that in Horace's ode on the golden mean (Odes 2.10 ll. 11–12) which Surrey translated 'Lightninges assault the hie mountains and clives [cliffs]' (Jones no. 39). Although selecting lines from, rather than translating, the Senecan chorus, Wyatt imitates the terse didacticism of the original:

> The high mountains are blasted oft,
> When the low valley is mild and soft.
> Fortune with health stands at debate.
> The fall is grievous from aloft.
> And sure, *circa Regna tonat*.
>
> (ll. 6–10)

Wyatt has selected only the plainest of Seneca's images. Imagery of the winds, mythological names and other details are rejected.[33] Each of Wyatt's end-stopped lines bears its own terse warning, like a brief adage. Wyatt carries Seneca's opening image of Fortune's wheel into stanza 3, but the stern, generalized injunctions are suddenly transformed into a voice of personal experience:

These bloody days have broken my heart.
My lust, my youth did them depart,
And blind desire of estate.
Who hastes to climb seeks to revert.
Of truth, *circa Regna tonat.*

The bell tower showed me such sight
That in my head stick day and night.
There did I learn out of a grate,
For all favour, glory or might,
That yet *circa Regna tonat.*

(ll. 11–20)

The generalized locations of the Senecan original, high seats and a humble cottage, are replaced by the personal and specific, the Bell Tower in the Tower of London which was used to house prisoners, probably Wyatt himself in 1536. The nature of the place gives an ironic twist to the conventional imagery of the gate of preferment's castle, used in stanza 1, and the hasty climb of stanza 3 l. 14. For this speaker both have led to the Bell Tower, from which he sees a beheading that 'sticks' in his own head.[34]

The final stanza of the poem uses the speaker's personal experience to authorize its stoic lessons:

By proof, I say, there did I learn:
Wit helpeth not defence to yerne, *to yerne: to run smoothly*
Of innocency to plead or prate.
Bear low, therefore, give God the stern,
For sure, *circa Regna tonat.*

(ll. 21–5)

If the poem does, as it seems, refer to Wyatt's own imprisonment in 1536 at the time when Anne Boleyn and her 'lovers', all Wyatt's acquaintances, were executed, then undoubtedly, on this occasion, his own experience amply confirmed the wisdom he quoted from the past. The characteristic language, topics and tropes of the classical plain style nevertheless offered him a voice and gestures, ready to hand, with which to understand his own experience and to shape it for others. In the summer of 1536, when signs of ambition would have seemed particularly suspect and dangerous in Wyatt, the poem harnesses traditional virtue in the cause of personal rehabilitation, rewriting political failure and dependency as willing retirement and the renunciation of ambition.

More generally, the *gravitas* of a rhetoric of wisdom and judgement offered Wyatt and other ambitious courtiers a persona to offset the implication of lightweight effeminacy associated with the poems and practice of witty courtly dalliance. For a potential ambassador, as indeed for most of the offices in which ambitious courtiers might be employed, mastery of the rhetoric of wise counsel, as well as facility in social dalliance, were important assets. Like Gnatho's long gown with straight sleeves, a cultivated plain style could display its user as serious and learned, a man marked by sober experience.

WYATT'S SATIRES

A rhetoric of plain speaking, and personae who claim to be honest men made wise by experience, characterize Wyatt's three long satirical epistles. Although the first satire, 'Mine own John Poyntz', is derived from a contemporary Italian source, Wyatt's ultimate model for all three satires is Horace, whose use and combination of the two genres of epistle and satire provided the prototype of the form and a prestigious example of an urbane, conversational, plain style.[35] In all three of Wyatt's satirical epistles, as I shall hope to show, the honest speaker turns out to be less, or more, than he claims.[36]

The dates for composition of the satires are not known with any certainty, although internal references suggest 'Mine own John Poyntz' (Reb. cxlix) was written in 1536 after Wyatt's release from the Tower, and ' "A spending hand" ', addressed to Bryan (Reb. cli), was written in, or just after, the period from 1537 to 1539, when Wyatt was a fellow diplomat of Bryan's.[37] 'My mother's maids' (Reb. cl) is undatable from any internal references. Its speaking voice is less assured than is the case with the other two poems, and its language and thought is sometimes strikingly close to Wyatt's translation of *The Quyete of Mynde*. It may therefore be the earliest of the three, although it is possible that Wyatt went back to the consolations of *The Quyete of Mynde* for his own use during the crisis of May 1536, or later.

In spite of its first-person speaker, 'My mother's maids' offers us a number of different voices which remain still distinct and unreconciled at the poem's conclusion. It begins as though it were a retelling of the Aesopian fable of the town and country mice.[38] The tale is remembered as it was sung by the speaker's 'mother's maids when they did sew and spin' (l. 1). The child-like simplicity with which the tale is told represents the women as unsophisticated and innocent, voices recollected nostalgically from the speaker's childhood. Aesop's fables seem to have had an association with children and women. Horace referred to the fable in *Satire* II.vi as an old wives' or grandmother's tale' ('anilis . . . fabellas', ll. 77–8), and Sir Thomas Elyot, in *The Book named The Governor*, advised the reading of Aesop 'in which argument children much do delight' as one of the first exercises in an educational system which, at the age of seven, removed the young gentleman from the company of women into that of the male tutor.[39]

Aesop's tales were moralized. For Henryson the tale taught that the mean estate was surest: 'The sweitest life thairfoir, in this cuntrie, / Is sickernes with small possesioun.'[40] In Horace's version, the tale is part of a celebration of the frugal pleasures of country living. When Tottel printed Wyatt's poem he entitled it 'Of the meane and sure estate written to John Poins'. The women who tell the story in Wyatt's poem do not, however, draw out a moral. In their version, the story seems partly about a domestic envy that is to some extent justified. The country mouse imagines that 'to live a lady' like her courtly sister is to sleep on featherdown and eat rare meats, free of both 'charge' and 'travail' (ll. 20–35). Her own domestic situation is imagined with particular horror, especially when it rains:

> when the furrows swimmed with the rain
> She must lie cold and wet in sorry plight
>
> . . .
>
> And when her store was 'stroyed with the flood,
> Then wellaway, for she undone was clean.
> Then was she fain to take in stead of food
> Sleep, if she might, her hunger to beguile.
>
> (ll. 7–8, 14–17)

The town mouse, on the other hand, is doing alright: 'Richly she feedeth and at the rich mans cost' (l. 23), although a note of harassed anxiety may be detected in the comic exchange of greetings when the country mouse first appears in town:

> 'Peep', quod the other, 'sister, I am here'.
> 'Peace', quod the town mouse, 'why speakest thou so loud?'
>
> (ll. 42–3)

Uniquely in Wyatt's version, the country mouse does not escape to enjoy her quiet security, but trips and is caught:

> At the threshold her silly foot did trip, *silly: helpless, defenceless*
> And ere she might recover it again
> The traitour cat had caught her by the hip
> And made her there against her will remain,
> That had forgotten her poor surety and rest
> For seeming wealth wherein she thought to reign.
>
> (ll. 64–9)

These lines conclude the fable and mark a transition to a new, markedly different voice, one that is male and authoritative, that of the poem's adult speaker addressing a male friend and drawing a moral from the women's story: 'Alas, my Poyntz, how men do seek the best / And find the worst . . . ' (ll. 70–1). The speaker's moral brings the fable into line with other male tellings. The simple, sympathetic narrative of the two mice is relegated to female chatter and situated in a nostalgic past, while in the present of the poem it is explained and moralized in masculine discourse.

For all his moral authority, the newly assertive masculine speaker has, in fact, a much less secure identity than those of the women whose song he reports. At first his voice is a reflective one, sharing sententious maxims with Poyntz, 'how men do seek the best / And find the worst by error as they stray!' Reflection, however, rapidly gives way to a more openly didactic stridency: 'O wretched minds, there is no gold that may / Grant that ye seek' (ll. 75–6). From line 70 to line 103, the poem veers from addressing Poyntz, to a generalized 'ye', to a single but unspecified 'thou', and back again.

As unstable as the sense of addressee and the tone of the speaker is the moral frame of reference, pagan or Christian. The problems are most evident in a passage which draws for its imagery on both the Plutarch essay which Wyatt had translated as *The Quyete of Mynde* and a passage from Luke's Gospel. In *The Quyete of Mynde* the foolishness of blaming fortune for what should never be attempted is illustrated by a series of impossibilities: 'as it were to be angry with fortune that thou canst not shoot an arrow with a plough, or hunt an hare with an ox, and that some cruell god should be against them that with vain endeavor hunt an hart with a drag net', while those who hope for what they cannot have are told: 'none of us sees a vine bear figs, nor an olive bear grapes' (M&T p 454 l. 32).[41] Some of these images and the moralizing application reappear in the verse satire:

None of ye all there is that is so mad
  To seek grapes upon brambles or briers,
  Nor none, I trow, that hath his wit so bad
To set his hay for conies over rivers; *conies: rabbits*
  Ne yet set not a drag-net for a hare.
  And yet the thing that most is your desire
Ye do mis-seek with more travail and care.

(ll. 85–91)

Appropriately, Plutarch's images of olives, figs and harts are changed to brambles, briars and conies to conform to the sodden English landscape inhabited by the two mice, but the alterations go further. In Plutarch the passages are philosophical: 'Surely the cause of this error is the naughty love of our self.' In 'My mother's maids', by contrast, the satirist, by attaching the grapes to brambles and briars rather than to an olive, invokes an apocalyptic biblical passage. Tyndale translates the relevant passage, in Luke 4.44: 'For every tree is known by his fruit. Neither of thorns gather men figs, nor of bushes gather they grapes.'[42] The biblical echo introduces the idea of judgement and of the absolute distinction between good and bad who will be known by their fruits.

The conflicts of tone and meaning between the two perspectives, pagan and Christian, produce one of the cruxes of the poem. Lines 97–103 of the satire echo another passage from *The Quyete of Mynde* in which Plutarch counsels us to be content with what we have in the present: 'for fools let good things pass though they be present, and regard them not when they perish, so much doth their thoughts gape greedily after things to come' (M&T p 455 ll. 22–4). In other words, we should be content with what we are and what we have. The relevant passage in 'My mother's maids' presents a problem with punctuation. In Wyatt's own, unpunctuated, Egerton MS the passage is as follows:

Then seke no more owte of thy self to finde
  the thing that thou haist sought so long before
  for thou shalt fele it sitting in thy minde
Madde if ye list to continue your sore
  let present passe and gape on time to com
  and diepe your self in travaill more & more

(ll. 97–102)[43]

The context of *The Quyete of Mynde* suggests that the meaning of lines 100–2 should be: you are mad if you wish to continue your anxious search for material happiness ('sore', *OED* 6), labouring for future gain rather than contenting yourself with the present. An orthodox Christian interpretation, appropriate for the country mouse, is, however, possible, in which we would be advised to raise our minds above the suffering ('sore', *OED* 1) of the present and long for ('gape', *OED* v. 4) eternity, accepting with good will the hardships of the journey of this life ('travail', *OED* sb. 1 and 4).

A Christian context of judgement and eternity seems confirmed by the speaker's invocation of 'the great God and . . . his high doom' (ll. 103, 105) and his apparent application of his own lessons to himself: 'Henceforth, my Poyntz, this shall be all and sum.' Far from rededicating himself, however, it is soon apparent that the speaker is washing his hands of others, the 'wretched minds . . . ye' (ll. 75–6) who have now become 'wretched fools . . . they' (ll. 104, 108). God's 'doom' (judgement) is invoked in a final prayer whose vehemence seems rather that of personal vengeance than Christian exhortation:

> None other pain pray I for them to be
> But when the rage doth lead them from the right,
> That looking backward, Virtue they may see
> Even as she is, so goodly fair and bright.
> And whilst they clasp their lusts in armes across,
> Grant them, good Lord, as thou mayst of thy might,
> To fret inward for losing such a loss.
>
> (ll. 106–12)

The re-entry of the feminine at the end of the poem, both fair Virtue and the illusory 'lusts', further destabilizes the voice of the masculine speaker. He prays that, as a punishment, Virtue 'goodly fair and bright' will be located for 'them' in a lost past. But this unavoidably reminds us of the speaker's own nostalgic memory of 'my mother's maids', innocent and virtuous, and the unjudging childhood they evoke. The false 'lusts' with which the speaker curses 'them' at the end of the poem seem not unlike those illusory desires which characterized all men, including the speaker, when, earlier, he shared his experience with his friend: 'Alas, my Poyntz, how men do seek the best / And find the worst by error as they stray' (ll. 70–1).

In striving for a voice of masculine knowledge and experience, this poem in fact fragments amongst a variety of authoritative discourses, classical and Christian. Interestingly, this loss of masculine control and identity occurs in a poem which tries to use female voices. The tale of the female mice, told by the maids, relates, in allegorical form, the dilemma of the young man attracted from his provincial, maternal home by the glittering, unstable, dependent and dangerous luxury of the court. The male speaker strives to differentiate his own masculine, authoritative voice from this fascinating and fearful tale, but cannot successfully do so. The life of the town mouse represents both a feminized place of luxury and dependence, the court, but also, paradoxically, the adult male world that took the well-born boy away from the simple, female, provincial world of childhood. By the end of the poem the maids' narrative seems, willy nilly, to control him, causing him to voice as a curse his own condition as a disillusioned exile from innocence and comfort, enticed by but always unable to grasp the feminized chimeras of satisfaction and quietness of mind.

A second satirical epistle to John Poyntz, 'Mine own John Poyntz' (Reb. cxlix), is a more assured and consistent performance. The John Poyntz to whom both epistles were addressed was a courtier at the Henrician court whose name appears with that of Wyatt in a joust of 1524.[44] Wyatt's use of the name of, we presume, a personal friend implies that the speaking voice of the epistle should be identified as that of the historical Thomas Wyatt. This is reinforced by allusions, towards the end of the poem, to Wyatt's own circumstances in 1536. The speaker mentions a 'clog' (manacle) at his heel (l. 86), in spite of which he claims to enjoy his retirement 'in Kent and Christendom' (l. 100). Wyatt's own estate was, of course, in Kent, at Allington. It was here that Wyatt was sent, into his father's charge, when he was released from prison in May 1536, with a warning from the king 'to adres him better' ringing in his ears (*LL* p 35). During the summer months of 1536 he was in Kent on probation, and the 'clog' seems to refer to these circumstances.

'Mine own John Poyntz' thus invites us to identify its first-person speaker with the writer, Wyatt. He is a plain speaker in the classical mould, a morally serious man of the world addressing another with reflections and wise counsels garnered from his experience and reading. As with other plain speakers, he claims to speak the truth transparently:

> My Poyntz, I cannot frame my tune to feign,
> To cloak the truth for praise, without desert,
>
> . . .
>
> I cannot with my words complain and moan
> And suffer naught, nor smart without complaint,
> Nor turn the word that from my mouth is gone.
>
> (ll. 19–20, 28–30)

Flattery, the craft of misnaming, turning 'the word that from my mouth is gone', is just what the speaker cannot do:

> As drunkeness good fellowship to call;
> The friendly foe with his double face
> Say he is gentle and courteous therewithal;
> And say that Favel hath a goodly grace
> In eloquence; and cruelty to name
> Zeal of justice, and change in time and place;
> And he that suffereth offence without blame
> Call him pitiful, and him true and plain
> That raileth reckless to every man's shame.
> Say he is rude that cannot lie and feign,
> The lecher a lover, and tyranny
> To be the right of a prince's reign.
> I cannot, I! No, no, it will not be!
>
> (ll. 64–76)

These lines are examples of the rhetorical figure *paradiastole*, calling one thing by the name of another, a term anglicized by George Puttenham, later in the century, as 'curry favel', drawing on an old proverb, 'he that will in Court dwell must needes currie favel'.[45] It is the quintessential figure of flattery, enacting the 'corrupt' potential of language to jumble what should be morally distinct. Castiglione used it to sum up the moral and linguistic confusion to which courtiers are prone: 'so everyone praises or condemns according to his own opinion, always camouflaging a vice under the name of the corresponding virtue, or a virtue under the name of the corresponding vice (cf. 'John Poyntz' l. 61)'.[46] The only antidote to this is the honest, transparent, artless speech practised, so he claims, by Wyatt's speaker.

But if *paradiastole* is the figure of courtly flattery, an attack on it had itself become a conventional literary topic.[47] The moral outrage of Wyatt's 'I' speaker has to be seen within literary contexts that contest his claim to artlessness. Indeed, the very language of transparent and artless honesty which Wyatt's speaker claims to use, 'I am not he such eloquence to boast, / To make the crow singing as the swan' (ll. 43–4), is artfully translated from a sophisticated continental model, a verse satire by an Italian poet resident in France, Luigi Alamanni, whose satires themselves partly imitate those of Horace.[48] Wyatt's honest speaker, masquerading in the poet's historical identity, ventriloquizes a voice, that of Alamanni addressing his friend Tommaso Sertini, that is not his own.

Alamanni (1495–1556) was a republican, an opponent of the princely Medici family in Florence, who was forced to live and write in exile in France. Wyatt has Englished Alamanni's highly cultivated, Italian republican voice with extraordinary skill and with his own distinctive emphases. The Wyatt speaker's protestation at his lack of 'eloquence' prefaces a passage which demonstrates Wyatt's careful selection and alteration of his source:

> I am not he such eloquence to boast,
> To make the crow singing as the swan,
> Nor call the lion of coward beasts the most
> That cannot take a mouse as the cat can;
> And he that dieth for hunger of the gold
> Call him Alexander, and say that Pan
> Passeth Apollo in music many fold;
> Praise Sir Thopas for a noble tale
> And scorn the story that the knight told;
> Praise him for counsel that is drunk of ale;
>
> (ll. 43–52)[49]

Alamanni's text puts less emphasis on the speaker's lack of eloquence. Indeed this passage, like the rest of the poem, provides a sustained display of classical learning:

> Io non saprei chiamar cortese & bello
> Chi sia Thersite, ne figliuol d'Anchise
> Chi sia di senno & di pietà rubello.
> Non saprei chi piu' l cor nell'oro mise
> Dirgli Alessandro, e' l pauroso & vile
> Chiamarlo il forte, ch'i Centauri ancise.
> Dir non saprei Poeta alto, & gentile
> Mevio, giurando poi che tal non vide
> Smirna, Manto, & Fiorenza ornato stile.[50]

> (I could not call a man courtly and refined who was a Thersites [a foul-speaking character in the *Iliad*], nor a true son of Anchises [Aeneas], one who had broken away from good sense and piety. I could not call a man an Alexander whose heart was all for money, nor name after the hero who slew the Centaurs [mythic figures, half man, half beast] a man who was a despicable coward. I could not say that Maevius [a minor poet attacked by Horace] was a great, distinguished poet, and swear that an equally polished style had never been found in Smyrna, Mantua or Florence [the cities, respectively, of Homer, Virgil and Dante].)

Wyatt retains a few classical allusions (Midas, Alexander, Pan and Apollo) but jettisons most of Alamanni's, referring instead to two of Chaucer's *Canterbury Tales* (ll. 50–1) and some Aesopian-sounding beast fables (ll. 44–6). The homely and demotic effect of such changes is increased by line 52, 'Praise him for counsel that is drunk of ale', which has no corresponding line in the Italian.[51] A similarly colloquial register is heard throughout the poem, as when Wyatt transforms a vow by the Italian satirist not to follow those who value fortune more than wisdom ('Ne quai Fortuna piu che 'l senno valse', l. 75) into the proverbial:

> This is the cause that I could never yet
> Hang on their sleeves that weigh, as thou mayst see,
> A chip of chance more than a pound of wit.
>
> (ll. 77–9)[52]

In some respects, then, Wyatt's speaker sounds more like an unrefined 'crow' or a country Pan rather than the 'swan' or Apollo of the polished poet. Such blunt vernacular and homely references seem appropriate for the bluff country gentleman described at the end of the poem who spends his time hunting and hawking, retiring to his book only in 'foul weather' (ll. 80–8).[53] On the other hand, this speaker is also a man who can use classical analogies when it suits him. The voice of Wyatt's 'I' speaker is very carefully balanced between the idiom of an honest provincial gentleman insufficiently sophisticated for the arts of the court, and that of an informed and educated commentator whose pointed barbs carry weight. The latter masquerades behind the naivety of the former.

The most dramatic of Wyatt's changes to his source alters a particularly clear instance of Alamanni's republicanism. Alamanni had written that he could not honour the dictators, Caesar and Sulla, while wrongfully condemning the republican, Brutus, and his peerless company:[54]

> Non di loda honorar chiara immortale
> Cesare & Sylla, condannando à torto
> Bruto, & la schiera che piu d'altra vale.
>
> (ll. 43–5)

Wyatt alters these lines, potentially dangerous ones in Henrician England, although he keeps the detailed reference to Roman history:

> I am not he that can allow the state
> Of high Caesar and damn Cato to die,[55]
> That with his death did 'scape out of the gate
> From Caesar's hands, if Livy doth not lie,
> And would not live where liberty was lost,
> So did his heart the common wealth apply.
>
> (ll. 37–42)

Commentators have puzzled over Wyatt's reference to Livy, who only briefly mentions Cato the Younger's death from suicide, and his failure to mention Plutarch who wrote a life praising his upright honesty.[56] Apart from considerations of metre, Wyatt's account may here be poised with political precision. The virtues that Plutarch made Cato stand for, plain speaking and an upright love of liberty and the common weal, are established by Wyatt's lines. The mention of Livy may serve to emphasize the historical outcome of his challenge to Caesar, his death. Cato's defence of liberty was noble but doomed. The satire's praise of him therefore comes hedged with warnings. Nevertheless the 'liberty' (l. 84) that the speaker himself finds within the liberties (*OED* 6 b, 'immunities or rights enjoyed by . . . grant') of his country estate, as well as his own claim to speak the truth, aligns Wyatt's speaker with Cato. He, too, suffers a penalty, the 'clog', which he acknowledges, but the poem manages to insinuate, in spite of the likely historical circumstances of Wyatt's rustication, that the speaker has been punished, like Cato, because he 'would not live where liberty was lost, / So did his heart the common wealth apply' (ll. 41–2).

The defence of plain speaking in 'Mine own John Poyntz' requires an extraordinarily artful and devious use of language. The poem makes use of two subtly different plain speaking voices, that of the blunt country gentleman and that of the knowledgeable political commentator, the barbs of the one hidden within the disarming honesty and the apparently voluntary retirement of the other. In a poem in which eloquence is synonymous with deceptive flattery, the fact that the poem is a fluent translation of an up-to-date and politically charged model, introducing for the first time into English the sophisticated and prestigious form of the classical satirical epistle, may constitute an in-joke. The facts of translation and classical imitation, of course, give the poem, as Greenblatt notes, 'deniability'; the voice and its views are not Wyatt's, but Alamanni's, and behind him lie the models of Horace and Juvenal.[57] 'Mine own John Poyntz' is highly adapted to its courtly place and time through its interweaving of display and camouflage. If the poem does belong to the summer of 1536, Wyatt, even as he quits the court under dubious circumstances, subtly represents that withdrawal as a sign of integrity and independence, and demonstrates how accomplished a performer the court may have lost by his, temporary, disgrace.

In fact Cromwell and Henry still had uses for Wyatt, and in January 1537 he was appointed to the crucially important post of ambassador at the court of the Emperor Charles V. In the midst of such political flux and royal changes of mind, a flexible persona and deniable words were undoubtedly an advantage. Wyatt's fellow ambassador at the court of King Francis I in France in 1537 was Sir Francis Bryan, to whom Wyatt addressed his third satirical epistle, ' "A spending hand" ' (Reb. cli), described by Catherine Bates as 'an extraordinarily perplexing, shifting poem . . . the most ironic of Wyatt's verse epistles'.[58]

> I thought forthwith to write,
> Bryan, to thee, who knows how great a grace
> In writing is to counsel man the right.
> To thee, therefore, that trots still up and down
> And never rests, but running day and night
> From realm to realm, from city, street, and town,
> Why dost thou wear thy body to the bones . . . ?
>
> (ll. 8–14)

The perplexing ironies of the poem are not immediately apparent. The voice of the speaker is one with which we are now familiar, a good counsellor and a plain speaker, addressing another man of affairs who knows what it is 'to counsel man the right'. Appropriately, as Cicero had recommended, he employs 'an abundance of apposite maxims' (see p 120 above):

> 'A spending hand that alway poureth out
> Had need to have a bringer-in as fast';
> And 'On the stone that still doth turn about
> There groweth no moss' – these proverbs yet do last.
>
> (ll. 1–4)

Diane Ross has pointed out, however, that the 'rolling stone' proverb

> quickly becomes a subject of debate . . . giving the lie to the "sure" place of proverbs. The speaker suggests that a mossy stone has the mineral equivalent of the good life – safe, rested, protected. Bryan, on the other hand, compares the mossy stone to a "fatted swine" wallowing in a filthy manger.[59]

The contested interpretation of the 'rolling stone' proverb sets a pattern for the entire poem, which is riddled with such conflicting proverbs and their interpretations. The proverbs of the poem's first speaker, who claims to use maxims of good counsel, are matched in Bryan's reply:

> Likest thou not this? 'No.' Why? 'For swine so groins
> In sty and chaw the turds moulded on the ground,
> And drivel on pearls, the head still in the manger.
> Then of the harp the ass do hear the sound.
> So sacks of dirt be filled up in the cloister
> That serves for less than do these fatted swine.'
>
> (ll. 18–23)[60]

As one plain speaker to another, the 'good counsellor' approves of Bryan's proverbs although they oppose his own: 'By God, well said' (l. 28). In fact, the counsellor's own commitment to retirement, deduced from his opening proverbs, turns out to be adaptable:

> but what and if thou wist
> How to bring in as fast as thou dost spend?
>
> (ll. 28–9)

The 'spending hand' proverb, it seems, can be used to argue both for spending less and for getting more. Echoing problematically behind this proverb may be a better known one, 'spend and God shall send', which offers a very different ideology and a subversive commentary on the counsellor's grasping advice.[61]

Echoes and fragments of conflicting proverbs recur throughout the poem: for example, proverbs on friendship and gold. At one point the counsellor urges Bryan:

> Thou know'st well, first, whoso can seek to please
> Shall purchase friends where truth shall but offend.
> Flee therefore truth: it is both wealth and ease.
>
> (ll. 32–4)

The counsellor's advice unpacks the adage 'Obsequium amicos, veritas odium parit' which Richard Taverner, in a popular selection of Erasmus's adages (published with 'newe addicions' in 1539 and repeatedly through the next few years), translated as 'flatterie and folowinge of mens mindes getteth frendes, where speaking of trouth gendreth hatred', relating it to vices of the court: 'He that will in Court dwell, must needes currie favel.'[62] This is the kind of proverb that caused Taverner considerable anxiety. On a related proverb, he commented: 'let no man thinke, that by this Proverbe is taught fowle and detestable flattery'.[63] The 'good counsellor' of ' "A spending hand" ', however, teaches precisely this lesson.

Implicit in the ambiguous syntax of line 34 are proverbs which reward truth with 'wealth' (= moral well-being) as opposed to 'wealth' (= worldly riches). For example, the biblical proverb,

'Aboundaunce of riches is not like a good name', to which Wyatt's Bryan alludes at lines 81–3:[64]

> Wouldest thou I should for any loss or gain
> Change that for gold that I have ta'en for best –
> Next godly things, to have an honest name?

The counsellor concludes his argument with the adage 'Be next thyself, for friendship bears no price' (l. 78).[65] Erasmus developed this adage, 'semper tibi proximus esto', in a different way: 'Doe so to thy friendes that thou be most frende unto thy self', in Taverner's translation.[66] Erasmus's formulation is itself profoundly ambiguous, supporting a counsel of self-interest as well as one of selflessness, as does another Erasmian adage lurking in Wyatt's line, 'Ubi amici, ibi opes', which exists in one English proverb as 'a true friend is a great treasure' and in another, cited by Taverner, as 'a friend in court is worth a penny in purse'.[67]

Wyatt's counsellor's discourse weaves together his own sententious style with actual proverbs, making distinction between the two difficult and lending to his own worldly experience the sagacious authority of traditional wisdom. Where he does draw on proverbs, those distillations of reason and custom, according to Erasmus, they are liable to speak like the Delphic oracle, with a forked tongue, endorsing and subverting at the same time.[68] More explicitly contestory is the voice of Bryan supporting his own position with his own arsenal of adages. Proverbs pepper the discourse of both men, providing authority for opposing views and moral positions, acting as 'evidence' for the smooth-tongued counsellor as readily as they support the terse Sir Francis.[69] Their effect of authority is self-evidently a rhetorical trope, infinitely flexible.

Not only are proverbs and adages, those marks of traditional authority and ornaments of a sagacious plain style, rendered unstable and problematic, but the moral positions and idioms of the speakers seem to confound classical and humanist ideals. Bryan, as the spokesman for moral integrity in the poem, is 'lean and dry without moisture' (l. 24), with a style to match; he may be liberal with gold but he is tight with words. The guttural brevity of his responses do not exemplify Erasmus's advice to 'interweave adages deftly and appropriately . . . to make the language as a whole glitter with sparkles'.[70] When Bryan exclaims: 'Then take me for a beast!' (l. 84), Thomas Wilson might have taken him at his word and included him among those ineloquent gentlemen who like 'some rich snudges having great wealth, go with their hose out at heels, their shoes out at toes, and their coats out at the elbows' (see p 115 above). It is possible that the counsellor's bequest to Bryan of a 'free tongue' (l. 87) is ironic in a poem that has depicted the king's 'orator' (the current term for an ambassador) as able to call a turd a turd, but verbally ill-equipped for the demands of diplomatic service.[71]

' "A spending hand" ' constitutes a critique of humanist eloquence and the duplicities of plain speaking, as much as of courtly service. A plain and authoritative style, grounded on truth and peppered with that quintessential expression of traditional wisdom, the adage or sentence, shapes a garment that can be turned to suit all wearers. The poem's use of proverbs criticizes the duplicity of a currently fashionable style, apparent, not least, in the long proverbial poem ascribed to Bryan, 'The Proverbes of Salmon'. If this is by Bryan, its 181 lines of proverbs align him more closely to the flexible prolixity of the counseller than to the terse Bryan of Wyatt's satire. No doubt knowledge of Bryan's, and Wyatt's, own reputations and spoken idioms, as well as the circumstances of the poem's writing, added considerably, in ways that we cannot now recover, to the satire's meaning and wit for contemporaries who read it in manuscript. It has been suggested that the poem was written in a spirit of friendship to its addressee, either at a time when Bryan himself was out of favour, or at a time when both ambassadors had reason to lament the poor rewards of royal service abroad.[72] Others have suggested that Wyatt was deliberately constructing a Bryan at odds with his contemporary reputation as 'the vicar of hell', a consummate and dissolute courtier whose extravagant gambling debts Wyatt was constrained to pay while they were both abroad.[73] Wyatt commented on the debt to Cromwell using the fashionable idiom: 'If the kinges honour more then his credit had not been afore min ies [mine eyes], he shold have pipid in an ive leff [ivy leaf] for owght off me.'[74] It would be entirely in keeping with Wyatt's politic skill with language had the nuances of the satire's treatment of Bryan been as undecidable by Wyatt's contemporaries as by us.

Wyatt's verse satires return again and again to the problem of reliable speakers, good counsel and the siren perfidy of language. Linguistic innocence and transparency are imagined and tentative attempts made to locate them: in a maternal past, from which they have to be appropriated and interpreted by uneasy male voices in 'My mother's maids', in the country with the not entirely honest translator of Alamanni in 'Mine own John Poyntz', or invested in the dubious figure of Sir Francis Bryan in ' "A spending hand" '. But the closer we look, the more elaborate the rhetorical construction, and the more problematic the innocence of such voices. Courtly vice in 'Mine own John Poyntz' and ' "A spending hand" ' are represented as primarily a matter of linguistic vice, due to the unfixedness of language's relation to truth; so often the man who succeeds at court is represented as the man who can 'frame [his] tongue to feign'. In that art, the verse satires show Wyatt to have been an accomplished performer.

SURREY'S SATIRES

Surrey certainly tried on the roles of the cultivated plain speaker in some of his poetry, as we have seen, but its dramatic effects of sagacious prudence and its gestures of submission to authority and fortune may not have suited his political self-presentation. In the two satires I now consider, Surrey turned to quite different models. Both 'Th'Assyrians king' (Jones no. 32) and 'London, hast thow accused me' (Jones no. 33) are invectives or denunciatory attacks. If either poem owes any debts to classical models, it is to the Roman satirist Juvenal (AD 55–*c.*140), who outspokenly attacked Rome and its citizens as effeminate, luxurious and corrupt.[75] 'Who / Could endure this monstrous city, however callous at heart, / And swallow his wrath?' asked Juvenal of Rome in his first satire, and invoked for his purposes the style of 'our outspoken / Ancestral bluntness, that wrote what burning passion dictated'.[76] In both the satires considered here, Surrey combines such a Juvenalian voice of moral and civic outrage with Christian models and biblical echoes to lend his speakers a prophetic resonance as they scourge vice and warn of divine judgement. Nevertheless in both poems the speaker's authority is open to question. In 'Th'Assyrians king', the highly wrought imagery of the sonnet threatens to implicate the morality of the speaker in the vices he condemns. In 'London hast thow', the combination of literary traditions and voices with the circumstances of the poem's composition produce a tirade whose tone and purpose have proved notoriously difficult to gauge.

Sardanapalus, the degenerate king attacked in 'Th'Assyrians king', was the type of the luxurious and effeminate ruler.[77] Surrey's formal models are Petrarch's series of ferocious anti-papal sonnets (*Rime* 114, 136, 137 and 138) which attacked the 'pagan' and degenerate papal court at Avignon as a second Babylon:

nido di tradimenti, in cui si cova
quanto mal per lo mondo oggi si spande:
de vin serva, di letti e di vivande,
in cui lussuria fa l'ultima prova.

(*Rime* 136 ll. 5–8)

(a nest of treachery, in which is hatched all the ill which nowadays spreads out through the world: served with wine, beds, and dishes; there luxury reaches its greatest excess)

Surrey's Sardanapalus is similarly a figure of corrupt luxury 'Who scace the name of manhode did retaine, / Drenched in slouthe and womanishe delight' (ll. 9–10). The poem strives to make an insistent differentiation between noble manliness and the effeminacy of Sardanapalus, to whom

The dent of swordes from kisses semed straunge,
And harder then his ladies side his targe;
From glotton feastes to sowldiers fare a chaunge,
His helmet far above a garlandes charge.

(ll. 5–8)

The effect of the promiscuous pairing of the sexual and the martial in these lines is disturbing. The eroticism of the one transfers itself to the other, as does, vice versa, the power of destruction. The penetrating sword, the hard, embracing shield, the soldier's fare and the crowning helmet 'far above a garlandes charge' take on an erotic potency, while the sword-like kisses and soft excesses of courtly feasting and whoring destroy by incapacitating their victims. Sardanapalus, too effeminate to make the weapons of war his own, yields to their force in the hands of others, a kind of martial rape in which he plays the woman's part. His only manly act, in the poem's final line, is finally to thrust his own sword into himself: 'Murdred him selfe to shew some manfull dede.' War is associated with a kingly heart, fire, and phallic erotic power, while the conditions of peace are dalliance, effeminacy and sloth.

It has been suggested that the sonnet alludes to Henry VIII through the figure of Sardanapalus, and the possible parallels between the fat, ageing, much-married Tudor monarch and the degenerate Assyrian king are sufficiently obvious to have been as much a potential frame of reference in the early 1540s as now. If Henry Tudor is a possible butt of the satire, he is only a figurehead. The poem expresses, with intensity, the conflict, which we explored in Chapter 2, between an increasingly outmoded ideology of active service in war as the defining mark of a man, and the perception of courtly service as a servitude to sloth, womanish delights and 'glotton feastes'. In Surrey's case this conflict is rendered particularly acute by his aristocratic genealogy, his ambitions, and possibly his own vainglory as a soldier (see Chapter 1, pp 26–29). Sardanapalus epitomizes the betrayal of that manly code by a degenerate monarch and court. However, as we have seen, the sonnet's enthusiasm for the physical rigours of the field, and the erotic charge of its prolonged comparison of things martial with things seductive, produce, in spite of its insistent differentiation, a contamination of one by the other. The superiority of the soldier's life seems based on the greater attractions of fantasized objects of homoerotic desire rather than on one of absolute moral difference.

The aristocratic disdain audible in 'Th'Assyrians king' is also apparent in 'London, hast thow accused me' (Jones no. 33). Surrey follows Wyatt's satires in using *terza rima* rhymes for this satire, but the effect he achieves could scarcely be further from the urbanity of Wyatt's satirical speakers in 'Mine own John Poyntz' and ' "A spending hand" '. Surrey's choice of a shorter tetrameter line helps to give a sustained vehemence to the prophetic and accusatory voice of his satire:

> London, hast thow accused me
> Of breche of lawes, the roote of strife?
> Within whose breast did boile to see,
> So fervent hotte thy dissolute lief,
> That even the hate of sinnes, that groo
> Within thy wicked walles so rife,
> For to breake forthe did convert soo
> That terrour colde it not represse.
>
> (ll. 1–8)

Here is the 'burning passion' with which Juvenal claimed to respond to the vices of first-century AD Rome, or with which Petrarch attacked the papal court at Avignon as a second Babylon. Behind Petrarch's sonnets lie biblical attacks on the city of Babylon itself as the nurse of idolatry and every vice. Surrey directly invokes such biblical passages, particularly warnings by the prophets Jeremiah and Ezekiel of imminent destruction to both the cities of Jerusalem and Babylon. Against Babylon, Jeremiah incited the 'archers':

> Go forth in your araye [as a cohort] against Babylon rounde about, all ye that can handle bowes: shute at her, spare no arowes, for she hath sinned against the Lorde . . . Yea vengeaunce shal be taken of her, and as she hath done, so shall she be dealt withall.[78]

Such a passage must lie behind Surrey's account of his actions:

> From justice rodd no fault is free;
> But that all such as wourke unright
> In most quiet are next ill rest.
> In secret silence of the night
> This made me, with a reckles brest,
> To wake thy sluggardes with my bowe:
> A figure of the Lordes behest,
> Whose scourge for sinn the Scriptures shew.
>
> (ll. 15–22)

On 1 April 1543, Surrey had been arraigned before the Privy Council for going on the rampage on one or more nights at the end of the previous January. Ruth Hughey gives a brief account of the circumstances:

> This satire on London was probably written in prison. On April 1, 1543, Surrey and two companions, Pickering and the younger Thomas Wyatt, were brought before the Privy Council on two charges: first, of eating meat during Lent, contrary to royal proclamation, and, second, of walking about the streets at night in an unseemly manner, and, most extraordinarily, breaking windows with stonebows. In answering Surrey said he had a license for eating meat, but that he had not used it as privately as he should have. He admitted his guilt in using the stonebows and submitted to punishment. He was then committed to the Fleet.[79]

The maidservant who was the principal source of information to the mayor and his investigative team reported that when rebuked by George Blage following one of these excursions, Surrey said that 'he had liever than all the good in the world it were undone, for he was sure it should come before the King and his Council; but we shall have a madding time in our youth, and therefore I am very sorry for it'.[80]

Modern commentators debate whether this episode is simply an example of upper-class vandalism, 'drunken aristocracy baying for broken glass', which Surrey's satire on London then tries to justify, either in mocking or preposterous terms, or whether it was, or was subsequently justified as, a serious gesture in defence of Reformist (i.e. evangelical, anti-Catholic) beliefs.[81] The most recent scholar to consider the facts, Susan Brigden, in her study *London and the Reformation*, follows H. A. Mason's view of the poem as a serious expression of Protestant Reformist views. She relates Surrey's escapade and subsequent prosecution to more general agitation by Reformers in the City of London in the early 1540s in opposition to a more conservative, pro-Catholic move within the Henrician church after 1539, and a fresh clamp-down on those sympathetic to Reformist views in the spring of 1543.[82] More recently, however, she has suggested that the poem is both serious and ironic; it was both 'a protestant call for justice' and it 'mockingly disguised his vandalism' in order to make a 'protest against the self-righteousness and inflexibility of both confessional sides'.[83] Brigden may here be bending over backwards to rescue Surrey from his own indiscretions.

H. A. Mason first pointed out that the idea of God's scourging the wickedness of the unregenerate, the role of the speaker in 'London hast thow', reappears in unquestionably serious contexts in Surrey's biblical paraphrases.[84] In the third chapter of Ecclesiastes, for example, scourges are interpreted as warnings:

> Ye be suche skourges sent that eache agrevid minde,
> Like the brute beasts that swell in rage and fury by ther kinde,
> His erroure may confesse, when he hath wreasteled longe;
> And then with pacience may him arme, the sure defence of wronge.
> (Jones no. 45 ll. 49–52)

Mason thinks it unlikely that ideas to which Surrey returned, with undoubted seriousness, in his biblical paraphrases, apparently written in the last year of his life, could have been used mockingly in 1543. It is possible, however, that Surrey was deliberately using in this satire a recognizably Reformed populist rhetoric for his own purposes, whether to justify his behaviour to Reformist friends or, conceivably, as a joke to be shared amongst his upper-class cronies. Such a rhetoric is found, for example, in Henry Brinklow's *The Lamentacyon of a Christen Agaynst the Cytye of London*, a treatise which had appeared the year before Surrey's escapade. Brinklow warns the city to repent in terms that anticipate Surrey's: 'Remember how he warned the citie of Jerusalem xi.yeares longe; and because they repented not but slew the prophetes by whom God warned them, he kept promes with them and scourged them accordinge to their deservings . . . Alas, alas, the great citie Babilon, that mightie citie, for at one houre is her judgement come.'[85] Brinklow blames London for 'the bourninge of Doctor Barnes and his fellowes', martyrs of the Reformed faith who died at Smithfield in 1540. It is to this event that Surrey's lines, 'Thy martires blood, by swoord and fire, / In Heaven and earth for justice call' (ll. 56–7) seem to allude. Five years after Surrey's poem, Bishop Latimer was to address London in similar vein in his 'sermon of the plough': 'I say, repent, O London; repent, repent. Thou hearest thy faults told thee, amend them, amend them.'[86] Petrarch's anti-papal sonnets, which Surrey echoes, also provided a rhetoric readily appropriated for Protestant use by later writers.[87]

In the political climate of 1543, a time of increasing religious conservatism and restriction on the circulation of the vernacular Bible, Surrey's satire, even if it was intended as a parody of Reformist rhetoric for his immediate circle, was bound to be understood beyond that circle as an attack on the conservative religious authorities, and was thus a characteristically reckless gesture on his part.[88] The poem, however, differs strikingly in one respect from such unambiguously Reformist diatribes against London as Brinklow's or Latimer's. Surrey, as the Reformers did, attacks London for generalized venial vices represented by the deadly sins (ll. 28–40 especially). Such attacks follow a long medieval tradition of complaints against the evils of the times which often take a socially conservative point of view. Social disorder, sometimes expressed in terms of the greed and pride of merchants, is seen as threatening the existing hierarchical social system. At the same time, such complaints are often used to attack social injustice to the poor and lack of charity by the rich.[89] Reformers typically inherited this tradition of social protest. Brinklow again provides an example:

> Ye abuse your riches, specially you that come to thoffice of the Citie, for ye spende unmeasurably. Uppon whome? Even uppon them that have no neade; as uppon the nobles and gentlemen of the courte; uppon the aldermen and other riche commoners, which have as great neade of your feastes as hath the see at the highest springe tide, of the pissinge of the wrenne; [and] the pore forgotten, except it be with a few scrappes & bones, sent to Newgate for a face.[90]

Surrey's satire shows no such concern with such social injustices. 'London, hast thow accused me' adopts the idiom of biblical and Reformist invective, and Surrey may well have shared some of the Reformers' views, but his particular targets seem chosen for socially conservative rather than morally Reformist reasons. The poem represents Surrey himself, identifiable by the autobiographical information the poem contains, as an agent of God who abrogates to himself the right, not only to preach to, but also to break the windows of, those whose commercial success epitomizes a new power and value system which seems to threaten the aristocratic prerogatives and ideals that he would defend.[91] Here the voice of the moralist, and the rhetoric of the Bible itself, seem hijacked to defend the class interests of a nostalgic nobleman whose anger is directed against a new social order and a new wealth. God's elect and social and intellectual elitism are confused in this poem, as they were to be in Surrey's final biblical paraphrases.

NOTES

1. Lanham, R. A. (1976) *The Motives of Eloquence: Literary Rhetoric in the Renaissance.* New Haven, Conn.: Yale University Press, p 22.
2. Elyot, Sir T. (1967) *Four Political Treatises.* Facsimile reproduction, intro. L. Gottesman. Gainesville, Fla.: Scholar Press Facsimiles & Reprints, pp 46, 47.
3. Elyot, Sir T. (1962) *The Book named The Governor,* ed. S. E. Lehmberg. Everyman Library. London: Dent & Co., p 76.
4. Inscribed on a monument in Bisham Church, Berkshire. Sir Philip was brother to Sir Thomas Hoby whose translation of Castiglione, *The Book of The Courtier,* was published in 1561.
5. Castiglione, B. (1976) *The Book of the Courtier,* trans. George Bull (2nd edn). Harmondsworth: Penguin, p 322.
6. Wilson, T. (1994) *The Art of Rhetoric (1560),* ed. P. E. Medine. Pennsylvania: Pennsylvania State University Press, p 192. References to this edition will be given in parentheses after quotations in the following discussion. For an account of Wilson's life and writings, see Medine, P. E. (1986) *Thomas Wilson.* Twayne English Authors Series. Boston: G. K. Hall & Co.
7. Roger Ascham attributes the saying to Aristotle: see Ascham, R. (1904) *The English Works,* ed. W. A. Wright. Cambridge: Cambridge University Press, p 298.
8. See Ch 3 p 77 above. The phrase is from Whigham, F. (1984) *Ambition and Privilege: The Social Tropes of Elizabethan Courtesy Theory.* Berkeley: University of California Press, p 33. Whigham discusses Wilson's *Art* on pp 1–3. For modern discussions of the suspicion of rhetoric, see especially Lanham (1976) esp. ch 1; Rhodes, N. (1992) *The Power of Eloquence and English Literature.* London: Harvester Wheatsheaf, esp. pp 33–40; and Crane, M. T. (1993) *Framing Authority: Sayings, Self and Society in Sixteenth-Century England.* Princeton, NJ: Princeton University Press, esp. pp 16–17. Graham, K. J. E. (1994) *The Performance of Conviction: Plainness and Rhetoric in the Early English Renaissance.* Rhetoric and Society. Ithaca, NY: Cornell University Press, has a chapter on Wyatt which comes to rather different conclusions from my own.
9. Jonson, B. (1975) *The Complete Poems,* ed. G. Parfitt. Harmondsworth: Penguin Books Ltd, p 435. For a discussion of the classical plain style and Jonson's use of it, see Trimpi, W. (1962) *Ben Jonson's Poems: A Study of the Plain Style.* Stanford, Ca.: Stanford University Press, p 65.
10. Jonson (1975) p 392. For the gendering of styles, see Parker, P. (1987) *Literary Fat Ladies: Rhetoric, Gender, Property.* London: Methuen, p 14; Wall, W. (1993) *The Imprint of Gender: Authorship and Publication in the Renaissance.* Ithaca, NY: Cornell University Press, esp. pp 240–2, and Ong, W. S. J. (1971) 'Latin language study as a puberty rite'. In *Rhetoric, Romance, and Technology: Studies*

in the Interaction of Expression and Culture. Ithaca, NY, and London: Cornell University Press, pp 113–41.

11. Cicero (1939) *Orator,* trans. H. M. Hubbell. Loeb Classical Library. Cambridge, Mass.: William Heinemann Ltd and Harvard University Press, pp 363, 365.
12. Ibid pp 319, 321.
13. For the *sermo*, see Trimpi (1962) p 6.
14. Mattingly, G. (1962) *Renaissance Diplomacy.* London: Jonathan Cape, pp 236–7.
15. For the association of a plain vernacular style with Protestantism, see Jones, R. F. (1942) 'The moral sense of simplicity'. In *Studies in Honor of F. W. Shipley*. Washington University Studies n.s. Language and Literature 14. St Louis, Mo., pp 265–87; King, J. N. (1982) *English Reformation Literature: The Tudor Origins of the Protestant Tradition.* Princeton, NJ: Princeton University Press, esp. pp 138–44; Mueller, J. M. (1984) *The Native Tongue and the Word: Development in English Prose Style, 1380–1580.* Chicago: University of Chicago Press, esp. ch 5. I am particularly indebted to Janette Dillon who allowed me to see chapters on the religious connotations of the vernacular from her book, provisionally entitled *Language and Stage in Medieval and Renaissance England*, forthcoming in early 1998 from Cambridge University Press.
16. See Skelton, J. (1983) *The Complete English Poems*, ed. J. Scattergood. New Haven, Conn.: Yale University Press, no. XIX l. 1088, and my discussion in Ch 3 p 73 above.
17. Quoted from Rollins 1 no. 238. Peterson, D. L. (1967) *The English Lyric from Wyatt to Donne: A History of the Plain and Eloquent Styles.* Princeton, NJ: Princeton University Press, p 24, discusses the poem as an example of the plain style. A paraphrase of Chaucer's lines would be: 'Flee from crowded [courts] and live with truth, let your goods however small be sufficient for you, because hoarding produces enmity and political success is uncertain, praise causes envy, and fortune is always blind.'
18. For an invaluable compilation of attitudes to the vernacular in the early modern period, see Jones, R. F. (1953) *The Triumph of the English Language: A Survey of Opinions Concerning the Vernacular from the Introduction of Printing to the Restoration.* Oxford: Oxford University Press. On p 200 n 71 Jones cites Bateson, F. W. (1961) *English Poetry and the English Language* (2nd edn). New York: Russell & Russell, who, in a note on p 31, reports that 'an analysis of 40 pages of the *Shorter Oxford Dictionary* has shown that of every 100 words in use before 1600, 39 were introduced between 1500 and 1600'.
19. The text is printed as Appendix B of M&T. Where it clarifies the sense, I have modernized the spelling and punctuation. The lines of the text are not numbered in M&T, but to help readers locate quotations in a dense text, I shall cite page and line references. These quotations are from pp 440 ll. 9–10 and 441 l. 5.
20. Quoted by Brilliant, A. N. (1971) 'The style of Wyatt's "The Quyete of Mynde" '. *Essays and Studies* 24: 1–21 (p 13).

21. Ibid pp 13–15. Thomson, P. (1964) *Sir Thomas Wyatt and His Background.* London: Routledge & Kegan Paul, pp 86–7, comments on how much more plain and unadorned Wyatt's translation is than those of later translators.

22. Brilliant (1971) p 15. Budé's Latin, given by Brilliant, is 'sciebam precarias me opes nec trabali clavo fixas (ut aiunt)'.

23. See Moss, A. (1996) *Printed Commonplace-Books and the Structuring of Renaissance Thought.* Oxford: Clarendon Press, and Crane (1993), who explores the widespread use of maxims in terms of an early modern anxiety about truth and meaning. See also my article ' "An Owl in a sack troubles no man". Proverbs, plainness and Wyatt', forthcoming in 1998 in *Renaissance Studies.*

24. Cicero (1939) p 365. I quote from Erasmus's introduction, 'What is a proverb?', to his huge compilation of classical proverbs in the *Adagia*: see Erasmus, D. (1982) *Adages I.i.1 to I.v.100,* trans. Margaret Mann Phillips. *Collected Works of Erasmus* vol. 31. Toronto: University of Toronto Press, p 12. Erasmus's *Adagia* was highly influential, and went through nine revised and augmented editions before 1536: see Phillips, M. M. (1964) *The "Adages" of Erasmus: A Study with Translations.* Cambridge: Cambridge University Press, Pt 1, where she traces the expanding editions through Erasmus's lifetime.

25. Quoted by Trimpi (1962) pp 16–19 from Martial's epigrams, Bk x no. 4. For similarities between the proverb and the epigram, see Manley, L. (1985) 'Proverbs, epigrams, and urbanity in Renaissance London'. *English Literary Renaissance* 15: 247–76, and between pithy sayings and the epigram, Crane, M. T. (1986) 'Intret Cato: authority and the epigram in sixteenth-century England'. In *Renaissance Genres: Essays on Theory, History, and Interpretation*, ed. B. K. Lewalski. Harvard English Studies 14. Cambridge, Mass.: Harvard University Press, pp 158–86.

26. Reb. p 373 identifies proverbs for ll. 2, 5 and 6–7.

27. Proverbs 8 (vv. 32–33). The quotation is from *The Bible in Englishe* . . . (1539) printed by Richard Grafton and Edward Whitchurch (the 'Great Bible'). This edition does not have verse numbers. I have added these in parentheses for ease of reference to other editions. For Thomas Radcliffe, Lord Fitswalter, later third earl of Sussex, 'Surrey's first cousin and companion-in-arms in France', see Brigden, S. (1994) 'Henry Howard, Earl of Surrey and the "Conjured League" '. *The Historical Journal* 37: 507–37, pp 533–34, and *DNB.*

28. Jones pp 128–9.

29. See Brigden (1994) p 534, who discusses the political implications of the warning.

30. Kinsman, R. S. (1978–9) ' "The Proverbes of Salmon Do Playnly Declare": a sententious poem on wisdom and governance, ascribed to Sir Francis Bryan'. *Huntington Library Quarterly* 42: 279–312 (l. 80). Kinsman p 312 argues that this line is the source of Wyatt's proverb, which was reused in the 'Defence' of 1541, 'For tho he hele the wounde yet the scharre shall remaine'.

31. I have modernized the spelling and punctuation.

32. The Latin can be found in M&T p 431.

33. For the Latin, see Seneca (1960–1) *Tragedies*, trans. Frank Justus Miller. Loeb Classical Library. 2 vols, Cambridge, Mass.: William Heinemann Ltd and Harvard University Press, 1 pp 410–11.

34. My discussion of this poem has benefited greatly from suggestions made by my colleague, Dr Ralph Houlbrooke. There is some difference of view about what Wyatt saw. Anne was beheaded within the Tower while her supposed 'lovers' were executed more publicly on Tower Hill. Southall, R. (1964) *The Courtly Maker: An Essay on the Poetry of Wyatt and his Contemporaries*. Oxford: Basil Blackwell, p 46, thought Wyatt could only have seen Anne Boleyn beheaded from the Bell Tower. Ives, E. W. (1986) *Anne Boleyn*. Oxford: Basil Blackwell, p 403, on the other hand, thinks he saw the execution of the 'lovers'.

35. The source of the tale of the country and town mouse in 'My mother's maids' is Horace's *Satires* II.6. Bates, C. (1993) ' "A mild admonisher": Sir Thomas Wyatt and sixteenth-century satire'. *Huntington Library Quarterly* 56: 243–58 (pp 246–7) discusses ' "A spending hand" ' in terms of its imitation of *Satires* II.5. The theme of withdrawal to a modest farm in the country from the corruptions of service in the city, the theme of 'Mine own John Poyntz', was one to which Horace often returned, e.g. *Satires* II.6 or *Epistles* I.10.

36. Bates (1993) p 245 suggests that Wyatt was especially drawn to the second book of Horace's satires (*sermones*) because there 'the authorial voice grows increasingly absent . . . [and] the narrative persona is . . . left open to attack, thus radically destabilizing the sort of authoritative voice that we find in sermones 1'. I am indebted to her discussion of Wyatt's satiric voices. Mermel, J. (1978) 'Sir Thomas Wyatt's satires and the humanist debate over court service'. *Studies in the Literary Imagination* 11: 69–79, usefully puts the satires in a tradition of debate about the virtue of courtly service and the vices of the court.

37. Mason, H. A. (1959) *Humanism and Poetry in the Early Tudor Period: An Essay*. London: Routledge & Kegan Paul, pp 203–4, suggests a date of 1541 on the basis of verbal echoes between the satire and the 'Defence'. Starkey, D. (1982) 'The court: Castiglione's ideal and Tudor reality, being a discussion of Sir Thomas Wyatt's satire addressed to Sir Francis Bryan'. *Journal of the Warburg and Courtauld Institutes* 45: 232–9 suggests a date between June 1538 and January 1539 when Bryan was in disgrace. Muir (*LL* p 251) suggests, on the dubious basis of the satire's position in the Egerton MS, that all three satires were written in 1536 before Wyatt went to Spain. On the difficulty of deducing a chronological order of composition from the Egerton MS, see Harrier, R. (1975) *The Canon of Sir Thomas Wyatt's Poetry*. Cambridge, Mass.: Harvard University Press, pp 3–5.

38. In Aesop's version the mice are male and disturbed by dogs, as is the case in Horace's retelling in *Satires* II.6. Robert Henryson retells it in the 'Taill of the Uplondis Mous and the Burges Mous', which was not published until 1570 but may have been known to Wyatt in manuscript. Henryson's mice are female, and they are threatened, although neither is killed, by a cat. For a discussion of Wyatt's possible sources, see Thomson (1964) pp 259–67.

39. Elyot (1962) pp 29, 19.

40. Henryson, R. (1958) *The Poems and Fables* (2nd revised edn), ed. H. H. Wood. Edinburgh and London: Oliver and Boyd, p 16 ll. 379–80, in the 'Moralitas' that follows the telling of the fable.

41. Brilliant (1971) pp 15–16 notes the debts of this satire to *The Quyete of Mynde.*

42. I quote Tyndale's translation from Tyndale, W. (1989). *New Testament: A modern-spelling edition*, ed. D. Daniell. New Haven, Conn.: Yale University Press. Mason, H. A., ed. (1986) *Sir Thomas Wyatt: A Literary Portrait.* Bristol: Bristol Classical Press, p 321 notes that Erasmus has the grapes part of this verse as a proverb in *Adagia.*

43. Quoted from Harrier (1975) pp 176–7. For discussions of the stoic thought in these lines, see Friedman, D. M. (1966) 'The "thing" in Wyatt's mind'. *Essays in Criticism* 14: 375–81; Daalder, J. (1985a) 'Seneca and Wyatt's second satire'. *Études Anglaises* 38(4): 422–6; and Daalder, J. (1985b) 'Wyatt and "liberty": a postcript'. *Essays in Criticism* 35: 330–6.

44. *LL* p 4. For evidence that Poyntz was in the service of Anne Boleyn, see Ives (1986) p 306.

45. Puttenham, G. (1968) *The Arte of English Poesie (1589).* Menston, Yorks: The Scolar Press Ltd, p 154. For the proverb, see Taverner, R. (1956) *Proverbes or Adages by Desiderius Erasmus: Gathered out of the Chiliades and Englished* (a facsimile of the 1569 edition). Gainesville, Fla.: Scholars' Facsimiles & Reprints, sig. 44^{v}, which glosses 'favel' as 'favour'.

46. Castiglione, B. (1976) *The Book of the Courtier*, trans. George Bull (2nd edn). Harmondsworth: Penguin, p 53.

47. Mason (1986) pp 283–5 and 287–8 gives examples of its use. Bryan uses it three times in *Dispraise*: see Guevara, A. de (1548) *A Dispraise of the life of a Courtier, and a commendation of the life of the labouring man*, trans. Sir Francis Bryan. London: R. Grafton, sigs. d.ii^{r}, g.ii^{v} and o.iii^{r}. Javitch, D. (1978) *Poetry and Courtliness in Renaissance England.* Princeton, NJ: Princeton University Press, pp 62–3 and Whigham (1984) pp 40–2 discuss the figure.

48. The satire Wyatt imitates was printed in Alamanni, L. (1532) *Opere Toscane.* 2 vols, Leyden: Sebast. Gryphius, 1 satire x (À Thommaso Sertini). Thomson (1964) p 248 comments that 'Alamanni's satires are . . . primarily Juvenalian, though not without Horatian interludes'. For Alamanni's life and work, see ibid pp 246–9.

49. Reb. puts inverted commas around 'the lion' in l. 45.

50. Alamanni (1532) 1 p 402 ll. 49–57. In the following discussion I quote from this edition, which has no line numbering. I insert them for convenience. The poem, in Italian with line numbering, is printed in M&T pp 347–9, and by Mason (1986) pp 264–5. The translation I give is by Mason. I have glossed some names, but the final note, on the three cities, is Mason's.

51. It may translate a much earlier line in Alamanni's poem, 'I malvagi consigli usar per buoni' [give bad counsel for good', 1. 32].

52. The last line may be proverbial: see Mason (1986) p 290.

53. Rather differently, the scholarly speaker of Alamanni's satire claims his great 'treasure', poor and alone in the country, are his inks and papers (ll. 76–7). Thomson (1964) p 249 describes Alamanni's style as 'grave and lofty'.
54. The translation is adapted from Mason (1986) p 264.
55. Reb. has 'him Caesar' in accordance with his use of the Devonshire MS as his copy text; 'highe' is used instead of 'him' in the Arundel MS and in *Tottel's Miscellany*.
56. See Mason (1986) pp 276–7.
57. Greenblatt, S. (1980) *Renaissance Self-Fashioning: From More to Shakespeare*. Chicago: University of Chicago Press, p 121 uses the term when discussing Wyatt's psalm translations. The anti-court topics of Wyatt's satire, and indeed its format, that of a letter to a friend, were frequently used throughout the Middle Ages. For this tradition see Heiserman, A. R. (1961) *Skelton and Satire*. Chicago: University of Chicago Press, pp 51–65.
58. Bates (1993) p 246. My own reading is indebted to Bates's article and a seminar she gave some years ago at Reading University.
59. Ross, D. M. (1987) 'Sir Thomas Wyatt: proverbs anbd the poetics of scorn'. *The Sixteenth Century Journal* 18(2): 201–12, p 211. She goes on to say that 'the poem destabilizes the genre of moralistic verse epistle, because the advice it gives runs counter to all homilitic tradition'. See also my article (forthcoming in *Renaissance Studies*), ' "An Owl in a sack troubleth no man" ' – proverbs, plainness and Wyatt'.
60. For the proverbs in this passage, see Whiting, B. J. and Whiting, H. W., eds (1968), *Proverbs, Sentences, and Proverbial Phrases from English Writings Mainly Before 1500*. Cambridge, Mass.: Harvard University Press, H 407–8 and S 534, 539 and 541. Also Tilley, M. P. (1950), *A Dictionary of Proverbs in England in the Sixteenth and Seventeenth Centuries*. Ann Arbor: University of Michigan Press, S 1042. Mason (1986) pp 326–43 provides examples of many current proverbs and sayings used by Wyatt. Reb. alters the 'to' of Wyatt's own Egerton MS version to 'do' in l. 21. It is possible, however, that the sense of these lines should be that the swine, with his head in the manger, is no more able than the ass to hear the sound of the harp. Both swine and asses were proverbially deaf to music: Tilley (1950) S 680.
61. 'Spend and God will send' was the opening line of at least one popular balet: see Whiting and Whiting (1968) G 261 and Habenicht, R. E., ed. (1963) *John Heywood's 'A Dialogue of Proverbs'*. Berkeley: University of California Press, l. 1729. Gascoigne uses the proverb, 'The common speech is spend and God will send', as the opening line of a satire that seems to owe a debt to Wyatt's satire to Bryan: see Gascoigne, G. (1907–10) *The Complete Works*, ed. J. W. Cunliffe. 2 vols, Cambridge: Cambridge University Press, 1 pp 64–6. While it seems probable that Wyatt is drawing on a current proverb for his poem's opening, no very close versions have been recorded: see Mason (1986) pp 328–9 and Whiting and Whiting (1968) S625 and S627.
62. Taverner (1956) sig. 44^{v}. See also Mason (1986) pp 287–8 and 333. For the Erasmian original, see Erasmus, D. (1991) *Adages II.vii.1 to III.iii.100*, trans.

R. A. B. Mynors. *Collected Works of Erasmus* vol 34. Toronto: University of Toronto Press, adage II.ix.53.

63. Taverner (1956) sig. 47^{r}.
64. I use the English translation of Proverbs 22.1, possibly by Bryan, in Kinsman (1978–9) p 292 (l. 101). See also Whiting and Whiting (1968) T 505 and Tilley (1950) P 525. Cf. the refrain of Chaucer's ballade 'Of Truthe' or 'Of Good Counsel': 'And trouth shall the deliver it is no drede' (Rollins 1 no. 238).
65. Reb. unaccountably has 'prize'. Manuscripts and Tottel have 'prise' or 'pryce'.
66. Quoted by Mason (1986) p 339 from Taverner's translation of Erasmus's *Catonis distichia* (1527).
67. Tilley (1950) F 719 and Taverner (1956) sig. 14^{r}. Erasmus comments: 'if anyone were to look at the ways of the world today, he would think the adage should be reversed: where there is wealth, there are friends': Erasmus (1982) p 256 (adage I.iii.24).
68. Erasmus (1982) pp 4–5.
69. For the view, deriving from Aristotle, that proverbs can be used as 'evidence' even in a legal case, see Erasmus (1982) pp 15–16 and Wilson (1994) p 111.
70. Erasmus (1982) p 17.
71. Starkey (1982) p 237 argues that Wyatt uses Bryan 'as a symbol or type of the courtier in general and Castiglione's idealization in particular'. My own position is close to that of Bates (1993) p 253, who argues that both speakers are undermined in the 'shifting and unstable texture of Wyatt's poem'.
72. Starkey (1982) and Brigden, S. (1996) ' " The Shadow That You Know": Sir Thomas Wyatt and Sir Francis Bryan at court and in embassy'. *The Historical Journal* 39(1): 1–31.
73. For example, Greenblatt (1980) pp 134–5. For the suggestion about gambling debts, see Brigden (1996) p 17.
74. *LL* p 86 and note. Wyatt was reclaiming the money from Cromwell. For the proverb, see Whiting and Whiting (1968) I 72 and Tilley (1950) I 110.
75. Sessions, W. A. (1986) *Henry Howard, Earl of Surrey*. Twayne English Authors Series. Boston: G. K. Hall, p 60 points to Juvenal as a model for 'Th'Assyrians king'.
76. Juvenal (1967) *The Sixteen Satires*, trans. Peter Green. Harmondsworth: Penguin Books Ltd, *Satire* 1 ll. 30–1 and 151–2. The second quotation is cited by Trimpi (1962) pp 15–16, who describes Juvenal's style as 'far more elevated' than the urbane plainness of Horace, but he sees the two as linked by their common programme of attacking contemporary vices.
77. Jones p 126, Rollins 2 p 157.
78. Jeremiah 50 (vv. 14–15). See also Jeremiah 51.3, and compare 'London, has thow accused me', ll. 20 and 51–68. For suggested echoes of Jeremiah, Ezekiel and Revelation, see the editions of Surrey's poem by Padelford p 191 and

Hughey, R., ed. (1960) *The Arundel Harington Manuscript of Tudor Poetry*. 2 vols, Columbus, Ohio: Ohio State University Press, 2 p 90.

79. Hughey (1960) 2 p 90. See *LP* xviii (1) 73, 315, 327, 347. See also Brigden (1994) pp 516–19 and Casady, E. (1938) *Henry Howard, Earl of Surrey*. New York: The Modern Language Association of America, pp 96–101. A 'stonebow' was a kind of catapult used for shooting stones (*OED*).
80. *LP* xviii (1) 327.
81. The quotation is from Mason (1959) p 243. Hughey (1960) 2 p 90, Casady (1938) p 160 and Padelford p 190 support the aristocratic prank theory. Nott 1 p liii and Mason (1959) pp 243–5 consider Surrey may have been a serious Reformer.
82. Brigden, S. (1989) *London and the Reformation.* Oxford: Clarendon Press, pp 340–4.
83. Brigden (1994) pp 518–19.
84. Mason (1959) p 243 cites the passage from Ecclesiastes 3. Brigden (1994) p 341 gives other examples from Surrey's biblical paraphrases. Surrey also used the idea of the scourge as a warning in his epigram to Radcliffe: see p 121 above.
85. Brinklow, H. (1874) *The Lamentacyon of a Christen Agaynst the Cytye of London, made by Roderigo Mors (1545 edition)*. Early English Text Society e.s. 22, ed. J. M. Cowper. London: Kegan Paul, Trench, Trübner & Co. Ltd, pp 95–6, 99. The first edition was published in 1542.
86. Latimer, H. (1906) *Sermons*. Everyman's Library. London: J. M. Dent and Co., p 58.
87. For Surrey's debts to Petrarch's anti-papal sonnets, see Jones p 128. Mason (1959) p 243 gives later examples of Protestant use of Petrarch's anti-papal sonnets.
88. Brigden (1994) p 517 points out that the poem was cited among other charges against him at the time of his arrest for treason in 1546 (citing LP xxi (2) 555(18)).
89. For example, Wright, T., ed. (1965) *Political Poems and Songs relating to English History* (1st edn 1859). 2 vols, Wiesbaden: Kraus Reprint Ltd, I p 271, II pp 353–5 and 252, and 285. See also Brant, S. (1874) *The Ship of Fools* (1509), trans. Alexander Barclay, ed. T. H. Jamieson. 2 vols, Edinburgh: William Paterson, 2 pp 167–9, 'Of Usurers and Okerers'.
90. Brinklow (1874) p 90.
91. Brigden (1994) p 517 suggests the gambling debts of some of Surrey's companions may have played a part in decisions about whose windows to break.

Chapter 5

The Word of Truth

THE PSALMS AND THE REFORMATION

As the maxims of classical thought and literature were memorized and the classical genres imitated to give shape and authority to the wise counsel of the royal servant, so increasingly, from the 1530s onward, quotation and imitation of the Bible in the vernacular characterized a new scriptural style that announced its speakers to be members of the Reformed faith, opposed to Roman Catholicism.[1] Particularly powerful as a model for poetry were the Psalms. In 1542, Thomas Becon dedicated his treatise, *David's Harp*, to Wyatt's brother-in law, Sir George Brooke, Lord Cobham.[2] Citing St Paul's words to the Ephesians, 'Be ye filled with the Spirit, speaking among yourselves in psalms, hymns, and spiritual songs, singing, and making melody in your hearts to the Lord', he exclaims: 'Ah would God that all minstrels in the world, yea, and all sort of persons, both old and young, would once leave their lascivious, wanton, and unclean ballads, and sing such godly and virtuous songs as David teacheth them.'[3]

The large number of psalm imitations and paraphrases through the sixteenth century testify that Becon's sense of the Psalms as lively sources of instruction and comfort, and as models for imitation, was shared by many.[4] They had been used throughout the Middle Ages as texts for private meditation, or repeated aloud in the liturgy. The seven penitential psalms paraphrased by Wyatt (6, 31, 38, 51, 102, 130 and 143 in modern numbering) appeared as a group in devotional handbooks and even in the primers used by schoolchildren as they began to learn Latin.[5] With the major shift from Roman Catholicism to Reformation thought from the early 1530s onward came a new emphasis. The subject matter of many of the Psalms, repentance, the experience of persecution and the avowal of faith in God as defender and justifier of his people, was particularly well suited to a Reformed theology of personal penitence, dependence on God's grace and the need for faithfulness in difficult times: 'David became for the Reformers both a preacher of the Promise, of the trust in justification by faith alone, and the man who experienced the revivifying spirit which spells the end of the flesh and sin.'[6]

The 1530s and early 1540s in England were difficult and confusing times in the crucial matter of religious belief.[7] It was clear by 1530 that Henry VIII's first wife, Katherine of Aragon, would never bear him the coveted son and heir, and this enhanced the attractions of the young Anne Boleyn as an alternative queen. The papacy's refusal to grant Henry the divorce he needed led to a decisive rejection of papal authority and the establishment, by the 'Reformation Parliament' of 1534, of an independent church in England with Henry himself as the Supreme Head. Henry's break from Rome was primarily political, not theological; it was not necessarily a challenge to the doctrinal beliefs of the Roman Catholic church. Nevertheless, Henry's need for the support and propaganda of Reformed scholars in England and abroad, who welcomed Henry's break for its furtherance of their own campaign against the doctrines and religious authority of the Roman Catholic church, meant that in the years following 1534, Henry was forced to appoint evangelical bishops and tacitly accept some degree of Reformed theology as orthodox within the English church. The presence and influence of highly placed Reformist sympathizers within the court was also a significant factor throughout the final decade and a half of Henry's reign. Notable were Queen Anne Boleyn before her execution in 1536; Thomas Cromwell, Wyatt's patron, and Henry's chief secretary until his execution in 1540; and, in the final years particularly, Dr William Butts, the royal physician, and Sir Anthony Denny, an influential member of Henry's Privy Chamber from 1539, and appointed its Chief Gentleman in October 1546. Henry's last queen, Catherine Parr, held strongly Reformist beliefs, although her political influence has been questioned.[8]

Henry took an active and interventionist role in the theology of his English church, and his own sympathies remained deeply conservative. Highly placed Reformist sympathizers at court could not overrule his will and often found themselves dangerously exposed when they were suspected of protecting others', or themselves holding, beliefs that were judged too extreme. The moderately Reformed statements of faith that defined orthodoxy in the latter half of the 1530s, the 'Ten Articles' of June 1536, approved by Henry and expanded in the 'Bishops' Book' or *The Institution of a Christian Man* (1537), which never officially received Henry's approval, gave way in the last years of the reign to much more traditionally Catholic expressions of orthodoxy: the 'Six Articles' of 1539 and, in 1543, *A Necessary Doctrine and Erudition for any Christian Man*, officially approved by Henry and called 'The King's Book'.[9] In July 1540, two days after Cromwell's execution, Henry's council burned three Catholics and three Lutherans in what appears to have been a symbolic gesture of royal determination to define and control orthodoxy. The last decade of Henry's reign was a particularly dangerous one in matters of religion, and, as Maria Dowling has pointed out, 'the dangers of the times meant that protestants rarely voiced their beliefs'.[10] A coded discretion in religious matters could be necessary for self-preservation.

From the point of view of the psalm and biblical paraphrases of Wyatt and Surrey, two particular aspects of Reformed belief and the disputes with Roman Catholicism need some explanation. The first is theological and concerns the relative importance for an individual's salvation of grace, faith and good works. In Roman Catholic practice and thought, formal confession to a priest and the performance of good works were necessary signs of penitence by the sinner and contributed to the work of God's grace. Thus, merit, earned by good works, was an active ingredient in the process of salvation.[11] Reformers, on the contrary, with varying clarity, emphasized the primacy of grace in man's salvation. The children of Adam and Eve, inheriting their progenitor's utter fallenness, were saved only by Christ's crucifixion which was the sufficient and only effective atonement. There were degrees of emphasis on repentance and good works, from the moderate position defined in the 'Ten Articles' and the 'Bishop's Book' that penitence and good works were the 'fruits' of repentance and necessary signs of the working of God's grace within the individual, to the more Lutheran emphasis on faith alone as the only necessary precondition of grace.

A second crucial element of Reformed belief was the need for translation of the Bible into the vernacular languages and its distribution as widely as possible. For the Reformers, salvation was a matter of the individual's personal relationship to God. The role of the Reformed priest was modelled on Christ's own image of the good shepherd, who made sure the sheep in his care were properly fed with the true Word of God and protected them from the subtle tricks and sleights of papist wolves dressed in sheep's clothing.[12] Access to the Bible, God's word, was therefore crucial. Notoriously, of course, the plain Word of God did not always appear to teach identical lessons to different worshippers and readers.

In a number of respects then, vernacular paraphrase of the Bible, and particularly the Psalms, dealing as many of them do with matters of penitence and persecution, and centring on the figure of David interpreted as an example of faithful trust in God, was a potentially political and controversial matter in the 1530s and 1540s. Becon's *David's Harp* was published at the height of the conservative clamp-down on evangelical thought in 1542. He had been arrested, recanted, and seen his books burned in 1541 before coming to Kent. His use of material from Psalm 73, one of those Surrey was to paraphrase, to express his sense of the persecuted condition of the godly, could scarcely fail to be political: ' "My feet were almost gone," saith David, "my treadings had nigh slipped. For I was sore grieved at the wicked to see the ungodly in such prosperity. For they are in no peril of death, but stand fast like a palace." ' Another timely recantation was to save him from the stake in 1543.[13] Even more outspoken was the evangelical martyr Anne Askew, for whom, also, the Psalms served as an authorization and model of resistance to Henrician religious orthodoxy. In his account of her examinations before she was burned on 16 July 1546, the Reformer John Bale reported Askew's replies to her examiners, calling attention to her frequent use of the Psalms: 'Well, well' she defied the conservative Bishop Gardiner, 'God will laugh your threatenings to scorn." Ps.ii.' At the end of her first examination, Askew's own paraphrase of Psalm 54 is printed:

> Lo, faithless men against me rise,
> And for thy sake my death practise . . .
> I wot thou wilt revenge my wrong,
> And visit them, ere it be long.[14]

The habit of reading contemporary political significance into the Psalms was not confined to Reformers. Henry VIII himself certainly approved of an implicit parallel between himself and David in a beautifully illustrated Latin manuscript psalter, probably presented to him before the break with Rome, for one of the illustrations shows God wearing a papal tiara. In a number of the manuscript miniatures, David appears unmistakably with the face of Henry himself.[15] Henry's own annotations to this manuscript, added possibly in the early 1540s, align himself with David as a righteous king whose God will uphold him and punish his enemies. John N. King notes that 'the king pointedly ignores his Hebrew predecessor's long-standing reputation as an archetype for the repentant sinner in the seven penitential psalms'.[16] It is King David, not David the penitent, who serves Henry as a model.

Henry's uxoriousness, however, left him vulnerable to parallels with that other, sinning, David. The Psalms had been frequently associated with David's penitence following his adultery with Bathsheba, particularly in illustrations to late fifteenth-century and early sixteenth-century versions of the Psalms.[17] It was this story that Wyatt used as a frame for his paraphrases of the seven penitential psalms. Praising Wyatt's psalm paraphrases, Surrey drew a lesson for kings in general, and almost certainly for one king in particular:[18]

> Where Rewlers may se in a mirrour clere
> The bitter frewte of false concupiscense,
> How Jewry bought Urias deathe full dere.
> In Princes hartes Goddes scourge yprinted depe
> Might them awake out of their sinfull slepe.
>
> (Jones no. 31 ll. 10–14)

Such a parallel was, as we have seen, by no means unprecedented in the period, but at a time when politic Reformers spoke and wrote discreetly, with 'certain words . . . used almost as ciphers', Surrey's tendentious appropriation of Wyatt's text pushed coded language almost to the point of foolhardiness.[19] Characteristically, Surrey 'blazed' his sonnet abroad, publishing it, with his other elegies on the death of Wyatt, in 1542.

Rather more discreet were Wyatt's own Reformist sympathies. The most serious charge against him at his imprisonment in 1541 was of possible collusion with the rebellious Roman Catholic Cardinal Pole 'by cawse of our opinions that are like and that I am papiste'. Wyatt adds: 'I thinke I shulde have more adoe with a great sorte in Inglande to purge my selffe of suspecte of a lutherane then of a Papist' (M&T pp 195–6).[20] Wisely, Wyatt corrects neither view, but simply says he braved the Inquisition by speaking against the Bishop of Rome. As I suggested in Chapter 1, Wyatt's wily and flexible control of language was his great strength as a diplomat; in his diplomatic letters and in his 1541 'Defence', as in his poetry, he adopts the plain and plaintive tones of innocence and honesty even as he discreetly removes or confuses the traces of incriminating guilt. He was, in Susan Brigden's words, 'a diplomat practised in the arts of concealment'.[21]

Wyatt's paraphrases of the seven penitential psalms are, I believe, distinctly Reformist, but their programme emerges subtlely from Wyatt's careful versions of his unimpeachably Catholic sources.[22] Their Reformed emphasis, usually a matter of implication rather than of bold statement, is, I shall argue, carefully consistent with the 'Ten Articles' which officially defined belief between 1536 and 1539. Equally discreet and evasive is the implied voice and attitude of the poet himself in a work in which the song of the psalmist is reported by a narrator who is himself a fiction borrowed and substantially translated from the Italian writer Aretino. Quite different are Surrey's biblical paraphrases, especially the three psalms (88, 73 and 55) normally associated with his last months and weeks of life, in which the voice of the psalmist is appropriated with the same risky boldness with which Surrey earlier commented on Wyatt's psalms. In Surrey's paraphrases the fictional voice of David is almost completely eradicated and the words of the psalm wrenched, with a sometimes raw immediacy, to serve Surrey's urgent purposes.

'BY MUSIC'S ART FORGED TOFORE AND FILED': WYATT'S SEVEN PENITENTIAL PSALMS

Readers of Wyatt's paraphrases (Reb. clii) have often detected either a personal confessional note or related the paraphrases to one of Wyatt's periods in prison, either in 1536 or 1541.[23] The narrative of David's adultery with Bathsheba could reflect on Wyatt's own adultery, perhaps with Elizabeth Darrell or even, if it occurred, with Anne Boleyn.[24] Surrey, as we have seen, saw Wyatt's David as reflecting on more conspicuous, crowned, sinners, a possibility briefly encouraged, in the first prologue, by the narrator's reflection on David's sensual sin which leads to lack of 'wisdom and forecast / (Which woe to realms when that these kings doth lack)' (ll. 17–18). As we have seen, an expectation that psalms could address the contemporary dilemmas of Christians, particularly those beleaguered by temporal or religious enemies, was widespread.

As Wyatt's paraphrases circulated in manuscript, they were no doubt read and applied differently by people who knew more or less about possible contexts. It is my argument, however, that they do not insist on, or even, beyond a few passingly suggestive phrases, invite, the identification of the psalmist or his enemies with particular persons or events. The paraphrases do engage closely with issues of Wyatt's own time, but they do so by developing the highly politicized issues of faith and salvation rather than by coded attacks on personal enemies. As we shall see, Wyatt's paraphrases of the seven penitential psalms are increasingly shaped as a critique of one of their major sources, the militantly Catholic *I Sette Salmi de la Penitentia di David*, written by Pietro Aretino and first published in Venice in 1534.

I Sette Salmi set the seven penitential psalms, through a series of prose prologues or links, in the context of the story of King David's adultery with Bathsheba, his destruction of Bathsheba's husband, Urias, the prophet Nathan's warning of God's displeasure, and the king's penitence. In Wyatt's version, Aretino's thoroughly Roman Catholic conversion narrative becomes a distinctly, but cautiously, Reformed one. In a dedication to Antonio da Leva, in charge of Charles V's Imperial troops, Aretino imagines his psalms being offered to Pope Paul III, and sees the printed edition playing its part in the fight against 'la diabolica setta de gli empi Heretici [the diabolical sect of impious heretics]'.[25] Wyatt reshapes Aretino's narrative of an exemplary repentance into a drama of David's remorse, the shattering of his penitential self, and his 'reconciling unto the Lord's grace' (Reb. clii l. 641), in which a continual stress on merit in the Italian original is replaced by an insistent emphasis on the primacy of grace.

At the same time, Wyatt's paraphrases question and probe man's art as opposed to God's word. Woven throughout his narrative is an implicit critique of Aretino's confident faith in the power of human artistry, apparent in his florid visual image-making and in his deployment of the key musical image of David's harp. Robin Kirkpatrick notes that 'Aretino was himself a close acquaintance of Titian; and the pictorial imagination which he displays in his *Penitential Psalms* can easily be seen to foreshadow the histrionic richness of Baroque spirituality'.[26] Aretino's faith in the power of human art to lift the soul to ecstasy and even redemption is most apparent at the end of his paraphrases when, in a final coda which Wyatt does not imitate, Aretino imagines David standing, his harp under his arm, listening to the angels repeat, with inexpressible sweetness, his own songs, and feeling the weight of his sins slip from him.[27]

Terrified by Nathan's warning, David is described in the first of Aretino's prologues as retiring into a cave under the ground, where he takes his harp and, modulating his playing and sighing, sings the Psalms. He is imagined in striking poses. In the prologue to Psalm 38 he stands with his eyes and hands elevated as though cut in stone.[28] In the same prologue, Aretino provides a dramatic image of light penetrating into the cave and striking off the chords of the harp into David's face, dazzling his eyes. Such visual effects culminate in the prologue to the last of the seven psalms (143), in which Aretino's David sees, 'quasi in visione [like a vision]', a tableau of Christ's life: the descent of the word of God from the sky, issuing from the mouth of an angel to become flesh in the Virgin; the birth of Christ; the crucifixion; the harrowing of hell to rescue David and his Old Testament forefathers; and finally the triumphant ascent into heaven.

Although many commentators have read in Wyatt's paraphrases the immediacy of the poet's own voice and personal anguish, Wyatt's imitation of Aretino's framing prologues follows his source in distancing the reader from David. We are positioned as observers of, and learners from, the spectacle of his dramatized penitence, and as Wyatt increasingly departs from his source, so we are invited to ponder words – both the dense textuality of Wyatt's paraphrases and the Word of God that speaks through the psalmist:

> he turneth and poiseth
> Each word that erst his lips might forth afford.
> He points, he pauseth, he wonders, he praiseth
>
> (ll. 518–20)

It has often been pointed out that Wyatt follows Aretino closely in the first two psalms and their prologues, but then increasingly alters or ignores his Italian source in favour of suggestions and phrasing from one or more of his other sources.[29] Both writers begin with David's sudden overwhelming lust for Bathsheba, whose bright eye-glances cause that total loss of self familiar in Petrarchan conceits. Bathsheba is now David's 'idol', 'the form that Love had printed in his breast / He honour'th it as thing of things best' (ll. 22 and 15–16). At the end of the prologue to the first psalm, we are given a visual image of David on his knees, his eyes turned up to heaven, his harp on his breast, its strings, his sighs and his voice attuned to one another. Wyatt follows Aretino closely, developing a pun (implicit in the Italian: 'toccando le *corde* con tenero fervore', p 260 – my emphasis) on strings or chords (*le corde*, Ital. = strings of the harp) and *cordis* (Lat. = heart):

> his cheer coloured like clay . . .
> His song with sighs, and touching of the strings
> With tender *heart*, lo, thus to God he sings.
>
> (ll. 69, 71–2; emphasis mine)

This pun will become increasingly crucial for Wyatt's paraphrase.[30]

It has been noted that at this point David seems more like a pleading lover than a sinner.[31] In the first of the penitential psalms that follow (Psalm 6), both writers use a language of supplication which belongs as readily to discourses of love as to the language of religious service: 'here hath my heart hope taken . . . at thy hand seek mercy . . . pity me . . . By nightly plaints instead of pleasures old / I wash my bed with tears continual' (ll. 73, 75, 92, 148–9). A histrionic quality in these passionate terms seems confirmed at the end of this prologue, when Wyatt foregrounds the human and technical effort that David puts into his song:

> His harp again into his hand he rought.
> Tuning accord by judgement of his ear,
> His heart's bottom for a sigh he sought,
> And therewithal upon the hollow tree
> With strained voice again thus crieth he.
>
> (ll. 212–16)

'Strained' (*OED* v. II 1. 'To extend with some effort', b. 'To tighten up (the strings of a musical instrument) so as to raise the pitch) translates the more spontaneous and musically neutral 'esclamò' of the Italian. The word suggests both passionate intensity and artful adjustment, reminding us of the strings (chords) of David's heart (Lat. *cor, cordis*). The 'strained voice' resonates discordantly against the word 'tree', translating Aretino's 'cavo legno [hollow wood]', but still in the sixteenth century used for the cross on which Christ died.[32] The words represent David as a Christ-like figure, crying out on the cross of his penitent afflictions, but they also undercut such an image with an insistent reminder of artful effort and the careful tuning of an instrument.

The harp which in Psalm 6 had been 'the faithful record of all his sorrows sharp' begins to play a more complex song in the second penitential psalm. Most strikingly, towards the close of the psalm David finds himself uttering God's words and not his own:

> 'I shall thee teach and give understanding
> And point to thee what way thou shalt resort
> For thy address, to keep thee from wand'ring.
> Mine eye shall take the charge to be thy guide.'
>
> (ll. 272–5)

Wyatt's version is here much closer to his scriptural source than to Aretino. However, in the subsequent (third) prologue, the effect of David's ventriloquizing of God's voice is registered by both Aretino and Wyatt in the image of a ray of light illuminating the cave and glancing across the chords of the harp, making the instrument glow like gold: 'The turn whereof into his eyes did start, / Surprised with joy by penance of the heart' (ll. 315–16). Wyatt is following Aretino closely, although he concentrates his reader's attention more fully on the harp and its instrumentality and, through compression of his grammar, on the identity of the beam of light and the sudden inner penitence that surprises the poet at the very moment the light 'starts' into his eyes.[33]

The divine art of such a sudden striking of the chords/heart is in marked contrast with another image which Wyatt borrows from Aretino in the third prologue. A few lines earlier, David, contemplating the words of God, had been compared to a statue carved in stone: 'Made as by craft to plain, to sob, to sigh' (l. 308). The image draws our attention to the power of ingenious human craft to mimic the outward signs of penitence. Aretino's florid visual images, which proliferate in his paraphrase, begin in Wyatt's more restrained version to seem discordant and problematic. At the end of this prologue to the third penitential psalm (Psalm 38), when Wyatt again foregrounds David's artfulness, his actions seem more appropriate to an amorous lutenist than a penitent harpist:

> He, then inflamed with far more hot affect
> Of God than he was erst of Barsabe,
> His left foot did on the earth erect,
> And just thereby remain'th the t'other knee.
> To his left side his weight he doth direct
> Sure hope of health and harp again tak'th he.
> His hand his tune, his mind sought his lay
> Which to the Lord with sober voice did say.
>
> (ll. 317–24)[34]

On this occasion, David's playing brings him no comfort. In the fourth prologue, we are told, he breaks off, weary, weeping and nigh insensible. His fingers still play over the chords of the harp but 'Without hearing or judgement of the sound' (l. 404). 'Judgement' is Wyatt's addition to the Italian and ironically recalls the confident artfulness that David brought to his harp playing in the prologue to the second psalm, 'Tuning accord by judgement of his ear' (l. 213). Increasingly, it is possible to detect a developing theme in Wyatt's use of the image of the harp. The instrument and the songs he has tuned to it have soothed his passions, voiced his penitence and raised ideas of mercy and grace which have given him hope, but his own best efforts and skill seem unable to take him further; indeed, his striking moment of joy so far comes from outside himself, the voice of God in the psalm, and the divine light striking on the chords of his heart/harp in sudden penitence.

The increasing problematizing of human song and effort, imaged in the playing of the harp, accompanies an increasing redefinition by Wyatt of his source. In Aretino's version, the emotional power and extravagance of David's penitence are efficacious: 'il merito', the merit or remission of punishment for his sins in purgatory that he earns through his repentance, repeatedly brings comfort: 'io ho sperato nel merito che mi apparecchia il patir mio; il quale sarà la salute delle anime [I have hope in the merit with which my suffering invests me; which will save my soul]' (p 284; sig. Fi^{r}).[35] As the drama of redemption develops, Aretino's David wavers between a sense of the merit he has earned and the fear that he has not yet been penitent enough. In the prologue to the fifth psalm (Psalm 102), for example, his David, measuring the hugeness of his error, trembles with fear and redoubles his penitential efforts. In Wyatt's version of this passage, David on the contrary sets the hugeness of his error against the hugeness of grace and finds comfort:

> he doth measure
> Measureless mercies to measureless fault,
> To prodigal sinners infinite treasure,
> Treasure termless that never shall default.
>
> (ll. 525–8)

In the prologue to the penultimate psalm (130), in which Aretino's David is still uncertain whether his penitence may yet have earned him sufficient remission for his sins: 'la penitentia fusse anchor giunta al termine della remissione del suo peccato' (p 309; sig. Kii^{v}), Wyatt departs entirely from his former source to elaborate on David's condition with a distinctly Reformed emphasis:

> But when he weigh'th the fault and recompense,
> He damn'th his deed and findeth plain
> Atween them two no whit equivalence;
> Whereby he takes all outward deed in vain
> To bear the name of rightful penitence,
> Which is alone the heart returned again
> And sore contrite that doth his fault bemoan,
> And outward deed the sign or fruit alone.
>
> (ll. 648–55)

This is clearly a Reformed statement.

An earlier crux in which Wyatt can be seen to be negotiating with care the theological niceties of a Reformed emphasis on the saving sufficiency of grace and a Roman Catholic emphasis on the importance of merit in the work of salvation occurs in the second penitential psalm (Psalm 32). The opening lines of Wyatt's translation are particularly difficult to follow. I give them with the punctuation they have in Wyatt's own manuscript copy:

> Oh happy are they that have forgivenes got
> Of their offence / (not by their penitence
> as by merit which recompenseth not
> although that yet pardon hath none offence
> Without the same/) but by the goodness
> Of him . . .
>
> (ll. 217–22)[36]

M&T paraphrase the meaning: 'Forgiveness "is not obtained by penitence but by grace . . . although no offence will obtain forgiveness without penitence" ' (p 366), which exposes the inherent contradiction in the lines. The equivalent lines in Aretino speak of the blessed who have gained pardon through grace, not through penitence or contrition: 'se ben senza esse le colpe nostre non hanno remissione [although without [penitence and contrition] our faults have no remission]' (p 18; sig. Ciii^{v}).[37] This makes sense in terms of Roman Catholic belief in the power of merit to earn remission for sins.

Wyatt complicates and alters Aretino's formulation by adding a line with a particularly Reformist emphasis: 'as by merit which recompenseth not'. Wyatt's twisting lines, acknowledging the importance of penitence but downplaying its efficacy, may be best explained by reference to the compromise position of a two-part penitence as set out in the 'Ten Articles' (which was repeated in the 'Bishops' Book'). Here the penitent is advised that he must

> conceive not only great sorrow and inward shame that he hath so grievously offended God, but also great fear of God's displeasure towards him, *considering he hath no works or merits of his own, which he may worthily lay before God, as sufficient satisfaction for his sins*; which done, then afterwards with this fear, shame and sorrow must needs succeed and be conjoined, the second part, viz. a certain faith, trust and confidence of the mercy and goodness of God, whereby the penitent must conceive certain hope and faith that God will forgive him his sins, and repute him justified, and of the number of his elect children, *not for the worthiness of any merit* or work done by the penitent, but for the only merits of the blood and passion of our Saviour Jesus Christ.[38]

Thus salvation is not gained by merit earned by penitence, although penitence, 'great sorrow and inward shame', must accompany faith in the saving power of Christ's passion. If Wyatt's lines seem contorted and contradictory, then so, it must be said, does the Bishops' formulation.[39]

In Wyatt's development of Aretino's prologues, or linking narratives between the psalms, David's agency in the work of redemption, especially that of his art, imaged by the playing of his harp and his tuning voice, is criticially scrutinized. At the end of the third penitential psalm, in which Wyatt's David had confidently harped to God 'inflamed with far more hot affect / Of god than he was erst of Barsabe' (ll. 317–18), his condition is at its lowest. He is described as a pilgrim who 'in a long way / Fainting for heat' lies down 'Under such shade as sorrow hath assigned' (ll. 395–6, 400). Very different is the state of mind of Aretino's pilgrim David, who, measuring the road in his mind, finds he has already come a good way ('misurando con la mente la lunghezza del camino, & havendone già buona parte fornito', p 287; sig. Fiii[v]). For Aretino, David's penitence is an inspiring spectacle of goodness which, had it reached his people, would have spurred them to run to comfort him (p 288). Wyatt does not imagine the response of his king's subjects, but emphasizes the privacy of his penitence: 'so close the cave was and uncouth / That none but God was record of his pain' (ll. 415–16). At the end of this prologue, when David again resumes his song, he seems to abandon his harp altogether, a detail to which Wyatt far more dramatically calls attention than Aretino's simple 'esclamando cantò':

> His voice he strains and from his heart outbrings
> This song that I not whether he cries or sings.
>
> (ll. 425–6)

The heart (*cordis*)/chord pun is again at work here, as is the pun on 'strains' (see p 162 above). But here, David is turning from his wooden instrument to a living one, his own heart, and his voice utters as much a cry as a song. The artful tuning and counterpoising of the earlier prologues has been abandoned.

David's power to praise God becomes a theme in the fourth penitential psalm (Psalm 51). In Wyatt's version, the power to sing God's praises emphatically follows salvation:

> My mouth shall spread thy glorious praises true.
> But of thyself, O God, this operation
> It must proceed by purging me from blood . . .
> Thou must, O Lord, my lips first unloose.
>
> (ll. 489–91, 494)

Aretino's David, by contrast, is confident that God has always been present in his praises: 'io in tutto il mio salmeggiare ti hò sempre dato & gloria, e laude [I have always given glory and praise to God in my psalms]'.[40]

God does open Wyatt's David's lips, because Psalm 51 ends with the most clearly evangelical expression of the importance of grace and the error of reliance on good works that we have had so far:

> But thou delights not in no such gloze
> Of outward deed as men dream and devise.
> The sacrifice that the Lord liketh most
> Is sprite contrite; low heart in humble wise
> Thou dost accept, O God, for pleasant host. *host: sacrifice*
> Make Zion, Lord, according to thy will,
> Inward Zion, the Zion of the ghost . . .
> Then shalt thou take for good these outward deeds.
>
> (ll. 498–504, 506)

The Calvinist Anne Lock, in her own later paraphrase of this psalm, in the form of twenty-one linked sonnets, introduces the redeeming power of Christ at this point: 'But thy swete sonne alone, / With one sufficing sacrifice for all / Appeaseth thee', calling Christ 'that sacred hoste'.[41] Her next few lines, particularly in their choice of the key rhyme words, suggest that she may have found in Wyatt's paraphrase a doctrinally sympathetic model:

> I yeld my self, I offer up my ghoste,
> My slaine delightes, my dyeng hart to thee.
> To God a trobled sprite is pleasing hoste.

In the prologue to the following (fifth) penintential psalm (102), Aretino's David continues to play his harp and fit his voice to the music, but Wyatt's has now not only abandoned the instrument, but moves away from control of his song. As he concludes the fourth penitential psalm, Wyatt's narrator comments:

> Of deep secrets that David here did sing,
> Of mercy, of faith, of frailty, of grace,
> Of God's goodness, and of justifying,

> The greatness did so astone himself a space, *astone: astonish*
> As who might say: 'Who hath expressed this thing?
> I, sinner, I! What have I said, alas?'
>
> (ll. 509–14)

David goes on to ponder silently 'Each word that erst his lips might forth afford' (l. 519), as though he were analysing some new, previously unseen text: 'He points, he pauseth, he wonders, he praiseth . . . ' (l. 521). Unlike his own 'lay' in the third penitential psalm, the result of a tuneful fitting of his hand and tune and mind (l. 323) which left him exhausted and despairing, this fifth psalm, in which David himself has become a passive instrument, gives him new and lasting hope.

Wyatt's development of the musical imagery in the Psalms has moved from the profanity of David's use of the harp in the manner of a lute in the first prologue to the metaphor, widespread in Christian thought, of the well-tuned body as an instrument upon which God or the soul can play. Thomas Becon, for example, evangelically insisted that 'without faith all the works that we do are unprofitable, glister they never so pleasantly . . . and whatsoever we sing after that sort is clean out of tune'.[42]

A new conceit of David as an instrument of God, not in Aretino, appears in the narrative link between Wyatt's fifth and sixth penitential psalms. David is imagined not as a harp, but as a wind instrument:

> he knew he hath alone expressed
> These great things that greater sprite complied,
> As shawm or pipe lets out the sound impressed,
> By music's art forged tofore and filed.
>
> (ll. 634–7)

Wyatt is like a pipe on which 'a greater sprite' plays: the forging and filing of human art has been superseded. His penitence has at least produced an instrument through which God's spirit can sound.

Wyatt's paraphrase of Psalm 130, the sixth penitential psalm, enacts a dialogue between David and God. The psalm begins with David's pleading repetitions of 'hear', 'ear' and 'voice':

> Thou in my voice, O Lord, perceive and hear . . .
> let by grant appear
> That to my voice thine ears do well intend . . .
> Hear then my woeful plaint.
>
> (ll. 668, 670–1, 674)

In the course of the psalm, however, David shifts from a petitioner to a prophet:

> Let Israel trust unto the Lord alway
> For grace and favour arn his property.
> Plenteous ransom shall come with him, I say,
> And shall redeem all our iniquity.
>
> (ll. 691–4)

'This word "redeem" that in his mouth did sound', the narrator tells us, 'Did put David . . . As in a trance to stare upon the ground / And with his thought the height of heaven to see' (ll. 496–7). The interplay of psalm paraphrase and narrative framework develops a drama of words: the psalmist's human words, superseded by divine words speaking through him, and finally, in the dramatic silence of the final linking narrative, the Word itself made flesh:

> he beholds the Word that should confound
> The sword of death by humble ear to be
> In mortal maid, in mortal habit made,
> Eternal life in mortal veil to shade.
>
> He seeth that Word, when full ripe time should come,
> Do way that veil . . .
> And leapeth lighter from such corruption
> Than glint of light that in the air doth lome. *lome: shine*
>
> (ll. 699–704, 706–7)

Wyatt's account of David's vision is woven together from scriptural passages. St John described Christ's coming in terms of the Word: 'And the word was made flesh and dwelt among us' (John 1.14). For St Paul, Christ's body is 'the veil, that is to say . . . his flesh' (Hebrews 10.20). Through the sacrifice of Christ's flesh and blood, 'in the twinkling of an eye, at the sound of the last trumpet . . . the dead shall rise incorruptible' (1 Corinthians 15.52).[43] Wyatt's image of the Word like a 'glint of light that in the air doth lome' (l. 707) may also recall the gift to the disciples of the Holy Spirit, who appeared like 'cloven tongues, like as they had been fire', giving to those he touched the ability 'to speak in tongues, even as the spirit gave them utterance' (Acts 2.3–4).[44] Where Aretino's corresponding prologue dwells on the traditional Roman Catholic iconic details of the angel of the annunciation, the Virgin, Christ's birth, the cross, the harrowing of Hell and the final ascent into Heaven, Wyatt's focuses attention on the revealed Word and its redemptive power, that 'can thereby convert / My death to life, my sin to salvation' (ll. 713–14).

Wyatt's focus on Christ as the Word is a distinctly Reformist one. Scripture is, in Becon's words, ' "the word of life," (Phil. ii) "the light of the world," (John viii) the only treasure of Christianity (Psalm xix) . . . abundantly "able to save the souls" (James i) of so many as hear it, believe it, and work thereafter'.[45] But David's prophetic vision of the Word made flesh and the glint of light in the air seems to take him beyond language to a more immediate access to truth through the agency of the Holy Spirit: 'to behold Christ crucified, in sprite, is the best meditacion that can be', wrote Katherine Parr. 'I certainly never knewe mine own miseries and wretchednes so wel by booke, admonicion, or lerning, as I have done by loking into the spiritual boke of the crucifix.'[46]

Wyatt's emphasis on the Word is the culmination of a Reformist critique of human words and human art and their limitations that has run throughout his paraphrase of the psalms. In the final prologue to the seventh penitential psalm, Wyatt gives no indication whether the psalm that follows (143) is sung, or even said aloud. The narrator tells us of David's unspoken words as he silently 'frames this reason [the significance of Christ's incarnation] in his heart' (l. 711), and the unvoiced monologue described in the prologue seems to continue into the psalm itself as David puts his suit, now 'with sured confidence' (l. 725), to God: 'Hear my prayer, O Lord, hear my request' (l. 727). Within the fiction of the poem, David has moved beyond the artifice of song, beyond even his own voice as an instrument, to an apparently unmediated communication with God.

Wyatt's imitation of Aretino's framed narrative of the seven penitential psalms systematically reshapes its source into a distinctly Reformed conversion narrative. At the same time, Wyatt's work engages with evangelical anxieties about human arts and their subordination to the Word. On one level, the psalms may be seen as a kind of palinode by the harping David, if not by Wyatt himself, in which the hidden secrets of 'lust posessed' (ll. 28–32) are rejected for the 'secret protection' of God's grace (l. 764), part of a project to replace secular poetry with spiritual songs and psalms which increasingly stirred evangelical moralists during the sixteenth century, and which saw some of Wyatt's own profane courtly lyrics rewritten as godly verses in John Hall's anthology *The Couurte of Vertue* (1565; see my Epilogue, p 193). 'Ah, would God that all minstrels of the world', wrote Thomas Becon, 'would once leave their lascivious, wanton, and unclean ballads, and sing such godly and virtuous songs as David teacheth them' (quoted above, p 155).

While there is no evidence that the paraphrases represent a genuine renunciation of his profane verse, Wyatt seems, through his use of the gradually displaced image of the harp, to be exploring the possibility of an unmediated language of truth, in which human artistry is discarded and man's voice or mind become passive channels for God's word. Such a transparent language attracted Reformers arguing for translation of God's word into a plain 'unrhetorical' English, clear to all, without the 'painted eloquence strength and authorite' associated with Latin and Roman Catholic glossing: 'For the Truthe is of suche power strength and efficacite, that it can neither be defended with wordes nor be overcome with any might.'[47]

Even as Wyatt's psalm paraphrases share with us their vision of a gradually purified communication through the divine Word and the spirit, the carefully crafted text that shapes the vision is obstinately before our reading eyes in all its materiality. While Wyatt increasingly simplifies and abbreviates the florid imagery of Aretino, the frameworks within frameworks which he borrows from the Italian are ever before us. The narrator draws our attention to the impossibility of what he shows us: 'for who had seen so kneel within the grave / The chief pastor . . .' (ll. 205–6); 'who had been without the cave's mouth / And heard the tears . . . / He would have sworn . . . / But that so close the cave was and uncouth / That none but God was record of his pain' (ll. 411–16). The narrator both gives us access to the secret drama of David and holds us at a distance from it, drawing our attention, by his intervening presence, to its artful fictionality. In the same way, the image of the harp focuses our attention on the initial artfulness of David, but also, through Wyatt's clever manipulation of it, on the witty craft of Wyatt himself.

An instance of such wit is evident even at the climactic moment of communion between David and God. In the prologue to the final psalm, David 'frames . . . in his heart' a reassurance based on the crucifixion:

> That goodness which doth not forbear his *son*
> From death for me and can thereby convert
> My death to life, my *sin* to salvation,
> Both can and will a smaller grace depart.
>
> (ll. 712–16, my emphases)

The 'smaller grace' David seeks is deliverance from his rebellious son, Absolon (the story is told in 2 Samuel 15–18):[48]

> Alas, my *son* pursues me to the grave,
> Suffered by God my *sin* for to correct.
> But of my *sin* since I my pardon have,
> My *son*'s pursuit shall shortly be reject.
>
> (ll. 721–4, my emphases)

David's apparent concern with his own domestic and political affairs at this crucial moment may seem at first sight disconcertingly temporal. One critic feels that 'his last request reveals that this David still operates within the train of lust; the order of Love and divine justice is beyond him'.[49] It seems to me, however, that Wyatt (David)'s wit is here playing on a patterning of 'son' and 'sin' in which David is paralleled with God. God's 'son' converts David's 'sin to salvation' (l. 714), but David's 'son' is a sign of his 'sin'. Now that David's sins are pardoned, 'My son's pursuit shall shortly be reject' (l. 724). M&T point out that in 2 Samuel 12, 'When Nathan tells David that God has "put away" his sin, he also prophesies that, as a result of it, his son by Bathsheba will die' (p 388). Although the son Nathan refers to is not Absolon, Wyatt seems to have conflated David's two sons, linking them to David's sin as its bodily image: David's son/sin is doomed by God's son, the redeemer of sin.

Wyatt's careful tracing of the process by which, in the words of the 'Ten Articles' of June 1536 and the 'Bishops' Book' of 1537, 'great sorrow and shame' of the sinner gives way to a 'certain hope and faith that God will forgive him his sins, and repute him justified . . . not for the worthiness of any merit or work done by the penitent, but only for the merits of the blood and passion of our Saviour Jesus Christ' (see p 165 above) would have made it particularly pleasing to his patron Thomas Cromwell. Indeed, a dating of the paraphrase to the summer and autumn of 1536, following publication of the 'Ten Articles', at a time when Wyatt's prospects seemed uncertain following his imprisonment in May, and at a time when the political and religious loyalties of courtiers were under particular scrutiny due to the Catholic uprising called the Pilgrimage of Grace, makes considerable sense. At such a time, a rendering of the penitential psalms into the vernacular, in a version which implicitly challenged the propagandist Roman Catholicism of Aretino and dramatized the relationship of penitence and grace in perfect conformity to the recently formulated religious orthodoxy, would have been a bold but well-judged enterprise. It is even possible to speculate that Wyatt's appointment in January 1537 to defend the point of view and the policies of Henry's new ecclesiastical order to his most Catholic Majesty, the Holy Roman Emperor Charles V, might owe some debt to such an initiative.

In spite of its thematic celebration of the transcendence of God's word over human language and art, Wyatt's paraphrase remains a carefully crafted, even a politically crafty, work, dependent for its effects on the careful redefinition of imagery. No more than the passionate 'I' of the courtly lyrics, or the sinuous 'I' of the satires, should the suffering and penitential 'I' of the psalms be taken at face value. The very art with which the drama of transcendence is enacted denies us access to an authentic penitence, least of all Wyatt's own.

'THE CURELESSE WOUND': SURREY'S BIBLICAL PARAPHRASES

If Wyatt's penitential psalms veil an authorial voice behind fictionality, translation, and the cautious selection of words and adjustment of emphases, Surrey's biblical paraphrases are powerful for quite opposite reasons. Especially in the paraphrases associated with his last six months of life and his imprisonment before execution, the voice of the biblical speaker disappears entirely before an insistent and personal 'I'.

Surrey paraphrased at least four psalms as well as five chapters from Ecclesiastes, the Book of the Preacher.[50] Of the psalms, the earliest seems to be his version of the eighth (Jones no. 47), which breathes a distinctly Renaissance confidence in man's capacity as of 'aungells substance' and gives thanks for the lavishness of God's gifts to men.[51] This paraphrase seems to have been an early exercise. It is possible that his paraphrases of the more sombre chapters from Ecclesiastes may also have begun as an exercise, perhaps to help discipline his mind after his sudden return from France in March 1546. The choice of Ecclesiastes, prolonged meditations in the voice of the wise King Solomon on the deceptive vanities of this world, may have seemed an appropriate text after the disappointments of Surrey's last months at Boulogne (see Chapter 1, pp 28–9). Surrey's own fear of the corrosive effects of inactivity, not only on his reputation, but on his own mind, would have made the exercise of reading and meditating on the Bible a laudable one.

Surrey's paraphrases, however, show less interest in meditating on his own shortcomings than in suggesting political and moral lessons for others. Given the contemporary practice of finding historical parallels between the Old Testament and the present, any references to persecuting kings, their godless power, or 'conjures' whereby 'the seade of kings is thrust from staate' (Jones no. 46 l 41) were potentially indiscreet, capable of being appropriated for contemporary application. That this happened is plain from the striking verbal similarity between some lines from Surrey's paraphrase of Ecclesiastes 3 and lines apparently written in prison by the evangelical martyr Anne Askew before she was burned in July 1546. Surrey's lines translate very freely the Vulgate Latin: 'Vidi sub sole in loco judicii impietatem, et in loco justitiae iniquitatem ... [I saw under the sun, impiety in the seat of judgement, and evil in the place of justice]':

> I saw a roiall throne wheras that Justice should have sitt;
> In stede of whom I saw, with fierce and crwell mode,
> Wher Wrong was set, that blody beast, that drounke the giltles blode.
> Then thought I thus: One day the Lord shall sitt in dome,
> To vewe his flock and chose the pure: the spotted have no rome.
> (ll. 44–8)

In Anne Askew's 'Ballad' the lines are used, as in Surrey's paraphrase, to articulate an apocalyptic vision:

> I saw a royal throne,
> Where justice should have sit,
> But in her stead was one
> Of moody, cruel wit.
>
> Absorbed was righteousness,
> As of the raging flood:
> Satan, in his excess,
> Sucked up the guiltless blood.
>
> Then thought I, Jesus Lord,
> When thou shall judge us all,
> Hard is it to record
> On these men what will fall.[52]

Although translating very freely, Surrey is following the thought and the sequence of Ecclesiastes 3, which makes it probable, but not certain, that Anne Askew had access to a manuscript text of Surrey's paraphrase before her death, and that it was she who was imitating him. Askew's contacts with courtly sympathizers were closely examined; her knowledge and use of Surrey's psalm could thus have been highly dangerous for him.[53]

To Askew's biographer, John Bale, the men on whom God's wrath would fall were certainly historically identifiable. Quoting Psalm 1 as he concluded his account of Askew's second examination and martyrdom, published on the continent on 16 January 1547, three days before Surrey's execution, he cited the Duke of Norfolk, then in prison with his indiscreet son, as an example of the 'ungodly and cruel enemies' whom God would 'as dust in the wind . . . scatter . . . from the face of the earth'.[54] The historians Susan Brigden and Maria Dowling in particular have traced the complex political rivalries of the last months of Henry VIII's reign in which religious and doctrinal fears and sympathies at court became bound up with manoeuvrings over who would control the old king's will and favour, and more particularly over who would control the new king, then scarcely ten years old. As the head of the premier family in England after that of the king, the Duke of Norfolk should have been a strong candidate for regent, and Surrey certainly felt this was his due. Norfolk's sympathies, whatever those of his son, were, however, strongly conservative in matters of religion, and he was viewed with anathema by the Reformers at court: 'rather than that it shuld come to passe that the prince shuld be under the governement of yor father or you, I woulde bide the adventure to thrust this dagger in you', the evangelical Blage told Surrey.[55] It may be that men such as Blage, Sir Anthony Denny, Edward Seymour (Earl of Hertford) and Surrey's one-time ally William Paget feared Surrey's arrogance and volatile judgement almost as much as they feared his father's religious conservatism. By December 1546, Hertford and the Reformist faction had gained control, and Surrey and his father were removed as rivals by means of imprisonment and charges of treason.

In Surrey's biblical paraphrases it is impossible to disentangle the feverish expressions of evangelical belief from, on the one hand, politic moves on Surrey's part to win over potential allies among the Reformers at court, and on the other an increasingly Davidic sense of his own unjust betrayal.[56] At the end of his paraphrase of Ecclesiastes 4 and the beginning of Ecclesiastes 5, Surrey clearly turned to his copy of Wyatt's psalm paraphrases, echoing them in a number of places, but particularly the key Reformist passage of the prologue to the sixth penitential psalm (Reb. clii ll. 651–5), in which, I suggested, Wyatt carefully conforms to the statements of faith contained in the 'Ten Articles' of 1536 and the 'Bishops'

Book' of 1537 (see p 164 above). The first of Surrey's lines quoted below, in its assertion of faith alone as the basis of grace, is a much bolder statement than Wyatt's careful weighing of grace and works:

And simple faith; the yolden hoost his marcy doth require — *yolden hoost: the spirit sacrificed to God*
Wher perfectly for aye he in his woord dothe rest,
With gentill care to heare thy sute and graunt to thy request.
In boost of owtwarde works he taketh no delight, — *boost: boast*
Nor waste of wourds; suche sacrifice unsavereth in his sight. — *unsavereth: is distasteful*
Eccles. Capitulo 5.
More shall thie penitent sighes his endlesse mercie please
Then their Importune sutes, which dreame that wordes Gods wrathe appease.
For hart contrite of fault is gladsome recompence,
And prayer frute of faith, whearby God doth with sinne dispence.[57]

The emphasis in these lines, on the true sacrifice of faith rather than outward works or words, signals both Surrey's Reformed sympathies and that he was an attentive reader of Wyatt's psalms. In his elegy on Wyatt published in 1542, Surrey had praised him as 'that simple soul' who fled to the heavens, leaving to the faithful remnant ('such as covet Christ to know') the 'witness' of both his life and his psalms, 'Witnesse of faith that never shall be ded' (Jones no. 28 ll. 33–5). By thus elegizing the older poet, Surrey emphasized, and explicitly aligned himself with, a Wyatt who is represented as an exemplary and fearless Reformer, indeed one more doctrinally Reformed than his own words authorize. Is such appropriation of a revered model a way of defining his own beliefs and placing himself within an honourable tradition? Or may Surrey be using Wyatt, explicitly in the elegy and implicitly in the lines from Ecclesiastes, to signal at key moments the political and religious positions he wishes to take up? In 1546 some of the influential Reformers at court, particularly George Blage, a gentleman of the Privy Chamber, had been friends and associates of Wyatt. May Surrey be attempting to reassure them that his political ambitions do not represent a threat to Reformed beliefs? It is impossible to recover Surrey's motives, and at least possible that Surrey himself was unclear about what they were.

Two of Surrey's psalm paraphrases were sent to powerful members of the Reformed faction at court, George Blage and Sir Anthony Denny, during Surrey's imprisonment on charges of treason in December 1546 and early January 1547.[58] In the prefatory poems he addressed to the two men, Surrey again draws on the model of Wyatt and implicitly makes allusion to his own patronage of Wyatt. A *strambotto* by Wyatt (Reb. cclxvii) is copied into the Arundel-Harington manuscript after Wyatt's paraphrase of Psalm 37 (Reb. cclxvi), not one of the penitential psalms, and before a folio which is now missing from the manuscript. The early editor of Wyatt and Surrey's poetry, G. F. Nott, plausibly suggested the *strambotto* was addressed to Surrey and was a dedicatory poem for a psalm paraphrase, probably written when Wyatt was in prison.[59] In it, Wyatt puts his confidence in God, but also suggests to the dedicatee that his doubts of other men's malice puts him in need of powerful friends:

> Mine Earl, this doubt my heart did humble then,
> For error so might murder innocents. *innocents: innocence?*
> Then sang I thus in God my confidence.

In his own troubles Surrey followed Wyatt's strategy. The dedicatory poem for Psalm 88, one of Surrey's few *strambotti*, is addressed to Sir Anthony Denny, who in October 1546 had become the powerful Chief Gentleman of the Privy Chamber. Surrey attributes his own 'errour' to 'rechles youthe . . . set on by wrath, revenge and crueltie' and takes 'David, the perfit warriour' as his model (Jones no. 36). The psalm that follows (88) is a psalm of repentance which nevertheless holds out the possibility that were God (perhaps by means of his servant Denny) to spare this sinner, then 'in the mouthe of thy elect thy mercies might be spredd' (l. 22). Surrey too, the paraphrase implies, might become a powerful furtherer of the cause of Reform.

Surrey again invokes the example of David in dedicating his paraphrase of Psalm 73 to Blage, with whom he had quarrelled earlier in 1546 but who might now, as a prominent Reformer at court and ally of those in the ascendant in the king's Privy Chamber, prove a useful friend. In spite of its initial hubris, the poem appears to make some gestures of penitence:

> For I, that on the noble voyage goo
> To succhor treuthe and falshed to assaile,
> Constrained am to beare my sailes ful loo
> And never could attaine some pleasaunt gale . . .
> But now my Blage, mine errour well I see:
> Such goodlie light King David giveth me.
>
> (Jones no. 37 ll. 3–6, 11–12)

The psalm that follows (73) makes it clear, however, that the poet's 'errour' has merely been a momentary hesitation in the 'noble voyage' of inveighing against vice in high places:

> Yet whiles the faith did faint that shold have ben my guide,
> Like them that walk in slipper pathes my feet began to slide.
>
> (Jones no. 49 ll. 3–4)

The image of slippery ground and feet sliding is in the Vulgate Latin of the psalm, but Surrey may also be penitentially recalling lines in Wyatt's paraphrase of Psalm 37, the psalm possibly sent to Surrey when Wyatt himself was in the Tower, in which Wyatt had written:

> With wisdom shall the wise man's mouth him able;
> His tongue shall speak alway even as it ought.
> With God's learning he hath his heart stable;
> His foot therefore from sliding shall be sure.
>
> (Reb. cclxvi ll. 81–6)[60]

Surrey/David had temporarily doubted God's promise to his elect, but he will be guilty of such sliding no more. The psalmist's voice is appropriated to represent the poet as one of the suffering vanguard of the 'just' who fight against fleshly power in high places:

> In terrour of the just thus raignes iniquitie,
> Armed with power, laden with gold, and dred for crueltie.
> Then vaine the warr might seme that I by faithe maintaine
> Against the fleshe, whose false effects my pure hert wold distaine.
> For I am scourged still, that no offence have doon,
> By wrathes children; and from my birth my chastesing begoon.
>
> (Jones no. 49 ll. 27–32)

Where, in Wyatt's paraphrases of the seven penitential psalms, the enemy seemed primarily to be internal, aspects of David's fallen self, in Surrey's paraphrase the ambiguity seems rather to resolve itself in favour of external foes, the worldly enemies of the godly. Lines 29–30 suggest that the psalmist's battle is that of the spirit against the flesh, but lines 27–8 suggest instead more historically identifiable embodiments of the powers of darkness. Perhaps even more specific are lines earlier in the paraphrase directed at those

> Whose glutten cheks slouth feads so fatt as scant their eyes be sene
> Unto whose crewell power most men for dred ar faine
> To bend and bow with loftie looks, whiles they vawnt in their raine.
>
> (ll. 14–16)

Susan Brigden has described Henry's bloated physique in his last year as 'moved by machines now, and physically repellent', and Sessions compares Surrey's line to the last known portrait of Henry by Cornelys Mastys in which the king's tiny eyes disappear into the fat of his broad cheeks.[61]

Surrey's appropriation of the psalmist's voice and imagery, and his eradication of any fictional or historical distance between himself as writer and David, invites the reader to identify the elect and suffering 'I' of the psalmist as Surrey himself. Surrey/David is a personal witness of persecution by the powerful:

> Alas, how oft my foes have framed my decaie . . .
> I, that in thy worde have set my trust and joie,
> The highe reward that longs therto shall quietlie enjoie.
> And my unworthie lipps, inspired with thy grace,
> Shall thus forspeke thy secret works in sight of Adams race.
>
> (ll. 53, 63–6)

Bale, concluding his *The First Examination of Mistress Anne Askewe*, published in Germany in November 1546, represented his subject in very similar terms: ' "God standeth by the generation of the righteous." Ps. xiii.'[62] As Surrey promises to 'forespeke thy secret works' and so serve the evangelical cause if he survives (through Blage's intercession), so Bale publishes the testimony of Askew so that 'the glory and power of the Lord, so manifestly appearing in his elect vessels, may not perish at all hands, and be unthankfully neglected, but be spread the world over as well in Latin as English, to the perpetual infamy of so wilfully cruel and spiteful tyrants'.[63]

It is improbable, though not impossible, that Surrey saw a copy of Bale's *First Examination*.[64] It would be an ironic twist of fate if Surrey, whose paraphrase of Ecclesiastes 3 provided lines imitated by Askew, had found in Askew herself a model for his own self-representation in his paraphrase of Psalm 73. He need not, however, have read Bale's work or known of Askew's writing and testimony to have recognized in the Psalms a ready language for those suffering religious persecution and even martyrdom, nor to have understood the importance to the Reformers of fearless witness. He would have known, too, how vividly martyrdom must have figured in the imagination of Blage. Blage himself had been arrested for heresy on 11 July 1546, five days before Askew was burned. He too had been condemned to the flames but saved, at the last moment, by the intervention with the king of his friends in the Privy Chamber. Greeted by the king, who used Blage's nickname of 'pig', on his return to court, Blage replied: 'if your Majesty had not been better to me than your bishops were, your pig had been roasted ere this time'.[65]

Anticipating his own martyrdom, Blage had himself composed two psalm-like poems:

> And I, o lord, in to thy handes do yield
> My faithefull soul, apointed now of the[e]
> This liffe to leve, thoro fier, in Smithefild.[66]

The language and imagery of Blage's 'psalms' draw on similar biblical imagery to that of Surrey's paraphrase. Where Surrey's foes 'sucke the fleshe of thy elect and bath them in their bloode' (l. 24), Blage accuses the conservative bishops, 'this blowdy Baals broud', of causing 'the elect to dy'. To Blage, the bishops, 'whiche by thy wourde cleime [claim] shepeherdes for to bee / Thy flok klene to kepe witheout spot or wem', are in fact wolves in sheep's clothing,

> for on ther bakkes our skinnes thes woulpfes do wer
> And for our fleece foul ofte would have us ded.

Surrey's version of the same biblical imagery describes the false sheep as covered by a 'golden fleece' which, when shorn, 'The spotts that under neth wer hidd, thy chosen shepe shall skorne' (l. 48). Surrey's 'chosen shepe' are the equivalent of 'thi littel flok' whom Blage appeals to God to save, but against whom God seems at present (in an image that seems to recall Surrey's satire 'London hast thow') his 'wrathefull boue . . . [to] bende'.[67]

Similarities of phrasing and thought do not establish that Surrey knew Blage's 'psalms' or was directly drawing upon them for his own. Surrey is, however, using a kind of discourse closely identified with those who felt themselves to be suffering witnesses and martyrs for the Reformed faith. Surrey seems audaciously in the three psalm paraphrases he wrote in prison (Psalm 88, addressed to Denny, particularly Psalm 73 addressed to Blage, and Psalm 55) to be drawing a parallel between the sufferings of recent Reformers and his own present imprisonment, which was in fact for treason but which he represents as the result of fearless godly witness. For Surrey, there seems no distinction between the 'noble voyage . . . To succhor treuthe' on which he described himself embarked in the dedicatory poem to Blage (Jones no. 37 ll. 3–4) and the voyage of the righteous psalmist which will lead, eventually, to heavenly reward:

And in eache voyage that I toke to conquer sinne,
Thow wert my guyd, and gave me grace to comfort me therin . . . *guyd: guide*
  And suche for drede or gaine, as shall thy name refuse,
Shall perishe with their golden godds that did their harts seduce.
  Where I, that in thy worde have set my trust and joye,
The highe reward that longs therto shall quietlie enjoie.
(ll. 55–6, 61–4)

In the final lines, Surrey hints, he might yet be saved by 'thy grace' and 'secret works' (ll. 65–6), perhaps addressing himself as much to a merciful Blage as to God himself.

Surrey's paraphrase of Psalm 55, generally agreed to be his last, and apparently unfinished, has no dedicatee. Unlike Surrey's previous psalm paraphrases, this one uses unrhymed alexandrines, and the metre gives the often colloquial language great power:

My fooes they bray so lowde, and eke threpe on so fast, *eke threpe: also thrust*
Buckeled to do me scathe, so is their malice bent. *Buckeled . . . scathe: armed to do me harm*
Care perceth my entrailes and traveileth my sprite; *traveileth: torments*
The greslie feare of death environeth my brest.
(ll. 3–6)

Quoting these lines, Sessions analyses with precision the technical skill that is the basis of their power: the 'drumming end-stopped lines' combined with 'alliterative Anglo-Saxon diction, strong verbs, and a terrifying combination of abstract subjects with concrete modifiers', rendering 'the basic image of the trapped animal'.[68] But here, even more than in the paraphrases of 88 and 73, it is not the craft but the drama of the psalmist/poet's condition that seizes the reader's attention.

Surrey elides his voice and situation completely with that of the psalmist as he represents himself betrayed by friends, surrounded by enemies, and living in guileful times. At line 30, there is another echo of Wyatt's David who, with 'heart contrite' (Reb. clii l. 223), had begun his third penitential psalm with 'far more hot affect' (Reb. clii l. 317). Wyatt's distancing devices are, however, lost in Surrey's version, where the words serve to intensify the speaker's urgency: 'With words of hott effect, that moveth from hert contrite.'

Interestingly, Surrey seems to have been working with a copy of Coverdale's version of the Psalms in the 'Great Bible' of 1539 (whose circulation had been restricted to the upper classes by statute in 1543) before him.[69] For Coverdale, verse 55, 'The wordes of his mouth were softer then butter, havinge warre in his hart: his wordes were smother then oile, and yet be they very swerdes', refers to God's words, as it does for Surrey:

> Butter fales not so soft as doth his pacience longe,
> And over passeth fine oile, running not half so smothe.
> But when his suffraunce finds that bridled wrath provoks,
> He thretneth wrath, he whets more sharppe then any toole can file.
> (ll. 38–41)

Both the Vulgate Latin and the commentary by Campensis that Surrey was using attribute these words, described simply as oily ('super oleum'; 'unquento'), to the hypocritical enemies of God.

As Surrey moves between the Latin and English versions of the psalm, the Vulgate's attribution of hypocrisy to God's enemies provokes Surrey to add to the biblical psalm a passionate and personal attack on hypocrisy:

> Friowr, whose harme and tounge presents the wicked sort
> Of those false wolves, with cootes which doo their ravin hide, *cootes: coats*
> That sweare to me by heaven, the fotestole of the Lord,
> Who though force had hurt my fame, they did not touche my life:
> Such patching care I lothe as feeds the welth with lies.
> But in th'other Psalme of David find I ease:
> Iacta curam tuam super dominum et ipse te enutriet.
> (ll. 42–48)

The thought of his enemies causes Surrey to lose sight of the text he is following, and the references seem to become personal. Brigden has ingeniously suggested a possible identification of the mysterious 'Friowr' as a Dr John Fryer, with whom Surrey may have discussed his religious doubts ('And in his bosome hide my secreat zeale to God', l. 25).[70] However, the representation of friars as hypocrites, wolves in sheep's clothing, was commonplace in anti-ecclesiastical satire.[71] As we have seen, Blage applied the image to false bishops in the poem he wrote anticipating his burning. The image of disguised wolves who 'raven' the innocent sheep has its source in Christ's warning against 'false prophets' in Matthew 7.15.

It may be that Surrey's mind, pondering the hypocrisy and lies of those he counted his erstwhile friends, has slipped from Psalm 55 to another psalm, perhaps such as 62, in which the psalmist also attacks hypocrisy ('their delite is in lies: they geve good wordes with their mouth, but curse with their hert') before putting his trust in God.[72] Surrey may thus have been led back to Psalm 55, 'th'other Psalme of David' (l. 47), and to the line that follows the one at which he broke off. This he quotes in the Latin of the Vulgate: 'Iacta curam tuam super dominum et ipse te enutriet'.[73] Or it may be that, moving between the English and Latin versions of the Psalms (differently numbered – the Vulgate numbers the psalm 54), he comes to think of them as separate psalms. The final recourse to Latin suggests that at the end of this, probably his last psalm, the evangelical display, so much in evidence in the paraphrases of Psalms 88 and 73, 'that in the mouthe of thy elect thy mercies might be spredd' (Jones no. 48 l. 22), may be giving way to the need for the private reassurance of the old, familiar biblical language of the Latin Vulgate.

In Chapter 3, I contrasted the characteristically stable moral voice of Surrey's first-person speakers, defined against the faithlessness and mutability of others, with the splintered ironies and ambivalences of Wyatt's sonnet lovers. In the biblical paraphrases of the two poets, the comparison may be to some extent reversed. The carefully dramatized voice of Wyatt's psalmist is contained within a coherent narrative in which communication is imagined as moving beyond human agency, although, of course, Wyatt's shaping craft remains always, even ostentatiously, in evidence. In Surrey's final paraphrases, the morally stable 'I' speaker that was so central to the strategy of his secular poems is lost. Surrey appropriates the voice of the psalmist, and sometimes the voice and strategies of Wyatt, but rather than providing a consistent, expressive language, there is a sense of contradiction and divided purpose. Repentance and the topics of spiritual battle are appropriated and redirected to launch attacks on factional enemies or express personal resentment and anger; the discourse of evangelical martyrdom is found in a poem which seems to be manoeuvring for political intercession; the exemplary prayers and meditations of David, the 'perfitt warriour', are interrupted by cries of betrayal and bitterness; and the vernacular English of a Reformation David is interrupted by recourse to the older Latin of a more certain past.

Such fracturing and contradiction are poignantly evident in Surrey's final poem, 'The stormes are past, these cloudes are overblowne' (Jones no. 38).[74] This is not a psalm paraphrase but it appears in *Tottel's Miscellany* bearing a title which is a quotation from the Vulgate Latin of Psalm 118: 'Bonum est mihi quod humiliasti me' ('it is good for me that I have been in trouble' – Coverdale's translation in the 'Great Bible'). So different is the title from those normally invented by Tottel that in this case he may have authority for its use from the manuscript copy he is using. Surrey may here be composing his own psalm, as Blage had done, or as Sir Thomas Smith later composed 'Other Psalms' alongside his paraphrases during his own imprisonment in the Tower in 1549.[75] Once again, Surrey seems to be looking back to his old model Wyatt, for thought and language as well as for form, for the poem seems to represent an imperfect, or draft, attempt to write in *terza rima*, the form of Wyatt's psalm paraphrases.

If the form is undecided, the tone and thought of the poem are even more so. The poem seems to begin as a celebration of an achieved assurance:

> The stormes are past, these cloudes are overblowne,
> And humble chere great rigour hath represt;
> For the defaute is set a paine foreknowne,
> And pacience graft in a determed brest.
>
> (ll. 1–4)

This mood ends in lines 11–12 with a sudden, startling change:

> But when my glasse presented unto me
> The curelesse wound that bleedeth day and night.
> To think, alas, such hap should graunted be
> Unto a wretch that hath no hart to fight,
> To spill that blood that hath so oft bene shed
> For Britannes sake, alas, and now is dead.
>
> (ll. 11–17)

The 'curelesse wound' recalls Wyatt's epigram written to Bryan from prison, 'Sure I am, Brian, this wound shall heal again / But yet, alas, the scar shall still remain' (Reb. lxii), which Surrey had already echoed in his epigram to Radcliffe (Jones no. 34; see Chapter 4, pp 121–2).[76] His reuse of the image suggests the power its Christ-like image of betrayal and martyrdom had for him. But there is little trace of a Christ-like patience or humility. The thought that a cowardly 'wretch' would succeed in bringing low one who had shed his blood in gestures of aristocratic chivalric bravery on the fields of France was more than enough to destroy the patience and assurance Surrey had carefully written himself into in the first part of his final poem. The Surrey who tried to write his own epitaph just before execution constructs himself as a shattered man, riven by contradictions.

NOTES

1. For useful discussions of ecclesiastical reform and changes in religious beliefs in this period, see especially Haigh, C. (1993) *English Reformations: Religion, Politics, and Society under the Tudors*. Oxford: Clarendon Press; Duffy, E. (1992) *The Stripping of the Altars: Traditional Religion in England c. 1400–c. 1580*. New Haven, Conn.: Yale University Press, pp 379–423; and Rex, R. (1993) *Henry VIII and the English Reformation*. British History in Perspective. Basingstoke: Macmillan. For a discussion of the scriptural style favoured by Reformers, see Mueller, J. M. (1984) *The Native Tongue and the Word: Development in English Prose Style, 1380–1580*. Chicago: University of Chicago Press, esp. ch 5.
2. In Becon, T. (1843) *The Early Works*, ed. J. Ayre. The Parker Society. Cambridge: Cambridge University Press, pp 264–303. Becon, a leading Reformer, was incumbent of a Kentish parish, Brenzett, from approx. June 1541 to July 1543, and dedicated *The New Pollicie of Warre* (August–September 1542) to Wyatt himself. For Cobham's Reformist sympathies, see MacCulloch, D. (1996) *Thomas Cranmer: A Life*. New Haven, Conn.: Yale University Press, p 203.
3. Becon (1843) p 266.
4. See Zim, R. (1987) *English Metrical Psalms: Poetry as Praise and Prayer, 1535–1601*. Cambridge: Cambridge University Press. The appendix lists printed psalm versions in the period. Manuscript versions are listed on p 260 n 6.
5. Ibid pp 27–31; Reb. p 453.
6. Gosselin, E. A. (1976) *The King's Progress to Jerusalem: Some Interpretations of David during the Reformation Period and their Patristic and Medieval Background*. Malibu: Undena Publications, p 70.
7. For the material in this paragraph, see especially Haigh (1993) ch 7 and Rex (1993) pp 144–53. Dowling, M. (1987) 'The gospel and the court: Reformation under Henry VIII'. In *Protestantism and the National Church in Sixteenth-Century England*, eds P. Lake and M. Dowling. London: Croom Helm, pp 36–77 (p 36) suggests that the use of the word 'protestant' to describe the Reformers is anachronistic at this time of fluid definitions of belief. I adopt the terms 'evangelical' and 'Reformed' as alternatives.
8. For the roles of Catherine Parr and courtly Reformers, see Dowling (1987).
9. The documents may be found together in Lloyd, C., ed. (1856) *Formularies of Faith, put forth by authority during the reign of Henry VIII*. Oxford: Oxford University Press.
10. Dowling (1987) pp 36, 39.
11. For a brief account of key doctrinal differences, see Doran, S. and Durston, C. (1991) *Princes, Pastors and People: The Church and Religion in England, 1529–1689*. London: Routledge, pp 3–17. See also Duffy (1992) pp 379–423.
12. For example, the Reformer William Turner's treatise of 1555, *The Huntying of the Romyshe Wolfe*.
13. Becon (1843) p 288 and Bailey, D. S. (1952) *Thomas Becon and the Reformation of the Church in England*. Edinburgh and London: Oliver and Boyd, pp 15, 30.

14. In Bale, J. (1849) *Select Works.* The Parker Society. Cambridge: Cambridge University Press, p 184.

15. The psalter is described and discussed by Tudor-Craig, P. (1989) 'Henry VIII and King David'. In *Early Tudor England: Proceedings of the 1987 Harlaxton Symposium*, ed. D. Williams. Woodbridge, Suffolk: Boydell Press, pp 183–205, and King, J. N. (1994) 'Henry VIII as David: the king's image and Reformation politics. In *Rethinking the Henrician Era: Essays on Early Tudor Texts and Contexts*, ed. P. C. Herman. Urbana and Chicago: University of Illinois Press, pp 78–97, who challenges Tudor-Craig's dating of 1540.

16. King (1994) p 85.

17. Zim (1987) p 43.

18. Surrey's poem was copied out at the head of Wyatt's own manuscript of his paraphrases of the seven penitential psalms, probably by John Harington of Stepney, a member of Henry VIII's household from about 1538 to 1545, who came into possession of the manuscript some time after Wyatt's death. See Hughey, R., ed. (1960) *The Arundel Harington Manuscript of Tudor Poetry*. 2 vols, Columbus, Ohio: Ohio State University Press, 1 pp 63–7.

19. The quotation is from Dowling (1987) p 40.

20. For a letter by the future bishop John Hooper which mentions Wyatt as one of the 'chiefe upholders of the gospel', see Dowling (1987) p 40.

21. Brigden, S. (1994) 'Henry Howard, Earl of Surrey and the "Conjured League" '. *The Historical Journal* 37: 507–37, (p 509).

22. My view of the psalm paraphrases is close to that of Reb. p 454: 'Wyatt departs from Aretino in order . . . to create a shape for the whole work that presents a Reformed Christian's view of the individual's experience of redemption rather than a Roman Catholic's.' Discussions of Wyatt's psalms, and his use of Aretino, may be found in Mason, H. A. (1959) *Humanism and Poetry in the Early Tudor Period: An Essay*. London: Routledge & Kegan Paul, pp 212–13; Twombly, R. G. (1970) 'Thomas Wyatt's paraphrase of the penitential psalms of David'. *Texas Studies in Literature and Language* 12: 345–80; Zim (1987) pp 43–70; and Halasz, A. (1988) 'Wyatt's David'. *Texas Studies in Literature and Language* 30: 320–44.

23. See, for example, Mason (1959) p 204; *LL* p 256; Greenblatt, S. (1980) *Renaissance Self-Fashioning: From More to Shakespeare*. Chicago: University of Chicago Press, p 121.

24. Fox, A. (1989) *Politics and Literature in the Reigns of Henry VII and Henry VIII*. Oxford: Basil Blackwell, pp 280–5 argues that the context for the paraphrases is Wyatt's enforced repudiation of Elizabeth Darrell in 1541.

25. Aretino (1536) *I Sette Salmi*. Venice: Francesco Marcolini da Forli, sig. Aiii^{v}.

26. Kirkpatrick, R. (1995) *English and Italian Literature from Dante to Shakespeare: A Study of Source, Analogue and Divergence*. London: Longman, p 138.

27. Aretino (1536) sig. Mii^{v}.

28. Throughout my discussion of Wyatt's psalms, I am indebted to the edition by Baron, H. V. (1977) 'Sir Thomas Wyatt's seven penitential psalms: a study of

textual and source materials' (unpublished doctoral thesis: University of Cambridge). Most of my quotations from Aretino, and all of those from Wyatt's other sources, are taken from her edition of the psalm paraphrases, which usefully cites sources in footnotes below the text. References to this edition will be given in parentheses in my text after quotations from Aretino. Passages from Aretino not given by Baron will be taken from the 1536 Venice edition of *I Sette Salmi*. For ease of reference, I shall give signature references to this edition in parenthesis after references to Baron's thesis. All translations from Aretino are mine. The passage referred to here is on p 278 of Baron's edition, and sig. D.iv^{r} of the 1536 edition.

29. Wyatt's main sources, apart from Aretino, have been identified as Johannes Campensis's *Enchiridion Psalmorum* (1st edn 1533), Cardinal Cajetan's *Psalmi Davidici* (1st edn 1530), and Bishop John Fisher's (attr.) *This treatise concernynge the fruytfull saynges of Davyd* (1st edn 1508). Mason (1959) first pointed out the importance of Campensis as a source. Baron (1977) discovered the significant contribution of Cajetan's commentary. Her edition contains an introduction, carefully reviewing sources and possible editions that Wyatt may have used.
30. For an earlier version of my argument about David's harp, see Heale, E. (1996) 'Lute and harp in Wyatt's poetry'. In *Sacred and Profane: Secular and Devotional Interplay in Early Modern British Literature*, eds H. Wilcox, R. Todd and A. MacDonald. Amsterdam: VU University Press, pp 3–15.
31. On the eroticism of Aretino's vocabulary, see Twombly (1970) p 354 and Greenblatt (1980) pp 122–3, and for Wyatt's, see Foley, S. M. (1990) *Sir Thomas Wyatt*. Twayne English Authors series. Boston: G. K. Hall & Co., p 88.
32. For example, William Cecil in his preface to Parr, K. (1548) *The Lamentacion of a sinner, made by the moste vertuous Lady quene Catherine, bewailing the ignoraunce of her blind life*. London: Edwarde Whitchurch, sig. A vi^{r}: Christ 'hath . . . borne our sinnes in his body, upon the tree, that we should be delivered from sinne.'
33. The relevant passage by Aretino is 'e percuotendo su le corde della cetera che egli si havea riposta in grembo, la fece lampeggiare nella guisa che lampeggia l'oro al cui splendore accresce luce il lume; e feriti i suoi occhi dal lampo, sentì da quello confortarsi l'anima, tutta lieta per il contritione del core (and striking on the strings of the harp which he had placed in his lap, it made them flash as gold flashes, whose brilliance makes light brighter, from which his soul drew comfort, joyful for his penitence)'. Baron (1977) p 279; Aretino (1536) sig. Div^{r}.
34. I have removed Reb.'s punctuation in ll. 321–2, to bring it closer to the unpunctuated manuscript.
35. See also 'il merito della sua penitentia', which Wyatt translates as 'pardon of his passed offence' (l. 302: Baron (1977) p 278; Aretino (1536) sig. Div^{r}), and the prologue to Psalm 143, where Aretino has David 'sanctificato ne suoi meriti' (p 313; sig. Li^{r}. There is no equivalent in Wyatt).
36. Harrier, R. (1975) *The Canon of Sir Thomas Wyatt's Poetry*. Cambridge, Mass.: Harvard University Press, p 224.

37. The full passage from Aretino reads: 'O Beati Coloro le cui iniquità perdona Iddio, lasciandole impunite, non per le opere della conritione, ne della penitentia, se ben senza esse le colpe nostre non hanno remissione, ma per benificio della gratia sua (O blessed is he whose sins are pardoned by God, leaving him unpunished, not through the works of contrition, nor penitence, although without them our sins have no remission, but by the benefit of his grace).'
38. Lloyd (1856) p 9 and cf. p 97 (my emphases).
39. See MacCulloch (1996) pp 161–5, 185–93 for the disputes surrounding formulation of the 'Ten Articles' and the 'Bishops' Book'.
40. See Baron (1977) p 294 for Cajetan's commentary (praise 'est fructus conversionis iniquorum ad deum'), and for the passage from Aretino (1536) sig. Giv^{v}. For the extent and significance of Wyatt's use of Cajetan, see Baron (1977) pp 246–7.
41. Lock, A. (1560) 'A Meditation of a Penitent Sinner: Written in maner of a Paraphrase upon the 51. Psalme of David'. Appended to her translation of *Sermons of John Calvin, upon the Songe of Ezechias*. London: John Daye, sig. A7^{v}.
42. Becon (1843) p 269.
43. All the biblical quotations are from Tyndale, W. (1989) *New Testament: A modern-spelling edition*, ed. D. Daniell. New Haven, Conn.: Yale University Press, pp 133, 356, 259. Tyndale's translation is not divided into verses. I use modern verse numbering. Baron (1977) p 313 cites the passages from Hebrews and Corinthians as sources.
44. Tyndale (1989) p 166.
45. Becon (1843) p 267. I have inserted the marginal identifications of biblical passages into the text in parentheses.
46. Parr (1548) sig. Dv^{v}.
47. Quoted from a work published in 1546 by the Reformer William Barlow, by Jones, R. F. (1942) 'The moral sense of simplicity'. In *Studies in Honor of F. W. Shipley*. Washington University Studies n.s. Language and Literature 14. St Louis, Mo., p 266. See also King, J. N. (1982) *English Reformation Literature: The Tudor Origins of the Protestant Tradition*. Princeton, NJ: Princeton University Press, pp 138–44.
48. Baron (1977) pp 247 and 314 shows that Wyatt is following a suggestion in Cardinal Cajetan's commentary.
49. Halasz (1988) p 334.
50. It is generally agreed that Surrey paraphrased five chapters of Ecclesiastes. There is also agreement that Surrey paraphrased four psalms: Psalm 8, which was probably written well before the events of 1546, and Psalms 88, 73 and 55, associated with Surrey's final imprisonment. In recent years it has been suggested that paraphrases of Psalms 31 and 51, also in Poulter's measure, printed in a collection of *c.*1550, may also be by Surrey. See Huttar, C. A. (1965) 'Poems by Surrey and others in a printed miscellany circa 1550'. *English*

Miscellany 16: 9–18, and Ruddick, M. (1975) 'Two notes on Surrey's psalms'. *Notes and Queries* n.s. xxii: 291–4. My own view is that these paraphrases are unlikely to be by Surrey, both from the point of view of their topics and the quality of their verse.

51. Appropriately, Pico della Mirandola, in his famous *Oration: On the Dignity of Man* (first published 1486), quotes from this psalm. See Davies, S., ed. (1978) *Renaissance Views of Man*. Manchester University Press, p 66 and n 7.
52. Bale (1849) p 240.
53. Mason (1959) p 244 first pointed out Askew's use of Surrey's paraphrase. For Anne Askew's trial and its significance, see Dowling (1987) pp 69–70, and Brigden (1994) p 525, who suggests a number of channels through which Surrey's paraphrase might have reached Anne Askew.
54. Bale (1849) p 238.
55. Brigden (1994) p 521.
56. My reading of the psalms agrees extensively with that of Sessions, W. A. (1996) 'Surrey's psalms in the Tower'. In *Sacred and Profane: Secular and Devotional Interplay in Early Modern British Literature*, eds H. Wilcox, R. Todd and A. MacDonald. Amsterdam: VU University Press, pp 16–31.
57. The lines from chapter 5 are quoted from Hughey (1960) 1 nos. 89 ll. 54–8 and 90 ll. 1–2, 5–8 (with my punctuation and some minor textual emendments). Jones's edition does not contain Surrey's paraphrase of Ecclesiastes 5. Mason (1959) pp 241–2 first pointed out the echoes of Wyatt's penitential psalms in these lines.
58. Hughey (1960) 2 pp 102–4.
59. Nott 2 p 580. Nott first pointed out that Surrey echoes lines from Wyatt's *strambotto* in Psalm 88. It is possible that the psalm this preface accompanied was in fact Psalm 37, but see Hughey (1960) 2 p 245.
60. While Surrey's lines echo Wyatt, they also follow closely at this point the imagery of Campensis's Latin commentary: see Jones's notes p 159.
61. Brigden (1994) p 524 and Sessions (1996) p 24. The portrait is British Museum Print 1868–8–22–2394. It is illustrated in Hind, A. M. (1952) *Engraving in England in the Sixteenth & Seventeenth Centuries*. 2 vols, Cambridge: Cambridge University Press, vol. 1 *The Tudor Period*, plate 9. Hind p 5 warns that, however suggestive the portrait might be, there is no evidence that Mastys visited England or saw Henry for himself.
62. Bale (1849) p 184.
63. Ibid p 140.
64. For connections between eminent court ladies, including the Duchess of Richmond, Bale and Askew, see Brigden (1994) p 525. Bennet, H. S. (1970) *English Books and Readers, 1475–1557. Being a Study of the History of the Book Trade from Caxton to the Incorporation of the Stationers' Company* (2nd edn). Cambridge: Cambridge University Press, pp 34–35 and 155, provides evidence of the quantity and speed with which books printed abroad found their way into England.

65. Quoted by Starkey, D. (1991) *The Reign of Henry VIII: Personalities and Politics*. London: Collins and Brown, p 140; see also his p 150.
66. Quoted from *LL* pp 273–6. Blage's poems were copied by the poet into the 'Blage MS': see O'Keefe, S. (1986) 'T.C.D.MS.160: a Tudor miscellany' (unpublished M. Litt. thesis, Trinity College, Dublin), pp 207–10. O'Keefe's view is that Muir's edition in *LL* runs two separate poems into one. In her edition, the first poem begins 'A voice I have' and the second 'Holde over us o lord'.
67. O'Keefe (1986) p 208 reads this line as 'thy wrathefull love apon us tho thou bende'. Muir's reading in *LL* seems the more likely.
68. Sessions (1996) p 26.
69. See Rex (1993) p 126. No more copies were printed after 1541, and its use for private reading was limited to the gentry, the clergy and merchants.
70. Brigden (1994) pp 535–6.
71. For example, Fals Semblant in Chaucer's translation of *The Romaunt of the Rose* refers to Frere Wolf, and claims that friars deceive the simple like wolves in sheep's clothing: Chaucer, G. (1974) *The Works*, ed. F. N. Robinson. Oxford: Oxford University Press, ll. 6259–71 and 6421–8. See also an example from Gower cited in Miller, R. P., ed. (1977) *Chaucer: Sources and Backgrounds*. Oxford: Oxford University Press, p 267.
72. The biblical quotation is from the 1539 'Great Bible'.
73. The copy of this paraphrase in the Arundel-Harington manuscript ends with an English translation of the Latin line: 'cast thie care upon the Lord and he shall norishe thee'. Hughey (1960) 1 no. 84.
74. Surrey's second son, Henry Howard, Earl of Northampton, identified this poem as 'the last thinge that he wrote before his ende': cited by Sessions (1996) p 27 fn 16. See Jones's note, pp 130–1.
75. Smith, Sir T. (1963) *Literary and Linguistic Works*. 3 vols. Stockholm Studies in English XII, ed. B. Danielsson. Stockholm: Amquist & Wiksell, vol 1 *Certaigne Psalmes or Songues of David Translated into English Meter by Sir Thomas Smith, knight*, pp 35–7. For a discussion of Smith's psalms, see Zim (1987) pp 98–103.
76. For Surrey's use of the image, see Brigden (1994) p 534 and idem (1996) ' "The Shadow That You Know" ': Sir Thomas Wyatt and Sir Francis Bryan at court and in embassy'. *The Historical Journal* 39(1): 1–31 (p 2).

Epilogue: Tottel and after

Much of the poetry of Surrey, Wyatt and a host of anonymous contemporaries was printed in Richard Tottel's *Songes and Sonettes* (usually known as *Tottel's Miscellany*) in June 1557. This volume was a crucial literary and cultural event, enjoying at least nine reprints before the end of the century, with three separate printings in the first year alone.[1] I shall conclude my study by briefly considering this transition from manuscript into print and its implications for subsequent perceptions of the poetry of Wyatt, Surrey and their generation of 'courtly makers'.

Tottel brought the manuscript texts he printed to a new audience, but he also subtlely altered their significance and, often less subtlely, their form. In Wyatt's case he polished the poems, rendering the diction more decorous, and altering irregular rhythms to produce regular iambic metres.[2] He also added titles to the poems he printed, fixing most of them in a context of conventionalized courtly devotion: 'The wavering lover willeth and dreadeth, to move his desire'; 'The lover hopeth of better chance'; 'The lover refused lamenteth his estate'. Such titles remove any suggestion of a political dimension to the poems.[3] The combined effect of such polishing and entitling is to transform the verse into glamorous examples and models of the kind of polite gestures and responses deemed current in the elegant pastime of cultivated courtiers. The social status of Surrey (whose name is the only one advertised on the title page of *Tottel's Miscellany*) was no doubt a shrewd selling point. As a recent scholar has argued, the *Miscellany* and its imitators 'marketed exclusivity . . . [they] functioned as conduct books . . . because they demonstrated to more common audiences the poetic practices entertained by graceful courtly readers and writers'.[4] Tottel's volume helped to inaugurate a new age of wider access to privileged knowledge and information, and in the process manufactured a romantic and fictive version of the elitism he disseminated.

Tottel's titles develop an embryonic persona, that of 'the lover', whose conventional amours appear to feed a growing desire in the mid- to later sixteenth century for erotic narratives in which the passion and plaint expressed in songs and sonnets are fictitiously presented as the passionate expressions of exemplary, even genuine, amorous liaisons.[5] Thus although the *Miscellany*'s titles appear to place the poems in the kind of social context within which they were produced, they actually distort the witty and essentially anonymous or generic nature of the poems within a system of manuscript exchange and sharing. Part of the success of *Tottel's Miscellany* may have been that while offering models of taste to its upwardly mobile customers, it made courtly culture more palatable to a growing Protestant suspicion of insincerity and verbal manipulation by constructing little narratives in which the poems play an apparently self-expressive role.

The influence of Tottel's packaging of courtly verse can be clearly seen in an important and influential volume, *A Hundreth Sundrie Flowres*, published anonymously in 1573 although it was in fact by the poet George Gascoigne. Like Tottel, Gascoigne's printed collection mimics aspects of a manuscript compilation, but adds circumstantial headnotes which pretend the poems are genuine overtures and responses in real courtly situations.[6] In a typical, but curiously improbable, combination, a version of Wyatt's witty and misogynist 'My lute awake' (Reb. cix; see Chapter 3, p 81) is introduced as 'A Lady being both wronged by false suspect, and also wounded by the durance of hir husband, doth thus bewray her grief'.[7] Phrases from Wyatt's poem find themselves combined with echoes of Surrey's complaint, in the voice of his wife, 'Good ladies, ye that have your pleasures in exile' (Jones no. 24), to produce the pathos of a patient Griselda:

> Good Ladies yet lend you me some relief,
> And beare a parte to ease me of my paine.
> My sortes are such, that wayng well *sortes: fates;*
> my trueth, *waying: weighing*
> They might provoke the craggy rocks to rueth . . . *rueth: pity*
> But thou my Lute, be still now take thy rest,
> Repose thy bones uppon this bed of downe:
>
> (ll.51–4, 57–8)

Here a provocative courtly balet is adapted to a taste for sentiment and sad stories of spurned virtue.

Despite, or perhaps because of, the effect of 'real' amorous occasions for which such poems strive, Gascoigne's 1573 volume stirred up that Reformist/Protestant disapproval of 'lascivious, wanton and unclean ballads' (see Chapter 5, p 154). In a preface to a second and chastened edition, Gascoigne acknowledged the hostility *A Hundreth Sundrie Flowres* had aroused among the graver sort and rearranged his materials to make the moral lessons they taught more evident.[8] A curious expression of such Reformed sobriety was John Hall's *The Couurte of Vertue* (1565), in which the courtly songs and sonnets disseminated by the likes of Tottel were less ambiguously reclaimed for the cause of virtue. In this volume Wyatt's 'My lute awake' is transformed into a godly song with the heading 'A song of the lute in the praise of God, and dispraise of Idolatrie'. It begins: 'My lute awake and praise the lord.'[9]

Tottel's packaging of the courtly balets of Wyatt, Surrey and other gentlemen fuelled a double desire by the upwardly mobile to imitate the cultural mannerisms of an elite and, at the same time, to misread the poetry as self-expressive and biographical. Courtly verse, in manuscript circulation or sung to an existing tune, is easily separated from its originating author and occasion, if any, but in mid-century printed versions the poems are characteristically presented as the genuine and unique expression of love or its refusal by a particular lover to his lady, or vice versa. Since such lyrics normally use the first person, persona and writer easily become confused, and a slippage occurs in which the poet becomes the amorous hero of his own poem.

The most dramatic example of this taste for poetic 'sincerity' and naive autobiography is the phenomenon of the love of the noble Earl of Surrey for the fair Geraldine.[10] In the first edition of *Tottel's Miscellany* one of Surrey's sonnets, an occasional poem to a nine-year-old child, is headed 'Description and praise of his love of Geraldine' (Rollins 1 no. 8). In 1594, Thomas Nashe's novel *The Unfortunate Traveller, or, The Life of Jack Wilton* turned this 'love' into an elaborate narrative of the love-sick earl's travels to Florence to defend Geraldine's honour against all comers. This ludicrous version of the supposed romance was modulated into a different key a little later by Michael Drayton in *Englands Heroicall Epistles* (1597–9), which contain a pair of verse letters in which Surrey addresses Geraldine from Florence and she replies. Here, as in Nashe's novel, Surrey is imagined spontaneously composing verse to his love and carving his lines on the trunk of a tree.[11] In his notes to the epistles, Drayton claims that a number of Surrey's poems are about his love for Geraldine. Even Wyatt's 'Tagus, farewell' is tentatively ascribed to Surrey to support the fictional narrative.[12]

Drayton's Surrey is an embodiment of a recurring late Elizabethan and early Stuart theme, that of the idealized nobleman whose chivalric courage and prowess are matched by high moral virtue and love of the muses, a synthesis which Mervyn James in his study of the changing honour codes of the sixteenth century has described as reaching its apotheosis in the late Elizabethan 'cult of honour' centred on such heroes as Sir Philip Sidney.[13] Sidney was in fact hailed as the true successor of Surrey in a lengthy poem of praise attached to an emblem linking fame, glory and poetry in Geoffrey Whitney's *A Choice of Emblemes* (1586).[14] It is probable that Surrey represented for Sidney a charismatic model of what Sessions has called a 'hero-poet', combining chivalric idealism and Renaissance eloquence.[15] For Sidney, *Tottel's Miscellany* was quite simply Surrey's book: 'in the Earl of Surrey's lyrics many things tasting of a noble birth, and worthy of a noble mind'.[16]

In his sonnet sequence *Astrophil and Stella* (*c.*1582), Sidney combines, with great sophistication, some of the characteristics of manuscript circulation with the new taste for poems as autobiographical, arising out of a sentimental narrative. The sequence tells the story of Astrophil's passion for Stella in which the courtly lyrics are presented as the spontaneous self-expression of Astrophil, but the relationship between writer (Sidney) and persona, historical fact and fiction, is teasingly and tantalizingly hinted at and veiled. The sequence, with its witty and ironic game-playing with its readers, belongs not to print culture but to coterie manuscript circulation in which personal knowledge of Sidney and Penelope Rich (Stella) would have added to the game of fact and fiction which is lost to a print readership. It was not, in fact, printed until 1592, after Sidney's death.

In spite of Sidney's admiration of Surrey's noble example, the technical achievement of the sonnets of *Astrophil and Stella*, with their use of irony, their colloquialisms and spoken rhythms and their often comic mimicking of a dramatic immediacy, suggest, in fact, at least as great a debt to Wyatt's example. However, it is not Sidney but John Donne who is closest in spirit to Wyatt in the late sixteenth century.[17] With Donne, whose secular poetry also circulated in manuscript among witty and ambitious men, conscious of themselves as an intellectual elite yet with an insecure hold on social success, we encounter once again the conditions that helped to shape Wyatt's courtly balets some half a century earlier. In Marotti's view, Donne's secular poetry works much as I have described Wyatt's as doing: 'by handling the role of courtly lyricist with a kind of critical daring and sophisticated assertiveness, Donne enacted a (wished-for) social autonomy even through the very literary vocabulary that signaled hierarchy and deference. . . . [poetic] persuasions to love reverse the passivity, dependence, and frustration competitive young men normally experienced'.[18]

Paradoxically, for all their teasing engagement with the reader and their ironizing of the relationship between writer and persona, the colloquial immediacy, irregular spoken rhythms and indecorums of the verse of Wyatt, Donne and the Sidney of *Astrophil and Stella* constitute precisely that '*energia*' or 'forcibleness' which Sidney praised as the rhetorical sign of sincerity and feeling and which he considered the amorous courtly lyric of his time had come to lack, rendering it lifeless.[19] May it be precisely that *energia*, an artful artlessness that mimics spontaneity, that has so successfully seduced so many modern readers into reading the poetic 'I' of Wyatt's verse in the same spirit that Drayton read Surrey's, as romance autobiography?

NOTES

1. Rollins 2 pp 7–36. Rollins provides a detailed account of the volume, its contributors and its history.
2. Rollins 2 pp 94–6. Compare, for example, 'Sometime I fled the fire' (Reb. lv, Rollins 1 no. 71) and the last lines of 'They flee from me' (Reb. lxxx and Rollins 1 no. 52).
3. Kamholtz, J. Z. (1979) 'Thomas Wyatt's poetry: the politics of love'. *Criticism* 20: 349–65 (p 351). Kamholtz gives the following examples of arguably political poems with amorous titles by Tottel: 'He is not dead' (Reb. xlii), 'Caesar when that the traitor of Egypt' (Reb. ix), 'The pillar perished' (Reb. xxix), 'It may be good' (Reb. lxxxv) and 'Whoso list to hunt' (Reb. xi). See my discussion on pp 53–4 above.
4. Wall, W. (1993) *The Imprint of Gender: Authorship and Publication in the Renaissance.* Ithaca, NY: Cornell University Press, p 97.
5. For discussion of medieval and sixteenth-century use of romance narrative to link courtly verse, see Gottfried, R. (1967) 'Autobiography and art: an Elizabethan borderland'. In *Literary Criticism and Historical Understanding. Selected Papers from the English Institute*, ed. P. Damon. New York: Columbia University Press, pp 109–34; Wartenkin, G. (1984) 'The meeting of the Muses: Sidney and the mid-Tudor poets'. In *Sir Philip Sidney and the Interpretation of Renaissance Culture: The Poet in His Time and Ours*, eds G. F. Waller and M. D. Moore. London: Croom Helm, pp 17–33; Boffey, J. (1985) *Manuscripts of English Courtly Love Lyrics in the Later Middle Ages*. Woodbridge, Suffolk: D. S. Brewer, p 66; Marotti, A. (1986) *John Donne, Coterie Poet.* Madison, Wisconsin: The University of Wisconsin Press, p 13, 295 n 36, and

idem (1995) *Manuscript, Print and the English Renaissance Lyric*. Ithaca, NY, and London: Cornell University Press, p 219.

6. For Gascoigne's imitation of aspects of a manuscript, see Wall (1993) pp 243–4 and Marotti (1995) pp 222–3.
7. Gascoigne, G. (1970) *A Hundred Sundry Flowers (1573)*. Menston, Yorks.: Scolar Press, p 330.
8. Disapproval may have been specifically directed against an erotic prose romance which Gascoigne included in *A Hundreth Sundrie Flowres*, 'The Aventures of Master F.J.', in which courtly balets are embedded in the form of letters and complaints by the chief protagonists.
9. Hall, J. (1961) *The Court of Virtue (1565)*, ed. R. A. Fraser. London: Routledge & Kegan Paul, p 169.
10. The evidence and development of the Geraldine myth are most fully explored in Rollins 2 pp 71–5.
11. Drayton, M. (1931–41) *The Works*, eds W. Hebel, K. Tillotson and B.H. Newdigate. 5 vols, Oxford: The Shakespeare Head Press, 2 p 283 ll. 215–26.
12. Ibid 2 p 287: 'Tagus, farewell' was 'done by the said Earle, or Sir Francis Brian'.
13. James, M. E. (1986) *Society, Politics and Culture: Studies in Early Modern England*. Cambridge: Cambridge University Press, p 392.
14. Whitney, G. (1969) *A Choice of Emblemes (1586)*, ed. J. Horden. English Emblem Books No. 3. Menston, Yorks.: Scolar Press, pp 196–7. Whitney dedicated his book to Sidney's uncle, the Earl of Leicester.
15. Sessions, W. A. (1994) 'Surrey's Wyatt: Autumn 1542 and the new poet'. In *Rethinking the Henrician Era: Essays on Early Tudor Texts and Contexts*, ed. P. C. Herman. Urbana and Chicago: University of Illinois Press, p 189. Sessions explores Surrey's part in developing this ideal. See especially pp 178–9 for his discussion of Surrey's influence on Sidney.
16. Sidney, Sir P. (1973) *An Apology for Poetry, or The Defense of Poesy*, ed. G. Shepherd. Manchester: Manchester University Press, p 133.
17. See Chambers, E. K. (1933) *Sir Thomas Wyatt and Some Collected Studies*. London: Sidgwick & Jackson, p 130 and Thomson, P., ed. (1974) *Wyatt: The Critical Heritage*. London: Routledge & Kegan Paul, p 148. See also Marotti (1986) pp 11–12. Note that the title *Songs and Sonnets* was not given to Donne's shorter erotic lyrics until the second posthumous edition of 1635.
18. Marotti (1986) pp 88–9.
19. Sidney (1973) pp 137–8 complained that 'many of such writings as come under the banner of unresistable love; if I were a mistress, would never persuade me they were in love; so coldly they apply fiery speeches, as men that had rather read lovers' writings . . . than that in truth they feel those passions, which easily (as I think) may be betrayed by that same forcibleness or *energia* (as the Greeks call it) of the writer'.

Bibliography

EDITIONS OF PRIMARY TEXTS AND DOCUMENTS

See p vii for abbreviations for and full details of frequently cited editions.

(1539) *The Bible in English*. London: Richard Grafton and Edward Whitchurch.

Alamanni, L. (1532) *Opere Toscane*. 2 vols, Leyden: Sebast. Gryphius.

Amyot, T. (1831) 'Transcript of an Original Manuscript, containing a Memorial from George Constantyne to Thomas Lord Cromwell'. *Archaeologia* 23: 50–78.

Anon. (1555) *The Institucion of a Gentleman*. London: T. Marshe.

Aretino (1536) *I Sette Salmi*. Venice: Francesco Marcolini da Forlì.

Ascham, R. (1904) *The English Works*, ed. W. A. Wright. Cambridge: Cambridge University Press.

Bale, J. (1849) *Select Works*. The Parker Society. Cambridge: Cambridge University Press.

Baron, H. V. (1977) 'Sir Thomas Wyatt's seven penitential psalms: a study of textual and source materials' (unpublished doctoral thesis: University of Cambridge).

Becon, T. (1843) *The Early Works*, ed. J. Ayre. The Parker Society. Cambridge: Cambridge University Press.

Bielby, N., ed. (1976) *Three Early Tudor Poets: A Selection from Skelton, Wyatt and Surrey*. Wheaton, Exeter: Wheaton Studies in Literature.

Brant, S. (1874) *The Ship of Fools* (1509), trans. Alexander Barclay, ed. T. H. Jamieson. 2 vols, Edinburgh: William Paterson.

Brinklow, H. (1874) *The Lamentacyon of a Christen Agaynst the Cytye of London, made by Roderigo Mors (1545 edition)*, ed. J. M. Cowper. Early English Text Society e.s. 22. London: Kegan Paul, Trench, Trübner & Co. Ltd.

Castiglione, B. (1976) *The Book of the Courtier*, trans. George Bull (2nd edn). Harmondsworth: Penguin.

Chaucer, G. (1532) *Workes*. London: William Thynne.

(1974) *The Works*, ed F. N. Robinson. Oxford: Oxford University Press.

Cicero (1939) *Orator*, trans. H. M. Hubbell. Loeb Classical Library. Cambridge, Mass.: William Heinemann Ltd and Harvard University Press.

Daalder, J., ed. (1975) *Sir Thomas Wyatt: Collected Poems*. Oxford: Oxford University Press.

Davies, S., ed. (1978) *Renaissance Views of Man*. Manchester: Manchester University Press.

Dowling, M., ed. (1990) 'William Latymer's chronicle of Anne Bulleyne'. In *Camden Miscellany* 30, Camden Society, 4th series, vol 39. London: Royal Historical Society, pp 23–65.

Drayton, M. (1931–41) *The Works*, eds W. Hebel, K. Tillotson and B. H. Newdigate. 5 vols, Oxford: The Shakespeare Head Press.

Elyot, Sir T. (1962) *The Book named The Governor*, ed. S. E. Lehmberg. Everyman Library. London: Dent & Co.

(1967) *Four Political Treatises*. Facsimile reproduction, intro. L. Gottesman. Gainesville, Fla.: Scholar Press Facsimiles & Reprints.

Erasmus, D. (1982) *Adages I.i.1 to I.v.100*, trans. Margaret Mann Phillips. *Collected Works of Erasmus* vol 31. Toronto: University of Toronto Press.

(1991) *Adages II.vii.1 to III.iii.100*, trans. R. A. B. Mynors. *Collected Works of Erasmus* vol 34. Toronto: University of Toronto Press.

Froissart, J. (1913) *The Chronicles*, trans. John Bourchier, Lord Berners, ed. G. C. MacCauley. London: Macmillan and Co.

Gascoigne, G. (1907–10) *The Complete Works*, ed. J. W. Cunliffe. 2 vols, Cambridge: Cambridge University Press.

(1970) *A Hundred Sundry Flowers (1573)*. Menston, Yorks.: Scolar Press.

Greene, R. L., ed. (1977) *Early English Carols*. Oxford: Clarendon Press.

Guevara, A. de (1548) *A Dispraise of the life of a Courtier, and a commendation of the life of the labouryng man*, trans. Sir Francis Bryan. London: R. Grafton

Habenicht, R. E., ed. (1963) *John Heywood's 'A Dialogue of Proverbs'*. Berkeley: University of California Press.

Hall, E. (1965) *Chronicle, Containing the History of England* (reprint of the 1809 edn). New York: AMS Press Inc.

Hall, J. (1961) *The Court of Virtue (1565)*, ed. R. A. Fraser. London: Routledge and Kegan Paul.

Hammond, E. P., ed. (1927) *English Verse between Chaucer and Surrey*. Durham, NC: Duke University Press.

Harrier, R. (1975) *The Canon of Sir Thomas Wyatt's Poetry*. Cambridge, Mass.: Harvard University Press.

Hawes, S. (1928) *The Pastime of Pleasure*, ed. W. E. Mead. Early English Text Society OS 173. Oxford: Oxford University Press.

(1975) *The Works*, intro. J. Frank Delmar, NY: Scolar's Facsimiles & Reprints.

Henryson, R. (1958) *The Poems and Fables* (2nd revised edn), ed. H. H. Wood. Edinburgh and London: Oliver and Boyd.

Horace (1988) *The Odes and Epodes*, trans. C. E. Bennett. The Loeb Classical Library. London: William Heinemann Ltd.

Hughey, R., ed. (1960) *The Arundel Harington Manuscript of Tudor Poetry*. 2 vols, Columbus, Ohio: Ohio State University Press.

Jansen, S. L. and Jordan, K. H., eds (1991) *The Welles Anthology: MS Rawlinson C.813*. Binghampton, NY: Medieval and Renaissance Texts and Studies.

Jonson, B. (1975) *The Complete Poems*, ed. G. Parfitt. Harmondsworth: Penguin Books Ltd.

Juvenal (1967) *The Sixteen Satires*, trans. Peter Green. Harmondsworth: Penguin Books Ltd.

Kerrigan, J., ed. (1991) *Motives of Woe. Shakespeare and "Female Complaint". A Critical Anthology*. Oxford: Clarendon Press.

Kinsman, R. S. (1978–79) ' "The Proverbes of Salmon Do Playnly Declare": a sententious poem on wisdom and governance, ascribed to Sir Francis Bryan'. *Huntington Library Quarterly* 42: 279–312.

Latimer, H. (1906) *Sermons*. Everyman's Library. London: J. M. Dent and Co.

Lloyd, C., ed. (1856) *Formularies of Faith, put forth by authority during the reign of Henry VIII.* Oxford: Oxford University Press.

Loades, D. M., ed. (1968) *Papers of George Wyatt Esquire of Boxley Abbey in the County of Kent*. Camden Fourth Series, vol 5. London: Royal Historical Society.

Lock, A. (1560) 'A Meditation of a Penitent Sinner: Written in maner of a Paraphrase upon the 51. Psalme of David'. In *Sermons of John Calvin, upon the Songe of Ezechias*. London: John Daye.

Lull, R. (1926) *The Book of the Ordre of Chyvalry*, trans. William Caxton. Early English Text Society, OS 168, ed T. P. Bayles. London: Oxford University Press.

Merrill, L. R., ed. (1969) *Nicholas Grimald: The Life and Poems* (2nd edn), reprinted Archon Books.

Miller, R. P., ed. (1977) *Chaucer: Sources and Backgrounds*. Oxford: Oxford University Press.

More, Sir T. (1965) *Utopia*, trans. G. C. Richards. In *The Yale Edition of the Complete Works of St. Thomas More*, vol 4, eds E. Surtz and J. H. Hexter. New Haven, Conn.: Yale University Press.

Muir, K. (1947) 'Unpublished poems in the Devonshire MS'. *Proceedings of the Leeds Philosophical Society: Literary and Historical Section* 6: 253–82.

(1961) *Unpublished Poems by Sir Thomas Wyatt and his Circle: Edited from the Blage Manuscript*. Liverpool: Liverpool University Press.

O'Keefe, S. (1986) 'T.C.D.MS.160: a Tudor miscellany' (unpublished M.Litt. thesis, Trinity College, Dublin).

Osborne, J. M., ed. (1962) *The Autobiography of Thomas Whythorne. Modern Spelling Edition*. Oxford: Clarendon Press.

Parr, K. (1548) *The Lamentacion of a synner, made by the moste vertuous Lady quene Catherine, bewailyng the ignoraunce of her blind life*. London: Edwarde Whitchurch.

Petrarca, F. (1951) *Rime, Trionfi, e Poesie Latine*, eds F. Neri, G. Martellotti, E. Bianchi and N. Sapegno. La Letteratura Italiana. Storia e Testi vol 6. Milano e Napoli: Riccardo Ricciardi Editore.

Puttenham, G. (1968) *The Arte of English Poesie (1589).* Menston, Yorks.: The Scolar Press Ltd.

Reed, E. B. (1910) 'The sixteenth-century lyrics in Add. MS. 18,752'. *Anglia* 33: 344–69.

Seneca (1960–1) *Tragedies,* trans. Frank Justus Miller. Loeb Classical Library. 2 vols, Cambridge, Mass.: William Heinemann Ltd and Harvard University Press.

Serafino (1516) *Opere.* Firenze: Philippo di Giunta.

Sidney, Sir P. (1973) *An Apology for Poetry, or The Defense of Poesy,* ed. G. Shepherd. Manchester: Manchester University Press.

Singer, S. W., ed. (1825) *The Life of Cardinal Wolsey by George Cavendish.* 2 vols, Chiswick, London: Harding, Triphook and Lepard.

Skelton, J. (1983) *The Complete English Poems,* ed. J. Scattergood. New Haven, Conn.: Yale University Press.

Smith, Sir T. (1963) *Literary and Linguistic Works.* 3 vols. Stockholm Studies in English XII, ed. B. Danielsson. Stockholm: Amquist & Wiksell, vol 1 *Certaigne Psalmes or Songues of David Translated into English Meter by Sir Thomas Smith, knight.*

Stevens, J., ed. (1962) *Music at the Court of Henry VIII.* Musica Britannica xviii. London: Stainer & Bell Ltd.

Taverner, R. (1956) *Proverbes or Adages by Desiderius Erasmus: Gathered out of the Chiliades and Englished* (a facsimile of the 1569 edition). Gainesville, Fla.: Scholars' Facsimiles & Reprints.

Tilley, M. P. (1950) *A Dictionary of Proverbs in England in the Sixteenth and Seventeenth Centuries.* Ann Arbor: University of Michigan Press.

Tydeman, W., ed. (1970) *English Poetry 1400–1580.* London: Heinemann.

Tyndale, W. (1989) *New Testament: A modern-spelling edition,* ed. D. Daniell. New Haven, Conn.: Yale University Press.

Vowell, J. (1840) 'The life of Sir Peter Carewe of Mohun Ottery, Co. Devon'. *Archaeologia* 28: 91–151.

Walton, I. (1973) *The Lives.* Oxford: Oxford University Press.

Whiting, B. J. and Whiting, H. W., eds (1968) *Proverbs, Sentences, and Proverbial Phrases from English Writings Mainly Before 1500.* Cambridge, Mass.: Harvard University Press.

Whitney, G. (1969) *A Choice of Emblemes (1586),* ed. J. Horden. English Emblem Books No. 3. Menston, Yorks.: Scolar Press.

Wilson, T. (1994) *The Art of Rhetoric (1560),* ed P. E. Medine. Pennsylvania: Pennsylvania State University Press.

Wright, T., ed. (1965) *Political Poems and Songs relating to English History* (1st edn 1859). 2 vols, Wiesbaden: Kraus Reprint Ltd.

SECONDARY STUDIES

Anglo, S. (1977) 'The courtier. The Renaissance and changing ideals'. In *The Courts of Europe. Politics, Patronage and Royalty 1400–1800,* ed. A. G. Dickens. London: Thames and Hudson, pp 33–53.

Atkins, J. W. H. (1968) *English Literary Criticism: The Renascence* (2nd edn). London: Methuen & Co. Ltd.

Bailey, D. S. (1952) *Thomas Becon and the Reformation of the Church in England*. Edinburgh and London: Oliver and Boyd.

Baron, H. (1989) 'The "Blage" manuscript: the original compiler identified'. *English Manuscript Studies* 1: 85–119.

(1994) 'Mary (Howard) Fitzroy's hand in the Devonshire Manuscript'. *Review of English Studies* n.s. 45: 318–35.

Barratt, A. (1992) *Women's Writing in Middle English*. London: Longman.

Bates, C. (1992) *The Rhetoric of Courtship in Elizabethan Language and Literature*. Cambridge: Cambridge University Press.

(1993) ' "A mild admonisher": Sir Thomas Wyatt and sixteenth-century satire'. *Huntington Library Quarterly* 56: 243–58.

Bateson, F. W. (1961) *English Poetry and the English Language* (2nd edn). New York: Russell & Russell.

Bennet, H. S. (1970) *English Books and Readers, 1475–1557. Being a Study of the History of the Book Trade from Caxton to the Incorporation of the Stationers' Company* (2nd edn). Cambridge: Cambridge University Press.

Bindoff, S. T., ed. (1982) *The House of Commons 1509–1558*. 3 vols. *The History of Parliament*. London: published for the History of Parliament Trust by Secker & Warburg.

Bloch, H. R. (1991) *Medieval Misogyny and the Invention of Western Romantic Love*. Chicago: University of Chicago Press.

Boffey, J. (1985) *Manuscripts of English Courtly Love Lyrics in the Later Middle Ages*. Woodbridge, Suffolk: D. S. Brewer.

(1993) 'Women authors and women's literacy'. In *Women and Literature in Britain, 1150–1500*, ed. C. M. Meale. Cambridge: Cambridge University Press, pp 159–82.

Bolgar, R. R. (1954) *The Classical Heritage and its Beneficiaries*. Cambridge: Cambridge University Press.

Bond, E. A. (1871) 'Wyatt's Poems'. *The Athenaeum* 2274: 654–5.

Boucher, F. (1967) *A History of Costume in the West*. London: Thames and Hudson.

Brigden, S. (1989) *London and the Reformation*. Oxford: Clarendon Press.

(1994) 'Henry Howard, Earl of Surrey and the "Conjured League" '. *The Historical Journal* 37: 507–37.

(1996) ' "The Shadow That You Know": Sir Thomas Wyatt and Sir Francis Bryan at court and in embassy'. *The Historical Journal* 39(1): 1–31.

Brilliant, A. N. (1971) 'The style of Wyatt's "The Quyete of Mynde" '. *Essays and Studies* 24: 1–21.

Brown, C. and Robbins, R. H. (1943) *The Index of Middle English Verse*. New York: Columbia University Press.

Buchanan, P. (1985) *Margaret Tudor, Queen of Scots*. Edinburgh: Scottish Academic Press.

Canning, M. (1936) *Costume in the Drama of Shakespeare and His Contemporaries*. Oxford: Clarendon Press.

Casady, E. (1938) *Henry Howard, Earl of Surrey*. New York: The Modern Language Association of America.

Caspari, F. (1954) *Humanism and the Social Order in Tudor England*. Chicago: University of Chicago Press.

Cazeaux, I. (1975) *French Music in the Fifteenth and Sixteenth Centuries*. Oxford: Basil Blackwell.

Chambers, E. K. (1933) *Sir Thomas Wyatt and Some Collected Studies*. London: Sidgwick & Jackson.

Clark, P. (1977) *English Provincial Society from the Reformation to the Revolution. Religion, Politics and Society in Kent, 1500–1640*. Hassocks, Sussex: Harvester Press.

Conway, A. (1932) *Henry VII's Relations with Scotland and Ireland 1485–1498*. Cambridge: Cambridge University Press.

Cooper, J. P. (1983) 'Ideas of gentility in early-modern England'. In *Land, Men and Beliefs. Studies in Early-Modern History*, eds G. E. Aylmer and J. S. Morrill. London: The Hambledon Press, pp 46–50.

Crane, M. T. (1986) 'Intret Cato: authority and the epigram in sixteenth-century England'. In *Renaissance Genres: Essays on Theory, History, and Interpretation*, ed. B. K. Lewalski. Harvard English Studies 14. Cambridge, Mass.: Harvard University Press, pp 158–86.

(1993) *Framing Authority: Sayings, Self and Society in Sixteenth-Century England*. Princeton, NJ: Princeton University Press.

Crewe, J. (1991) *Trials of Authorship: Anterior Forms and Poetic Reconstruction from Wyatt to Shakespeare*. Berkeley and Los Angeles: University of California Press.

Daalder, J. (1985a) 'Seneca and Wyatt's second satire'. *Études Anglaises* 38(4): 422–6.

Daalder, J. (1985b) 'Wyatt and "liberty": a postcript'. *Essays in Criticism* 35: 330–6.

Davies, B. M. (1959–60) 'Surrey at Boulogne'. *Huntington Library Quarterly* 23: 339–48.

Doran, S. and Durston, C. (1991) *Princes, Pastors and People: The Church and Religion in England, 1529–1689*. London: Routledge.

Dowling, M. (1986) *Humanism in the Age of Henry VIII*. London: Croom Helm.

(1987) 'The gospel and the court: Reformation under Henry VIII'. In *Protestantism and the National Church in Sixteenth-Century England*, eds P. Lake and M. Dowling. London: Croom Helm, pp 36–77.

Duffy, E. (1992) *The Stripping of the Altars: Traditional Religion in England c.1400–c.1580*. New Haven, Conn.: Yale University Press.

Einstein, A. (1949) *The Italian Madrigal*, trans. Alexander H. Krappe, Roger H. Sessions and Oliver Strunk. 3 vols, Princeton: Princeton University Press.

Elias, N. (1978) *The Civilizing Process*, trans. Edmund Jephcott. 2 vols. Oxford: Basil Blackwell, vol 1 *The History of Manners*.

Estrin, B. L. (1994a) *Laura: Uncovering Gender and Genre in Wyatt, Donne, and Marvell*. Durham, NC, and London: Duke University Press.

(1994b) 'Wyatt's unlikely likenesses: or, has the lady read Petrarch'. In *Rethinking the Henrician Era: Essays on Early Tudor Texts and Contexts*, ed. P. C. Herman. Urbana and Chicago: University of Illinois Press, pp 219–39.

Ferguson, A. B. (1960) *The Indian Summer of English Chivalry: Studies in the Decline and Transformation of Chivalric Idealism*. Durham, NC: Duke University Press.

Ferry, A. (1983) *The "Inward" Language: Sonnets of Wyatt, Sidney, Shakespeare, Donne*. Chicago: University of Chicago Press.

Foley, S. M. (1990) *Sir Thomas Wyatt*. Twayne English Authors series. Boston: G. K. Hall & Co.

Fox, A. (1989) *Politics and Literature in the Reigns of Henry VII and Henry VIII*. Oxford: Basil Blackwell.

Foxwell, A. (1911) *A Study of Sir Thomas Wyatt's Poems*. London: Hodder & Stoughton for University of London Press.

Frankis, P. J. (1956) 'The erotic dream in Middle English lyrics'. *Neuphilologische Mitteilungen* 57: 228–37.

Freccero, C. (1992) 'Politics and aesthetics in Castiglione's *Il Cortegiano*: Book III and the Discourse on Women'. In *Creative Imitation: New Essays on Renaissance Literature in Honor of Thomas M. Greene*, eds D. Quint, M. W. Ferguson, G. W. Pigman III and W. Rebhorn. Binghampton, NY: Medieval and Renaissance Texts and Studies, pp 259–79.

Friedman, D. M. (1966) 'The "thing" in Wyatt's mind'. *Essays in Criticism* 14: 375–81.

Gosselin, E. A. (1976) *The King's Progress to Jerusalem: Some Interpretations of David during the Reformation Period and their Patristic and Medieval Background*. Malibu: Undena Publications.

Gottfried, R. (1967) 'Autobiography and art: an Elizabethan borderland'. In *Literary Criticism and Historical Understanding. Selected Papers from the English Institute*, ed. P. Damon. New York: Columbia University Press, pp 109–34.

Graham, K. J. E. (1994) *The Performance of Conviction. Plainness and Rhetoric in the Early English Renaissance*. Rhetoric and Society. Ithaca, NY: Cornell University Press.

Greenblatt, S. (1980) *Renaissance Self-Fashioning: From More to Shakespeare*. Chicago: University of Chicago Press.

Greene, T. M. (1982) *The Light in Troy: Imitation and Discovery in Renaissance Poetry*. New Haven, Conn.: Yale University Press.

Gunn, S. J. (1987) 'The French wars of Henry VIII'. In *The Origins of War in Early Modern Europe*, ed. J. Black. Edinburgh: John Donald Publishers Ltd, pp 28–51.

(1990) 'Chivalry and the politics of the early Tudor court'. In *Chivalry in the Renaissance*, ed. S. Anglo. Woodbridge, Suffolk: The Boydell Press, pp 107–28.

(1991) 'Tournaments and early Tudor chivalry'. *History Today* 41: 15–21.

(1995) *Early Tudor Government, 1485–1558*. British History in Perspective. Basingstoke: Macmillan.

Haigh, C. (1993) *English Reformations: Religion, Politics, and Society under the Tudors*. Oxford: Clarendon Press.

Halasz, A. (1988) 'Wyatt's David'. *Texas Studies in Literature and Language* 30: 320–44.

Hanson-Smith, E. (1979) 'A woman's view of courtly love: the Findern Anthology: Cambridge University Library MS Ff.16'. *Journal of Women's Studies in Literature* 1: 179–94.

Harvey, E. D. (1992) *Ventriloquized Voices: Feminist Theory and English Renaissance Texts*. London: Routledge.

Heale, E. (1995) 'Women and the courtly love lyric: the Devonshire MS (BL Additional 17492)'. *Modern Language Review* 90: 296–313.

(1996) 'Lute and harp in Wyatt's poetry'. In *Sacred and Profane: Secular and Devotional Interplay in Early Modern British Literature*, eds H. Wilcox, R. Todd and A. MacDonald. Amsterdam: VU University Press, pp 3–15.

Hearn, K. (1995) *Dynasties. Painting in Tudor and Jacobean England, 1530–1630*. Tate Publishing.

Heartz, D. (1964) 'Les gouts réunis or the worlds of the madrigal and the chanson confronted'. In *Chanson and Madrigal 1480–1530*, ed. J. Haar. Cambridge, Mass.: Harvard University Press, pp 88–138.

Heiserman, A. R. (1961) *Skelton and Satire*. Chicago: University of Chicago Press.

Hind, A. M. (1952) *Engraving in England in the Sixteenth & Seventeenth Centuries*. 2 vols, Cambridge: Cambridge University Press, vol. 1 *The Tudor Period*.

Hollander, J. (1961) *The Untuning of the Sky: Ideas of Music in English Poetry, 1500–1700*. Princeton, NJ: Princeton University Press.

Holohan, M. (1993) 'Wyatt, the heart's forest, and the ancient savings'. *English Literary Renaissance* 23: 46–80.

Hunter, G. K. (1970) 'Drab and golden lyrics of the Renaissance'. In *Forms of Lyric: Selected Papers from the English Institute*, ed. R. A. Brower. New York: Columbia University Press, pp 1–18.

Huttar, C. A. (1965) 'Poems by Surrey and others in a printed miscellany circa 1550'. *English Miscellany* 16: 9–18.

Ives, E. W. (1986) *Anne Boleyn*. Oxford: Basil Blackwell.

James, M. E. (1986) *Society, Politics and Culture: Studies in Early Modern England*. Cambridge: Cambridge University Press.

Javitch, D. (1978) *Poetry and Courtliness in Renaissance England*. Princeton, NJ: Princeton University Press.

Jones, A. R. (1987) 'Nets and bridles: early modern conduct books and sixteenth-century women's lyrics'. In *The Ideology of Conduct: Essays on Literature and the History of Sexuality*, eds N. Armstrong and L. Tennenhouse. London: Methuen, pp 39–72.

Jones, R. F. (1942) 'The moral sense of simplicity'. In *Studies in Honor of F. W. Shipley*. Washington University Studies n.s. Language and Literature 14. St Louis, Mo., pp 265–87.

(1953) *The Triumph of the English Language: A Survey of Opinions Concerning the Vernacular from the Introduction of Printing to the Restoration.* Oxford: Oxford University Press.

Kamholtz, J. Z. (1979) 'Thomas Wyatt's poetry: the politics of Love'. *Criticism* 20: 349–65.

Kelly, J. (1984) *Women, History, and Theory.* Chicago: University of Chicago Press.

King, J. N. (1982) *English Reformation Literature: The Tudor Origins of the Protestant Tradition.* Princeton, NJ: Princeton University Press.

(1994) 'Henry VIII as David: the king's image and Reformation politics'. In *Rethinking the Henrician Era: Essays on Early Tudor Texts and Contexts*, ed. P. C. Herman. Urbana and Chicago: University of Illinois Press, pp 78–97.

Kipling, G. (1977) *The Triumph of Honour. Burgundian Origins of the Elizabethan Renaissance.* Leiden: Leiden University Press.

Kirkpatrick, R. (1995) *English and Italian Literature from Dante to Shakespeare: A Study of Source, Analogue and Divergence.* London: Longman.

Klein, L. M. (1992) 'The Petrarchism of Sir Thomas Wyatt reconsidered'. In *The Work of Dissimilitude: Essays from the Sixth Citadel Conference on Medieval and Renaissance Literature*, eds D. G. Allen and R. A. White. Newark: University of Delaware Press, pp 131–47.

Lanham, R. A. (1976) *The Motives of Eloquence: Literary Rhetoric in the Renaissance.* New Haven, Conn.: Yale University Press.

Lewis, C. S. (1954) *English Literature in the Sixteenth Century Excluding Drama.* Oxford History of Literature. Oxford: Oxford University Press.

Loades, D. (1992) *The Tudor Court* (2nd edn). Bangor: Headstart History.

MacCulloch, D. (1996) *Thomas Cranmer: A Life.* New Haven, Conn.: Yale University Press.

MacFie, P. R. (1987) 'Sewing in Ottava Rima: Wyatt's assimilation and critique of a feminist poetic'. *Renaissance Papers*: 25–37.

Manley, L. (1985) 'Proverbs, epigrams, and urbanity in Renaissance London'. *English Literary Renaissance* 15: 247–76.

Marotti, A. E. (1982) ' "Love is not Love" ': Elizabethan sonnet sequences and the social order'. *English Literary History* 49: 396–428.

(1986) *John Donne, Coterie Poet.* Madison, Wisconsin: The University of Wisconsin Press.

(1989) 'Manuscript, print and the English Renaissance lyric'. In *The New Cultural History*, ed. L. Hunt. Berkeley: University of California Press, pp 209–21.

(1995) *Manuscript, Print and the English Renaissance Lyric.* Ithaca and London: Cornell University Press.

Mason, H. A. (1959) *Humanism and Poetry in the Early Tudor Period: An Essay.* London: Routledge & Kegan Paul.

ed. (1986) *Sir Thomas Wyatt: A Literary Portrait.* Bristol: Bristol Classical Press.

Mattingly, G. (1962) *Renaissance Diplomacy.* London: Jonathan Cape.

Maynard, W. (1965) 'The lyrics of Wyatt: poems or songs?' *Review of English Studies* n.s. 16: 1–13 (pt 1) and 245–57 (pt 2).

McCoy, R. (1989) *The Rites of Knighthood : The Literature and Politics of Elizabethan Chivalry*. Berkeley and Los Angeles: University of California Press.

Medine, P. E. (1986) *Thomas Wilson*. Twayne English Authors Series. Boston: G. K. Hall & Co.

Mermel, J. (1978) 'Sir Thomas Wyatt's satires and the humanist debate over court service'. *Studies in the Literary Imagination* 11: 69–79.

Miller, H. (1986) *Henry VIII and the English Nobility*. Oxford: Basil Blackwell.

Molinier, H.-J. (1910) *Mellin de Saint-Gelays (1490?–1558): Étude sur sa Vie et sur ses Oeuvres*. Rodez: Imprimerie Carrère.

Moss, A. (1996) *Printed Commonplace-Books and the Structuring of Renaissance Thought*. Oxford: Clarendon Press.

Mueller, J. M. (1984) *The Native Tongue and the Word: Development in English Prose Style, 1380–1580*. Chicago: University of Chicago Press.

Mumford, I. L. (1957) 'Musical settings to the poems of Henry Howard, Earl of Surrey'. *English Miscellany* 8: 9–20.

(1963) 'Sir Thomas Wyatt's verse and Italian musical sources'. *English Miscellany* 14: 9–26.

(1971) 'Petrarchism and Italian music at the court of Henry VIII'. *Italian Studies* 26: 49–67.

Newman, J. (1957) 'An Italian source for Wyatt's "Madame, withouten many wordes" '. *Renaissance News* 10: 13–15.

Ong, W. S. J. (1971) 'Latin language study as a puberty rite'. In *Rhetoric, Romance, and Technology: Studies in the Interaction of Expression and Culture*. Ithaca, NY, and London: Cornell University Press, pp 113–41.

Parker, P. (1987) *Literary Fat Ladies: Rhetoric, Gender, Property*. London: Methuen.

Patch, H. R. (1927) *The Goddess Fortuna in Medieval Literature*. Cambridge, Mass.: Harvard University Press.

Pearsall, D. (1979) *John Lydgate*. London: Routledge & Kegan Paul.

Peterson, D. L. (1967) *The English Lyric from Wyatt to Donne: A History of the Plain and Eloquent Styles*. Princeton, NJ: Princeton University Press.

Phillips, M. M. (1964) *The "Adages" of Erasmus: A Study with Translations*. Cambridge: Cambridge University Press.

Prizer, W. F. (1989) 'North Italian courts'. In *The Renaissance*, ed. I. Fenlon. Man and Music Series. Englewood Cliffs, NJ: Prentice Hall, pp 133–55.

Reese, G. (1954) *Music in the Renaissance*. London: Dent.

Remley, P. G. (1994) 'Mary Shelton and her Tudor literary milieu'. In *Rethinking the Henrician Era: Essays on Early Tudor Texts and Contexts*, ed. P. C. Herman. Urbana and Chicago: University of Illinois Press, pp 40–77.

Rex, R. (1993) *Henry VIII and the English Reformation.* British History in Perspective. Basingstoke: Macmillan.

Rhodes, N. (1992) *The Power of Eloquence and English Literature.* London: Harvester Wheatsheaf.

Richardson, W. C. (1952) *Tudor Chamber Administration 1485–1547.* Baton Rouge, La: Louisiana University Press.

Richmond, H. (1981) *Puritans and Libertines: Anglo-French Literary Relations in the Reformation.* Berkeley: University of California Press.

Robinson, J. (1982) *The Dukes of Norfolk: A Quincentennial History.* Oxford: Oxford University Press.

Ross, D. M. (1987) 'Sir Thomas Wyatt: proverbs and the poetics of scorn'. *The Sixteenth Century Journal* 18(2): 201–12.

Rosso, A. (1980) *Serafino Aquilano e la Poesia Cortigiana.* Brescia: Morcelliana.

Ruddick, M. (1975) 'Two notes on Surrey's psalms'. *Notes and Queries* n.s. xxii: 291–4.

Salomon, L. B. (1961) *The Devil Take Her! A Study of the Rebellious Lover in English Poetry* (2nd edn). New York: Barnes & Co. Inc.

Scarisbrick, J. J. (1961) 'The first Englishman round the Cape of Good Hope?' *Bulletin of the Institute of Historical Research* 34: 165–77.

(1968) *Henry VIII.* London: Eyre & Spottiswoode.

Schmitz, G. (1990) *The Fall of Women in Early English Narrative Verse.* Cambridge: Cambridge University Press.

Seaton, E. (1956) 'The Devonshire Manuscript and its medieval fragments'. *Review of English Studies* n.s. 7: 55–6.

Sessions, W. A. (1986) *Henry Howard, Earl of Surrey.* Twayne English Authors Series. Boston: G. K. Hall.

(1991) ' "Enough Survives". The Earl of Surrey and European culture'. *History Today* 41(6): 48–54.

(1994) 'Surrey's Wyatt: Autumn 1542 and the new poet'. In *Rethinking the Henrician Era: Essays on Early Tudor Texts and Contexts*, ed. P. C. Herman. Urbana and Chicago: University of Illinois Press, pp 168–192.

(1996) 'Surrey's psalms in the Tower'. In *Sacred and Profane: Secular and Devotional Interplay in Early Modern British Literature*, eds H. Wilcox, R. Todd and A. MacDonald. Amsterdam: VU University Press, pp 16–31.

Smith, H. (1946) 'The art of Sir Thomas Wyatt'. *Huntington Library Quarterly* 9: 323–55.

Southall, R. (1964) *The Courtly Maker: An Essay on the Poetry of Wyatt and his Contemporaries.* Oxford: Basil Blackwell.

Sowerby, R. (1994) *The Classical Legacy in Renaissance Poetry.* London: Longman.

Spearing, A. C. (1985) *Medieval to Renaissance in English Poetry.* Cambridge: Cambridge University Press.

Spiller, M. R. G. (1992) *The Development of the Sonnet: An Introduction.* London: Routledge.

Starkey, D. (1982) 'The court: Castiglione's ideal and Tudor reality, being a discussion of Sir Thomas Wyatt's satire addressed to Sir Francis Bryan'. *Journal of the Warburg and Courtauld Institutes* 45: 232–9.

(1987) 'Intimacy and innovation: the rise of the Privy Chamber, 1485–1547'. In *The English Court: from the Wars of the Roses to the Civil War*, ed. D. Starkey. London: Longman, pp 71–118.

(1990) *Rivals in Power: Lives and Letters of the Great Tudor Dynasties*. London: Macmillan.

(1991) *The Reign of Henry VIII: Personalities and Politics*. London: Collins and Brown.

Stevens, J. (1961) *Music and Poetry in the Early Tudor Court*. London: Methuen.

Thomson, P. (1964) *Sir Thomas Wyatt and His Background*. London: Routledge & Kegan Paul.

ed. (1974) *Wyatt: The Critical Heritage*. London: Routledge & Kegan Paul.

Thornton, P. (1991) *The Italian Renaissance Interior*. New York: Harry N. Abrams Inc.

Trimpi, W. (1962) *Ben Jonson's Poems: A Study of the Plain Style*. Stanford, Ca.: Stanford University Press.

Tromley, F. B. (1980) 'Surrey's fidelity to Wyatt in "Wyatt Resteth Here" '. *Studies in Philology* 77: 376–87.

Tudor-Craig, P. (1989) 'Henry VIII and King David'. In *Early Tudor England: Proceedings of the 1987 Harlaxton Symposium*, ed. D. Williams. Woodbridge, Suffolk: Boydell Press, pp 183–205.

Twombly, R. G. (1970) 'Thomas Wyatt's paraphrase of the penitential psalms of David'. *Texas Studies in Literature and Language* 12: 345–80.

Utley, F. L. (1970) *The Crooked Rib: An Analytical Index to the Arguments about Women in English and Scots Literature to the End of the Year 1563* (2nd edn). New York: Octagon Press.

Vale, M. (1981) *War and Chivalry: Warfare and Aristocratic Culture in England, France and Burgundy at the End of the Middle Ages*. London: Duckworth.

Vickers, B. (1970) *Classical Rhetoric in English Poetry*. London: Macmillan.

Vickers, N. J. (1982) 'Diana described: scattered woman and scattered rhyme'. In *Writing and Sexual Difference*, ed. E. Abel. Brighton: Harvester Press, pp 95–109.

Walker, G. (1988) *John Skelton and the Politics of the 1520s*. Cambridge: Cambridge University Press.

Wall, W. (1993) *The Imprint of Gender: Authorship and Publication in the Renaissance*. Ithaca, NY: Cornell University Press.

Waller, M. (1989) 'The empire's new clothes: refashioning the Renaissance'. In *Seeking the Woman in Late Medieval and Renaissance Writings: Essays in Feminist Contextual Criticism*, eds S. Fisher and J. E. Halley. Knoxville: University of Tennessee Press, pp 160–83.

Ward, J. (1960) 'The lute music of MS Royal Appendix 58'. *Journal of the American Musicological Society* 13: 117–25.

Warnicke, R. (1991) *The Rise and Fall of Anne Boleyn: Family Politics at the Court of Henry VIII*. Cambridge: Cambridge University Press.

Wartenkin, G. (1984) 'The meeting of the Muses: Sidney and the mid-Tudor poets'. In *Sir Philip Sidney and the Interpretation of Renaissance Culture: The Poet in His Time and Ours*, eds G. F. Waller and M. D. Moore. London: Croom Helm, pp 17–33.

Whigham, F. (1984) *Ambition and Privilege: The Social Tropes of Elizabethan Courtesy Theory*. Berkeley: University of California Press.

Winn, J. A. (1981) *Unsuspected Eloquence: A History of the Relations between Poetry and Music*. New Haven, Conn.: Yale University Press.

Woodbridge, L. (1984) *Women and the English Renaissance: Literature and the Nature of Womankind, 1540–1620*. Hassocks, Sussex: Harvester Press.

Woods, S. (1984) *Natural Emphasis: English Versification from Chaucer to Dryden*. San Marino, Ca.: The Huntington Library.

Zim, R. (1987) *English Metrical Psalms: Poetry as Praise and Prayer, 1535–1601*. Cambridge: Cambridge University Press.

Zitner, S. (1983) 'Truth and mourning in a sonnet by Surrey'. *English Literary History* 50: 509–29.

Index

Notes: Modern commentators and end-of-chapter notes are not indexed. Titles of poems/works appear under author, where author is named in text. Titles of works by Surrey and Wyatt appear in a separate alphabetical sequence following their subject sub-entries, for ease of reference.